# YOUR POSITIVE PLAN FOR *LOVE &* HAPPINESS

TERRY:
MAY THE LORD BLESS YOU.
BILL CARLSON
3-15-97

# YOUR POSITIVE PLAN FOR *LOVE* & HAPPINESS

## How to Experience the Positive Attitudes that Will Transform Your life

---

TWO BESTSELLING WORKS COMPLETE IN ONE VOLUME

## THE BE (HAPPY) ATTITUDES

## BE HAPPY—YOU ARE LOVED

---

# ROBERT H. SCHULLER

**Inspirational Press • New York**

4299

# Acknowledgments

## The Be Happy Attitudes

I AM INDEED GRATEFUL to those friends and loved ones who have so graciously allowed me to share their stories in this book. They join with me in the hope and prayer that others will find the secret of the Be-Happy Attitudes. I also extend my gratitude to Sheila Schuller Coleman, the editor of my weekly Sunday messages, who collected and organized my thoughts and anecdotal material. Her help in compiling this manuscript was immeasurable. And to Betty Cornell—thank you for the diligent hours you gave in research and clerical assistance.

## Be Happy You Are Loved

THANKS TO MY WIFE, Arvella, and my daughter, Sheila, for their many hours of work collecting, editing, and correcting my work.

# The Be (Happy) Attitudes

*To the congregation of the Crystal Cathedral*
*and the millions of friends*
*in the Hour of Power television ministry—*
*the people with whom I've laughed, cried, and dreamed.*
*Together we have walked the walk*
*from sorrow to joy, from despair to victory,*
*Together we have seen and lived*
*the truth of our Lord's beautiful Be-Happy Attitudes.*

# Contents

## Be-Happy Attitude #5

# "I'm going to treat others the way I want others to treat me."

*"Blessed are the merciful, for they shall obtain mercy."*

122

## Be-Happy Attitude #6

# "I've got to let the faith flow free through me."

*"Blessed are the pure in heart, for they shall see God."*

146

## Be-Happy Attitude #7

# "I'm going to be a bridge builder."

*"Blessed are the peacemakers, for they shall be called children of God."*

166

## Be-Happy Attitude #8

# "I can choose to be happy—anyway!"

*"Blessed are those who are persecuted for righteousness' sake, for theirs is the kingdom of heaven."*

194

# Introduction

HAPPINESS! Elusive, isn't it?
How often have you thought:

- If only I had that car . . .
  then I'd be satisfied!
- If only I could find someone truly to love me . . .
  then I'd be happy!
- If only I wasn't under so much financial stress . . .
  then I'd be content!
- If only . . .
- If only . . .

The news I have for you today is: All the "If only's" in the world—*even if they all came true*—still could not guarantee your happiness!

As we all have discovered at one time or another, cars, houses, jewelry, and other material gains don't bring happiness for long. After the immediate rush of joy at receiving something we have longed for, we are hit with the unique problems that every gain brings.

I'll never forget the young man who longed for a Ferrari. He dreamed about it. He imagined himself behind the wheel. He could smell the soft, supple leather. He could feel the power of the engine as it hugged the road.

Then it happened. He got the promotion he wanted, and with the promotion came a good sized raise. At last he knew he could fulfill his fantasy.

Shining black, the Ferrari gleamed and glistened as he drove it away from the showroom floor. His dream had come true. He was ecstatic!

The car was magnificent to drive, and the young man loved all the attention he received from envious young men and lovely ladies. But the payments were steep. The entire raise and more was going into this car. The girls that the car attracted expected him to take them to expensive restaurants. They expected expensive gifts. And parking attendants expected fat tips.

Then it came time to have the Ferrari serviced. Wow! He had no idea that a mere lube job would cost so much. He managed to pay, although the high charges left him in the hole financially.

But it was worth it! He had a Ferrari—his dream car!

The young man enjoyed washing and waxing the Ferrari, rubbing the wax and watching the sun glint off the mirrored body. But after a few months he began to notice little nicks in the paint and scratches on the door.

He began to get tired of the attention and the demands that the car and its new friends made on him. In fact, he was beginning to wonder who the girls were going out with—him or his car!

That car—the young man's pride and joy, his source of happiness—was beginning to become a source of disappointment and depression, as well as a burden. This letdown was totally unexpected. He had thought he would be eternally happy once he had that car. But he wasn't.

Future shock overtook—and shook—him. Now he was haunted by the question: "Will I ever be happy? Will I ever be satisfied?"

Material gains will not bring happiness. People who search for happiness in terms of money, real estate, possessions, or investment portfolios are always in for a rude awakening. All the money in the world will not buy happiness.

I have known some *very wealthy* people, and they have

*"Attitudes are more important
than facts!"*

— *Karl Menninger*

just as many problems as you and I do. They are no happier than you or I. In fact, money frequently brings with it *more* problems and less happiness. Wealthy people are often lonely and suspicious of people's motives.

If wealth can't guarantee happiness, then how about fame?

I have known famous people and many of them live a life of despair. I'm sure that you can think of several movie stars and performers whose names were household words, who had achieved the highest level of fame, but who were so unhappy that they ended it all through suicide.

Where do you look to find happiness?

- *Riches?* It will take more than money.
- *Recognition?* Fame is fleeting!
- *Relationships?* Even those who love you will sometimes let you down.
- *Recreational drugs?* They create habits that spell nothing but trouble!

How, then, do you find happiness? Not in riches, recognition, relationships, or recreational drugs, but in *readjusted mental attitudes!*

That's what this book is about—*the life-transforming power of a readjusted mental attitude!* The good news is: Bad news can turn into good news if you readjust your attitude toward the tough times.

In this book:

- You'll meet people who did just that!
- You'll be introduced to eight spiritual laws, taught and lived out by Christ, that will help you realign and readjust your attitude!
- You'll be inspired to make the commitment to react positively to negative times!

This book will absolutely change your life—if you can learn to live by the Be-Happy Attitudes.

The Be-Happy Attitudes—what are they? You've probably heard of them as the "Beatitudes," the eight positive attitudes that come from the eight opening lines of Jesus of Nazareth's famous "Sermon on the Mount":

- "Blessed are the poor in spirit, for theirs is the kingdom of heaven."
- "Blessed are those who mourn, for they shall be comforted."
- "Blessed are the meek, for they shall inherit the earth."
- "Blessed are those who hunger and thirst for righteousness, for they shall be satisfied."
- "Blessed are the merciful, for they shall obtain mercy."
- "Blessed are the pure in heart, for they shall see God."
- "Blessed are the peacemakers, for they shall be called children of God."
- "Blessed are those who are persecuted for righteousness' sake, for theirs is the kingdom of heaven."

*Blessed* literally means "happy." So, whether you are winning or losing, succeeding or failing, enthusiastic or depressed, happy or suffering, you can be happy *if* you will discover the eight positive attitudes given to us by Jesus in the Beatitudes.

Architect Philip Johnson, who designed the Crystal Cathedral, says the most important part of any structure is the "Goesinto"—that part or place where a person "goes into" the experience.

What the "Goesinto" is to a building . . .

What the overture is to a symphony . . .

What the first serve is to tennis . . .

What the main entrance is to a facility . . .

What the glorious christening is to a ship . . .

What the opening salvo is to an argument . . .

What the first impression is to a new relationship . . .

What the opening number is to a program . . .

That's what these eight classic sentences are to the teachings of Jesus. Classic—they've passed the test of time. For over two thousand years they have transformed the minds, the moods, the manners of men and women.

What is their secret? Why have they proven unsurpassed as successful therapy to depressed minds? Now we know! The analysis is in. The secret is out. Each contains the spiritual motivation to alter a human being's attitude. What we really have here is a therapeutic exercise in replacing negative attitudes with positive attitudes! Yes, here—unsurpassed in helpful literature—are eight positive attitudes that will transform any life! Discover them! Apply them! Enjoy life with these "Be-Happy Attitudes."

Be-Happy Attitude #1

# "I need help—I can't do it alone!"

*"Blessed are the poor in spirit, for theirs is the kingdom of heaven."*
Matthew 5:3

**W**HO'S HAPPY TODAY? Everybody has so many problems!" she snapped.

I had watched the television reporter approach this woman on the streets of New York City. She was obviously over-rushed, over-tense. The interviewer had simply asked her if she was happy. Now all I could see on my screen was the miserable side shot of an ill-mannered, ill-tempered woman whose negative attitude rang in my ears.

I wanted to speak up: *"Wait a minute, whoever you are!* Happiness is not a question of having or not having problems. Everyone has problems, and not everyone is unhappy!"

Happiness is not dependent on whether or not we have problems, any more than it is dependent on whether or not we have material wealth. There are people who are happy even though they have very little. There are also people who are unhappy, even though they have the wealth of kings.

19

I have visited in the home and the office of a man whose personal fortune is measured in the tens of millions of dollars. And yet this man has financial problems. He has cash-flow problems. His wealth is all tied up in investments. He earns an awesome salary, but most of his paycheck goes into the equally awesome mortgage payments.

"Oh," but you say, "I'd gladly trade his financial security for my financial insecurity."

To that I reply, "*Nobody* is financially secure. The more you have, the more you can lose."

So, where do we find this elusive attitude of happiness? Where do we find escape from the entrapping problems that rob us of our joy? Where do we find the healing of our wounded hearts?

This question is all important, for too often, too many of us go to the wrong source for help.

I love the story of the man who went to his doctor. The doctor told him, "I'm sure I have the answer to your problem."

The man answered, "I certainly hope so, doctor. I should have come to you long ago."

The doctor asked, "Where did you go before?"

"I went to the pharmacist."

The doctor snidely remarked, "What kind of foolish advice did he give you?"

"He told me to come see you!"

We do go to the wrong places too often. If you have a medical problem, see your physician. If your problem is an unhappy spirit, then I have a spiritual doctor that I recommend. His name is Jesus Christ. Believe me, Jesus Christ was a joy-filled person. He had problems, but He knew how to handle them creatively and constructively.

Follow me through the next eight chapters. As we look upon the Beatitudes—the Be-Happy Attitudes—of Jesus Christ, you will discover our Lord's key to joyful living.

Joyous living is a grand possibility! Yes, even if we have

problems! Financial problems? Wait a minute! Our *reaction* to our financial condition is far more important than the *reality* of the financial position.

After all, poverty is not just a matter of finances! Every one of us faces some kind of poverty; we all have a need at some level of our lives. It may be *financial* poverty. But it may also be *occupational* poverty, either a lack of success in our chosen profession or merely a lack of direction, lack of a dream or a goal. It may be *intellectual* poverty or *emotional* poverty.

Jesus begins the Beatitudes with a tremendous principle that has to do with this question of poverty: *"Blessed are the poor in spirit, for theirs is the kingdom of heaven."* The secret of successful living is simple: You and I must discover our soft spot, our weak link, our ignorant area, our poverty pocket. And then we must become "poor in spirit" as well—face up to our poverty, humble our attitude, acknowledge our weakness, ask for help.

### OCCUPATIONAL POVERTY

Everybody is poor in his or her own way. Yours may be occupational poverty. If you are just starting out in life, you probably lack a dream. You need to know how to find a professional dream and how to pursue it. If you already have a goal toward which you're striving, you may lack an emotional support system which will carry you toward success.

If you are very successful, if you think you have arrived and you've got it made, you may also have a need. What is it? You may need to decide where you go from here and how you handle the success you have achieved.

If occupational success is eluding you, then the first Be-Happy Attitude verse is for you, for happiness will come when you surrender your arrogance and ask for help. Pride keeps us from crying out; greed also stops us. We want to take all the credit for our success. Let me share with you a valuable sentence I committed to memory long ago: "God can do tremendous things through the person who doesn't care who gets the credit."

If you are willing to accept this basic premise, then you are willing to hire highly qualified people in your company or your corporation. They will make your business venture a success. They may get the credit, but you will be a success—and you will have helped not only yourself, but also everyone else around you.

Poverty handled in a pleasant, positive manner, is an opportunity to involve good and generous people in our dreams, for often the strong welcome an opportunity to help the weak. The wealthy find meaning in their lives when they are given an opportunity to share in some worthy project or person. Today I enjoy the friendship of many wonderful people whom I met when I had to beg for their help to build a Crystal Cathedral or to spread a ministry via television.

I have been blessed because I have been poor—poor enough to swallow my pride and humbly ask for assistance. The result? Not merely success in reaching my occupational goals, but lasting friendships with those who saved the day for me.

So, don't become defensive about your lack by trying to gloss over it or pretending the problem doesn't exist. Chances are that such an attitude will end in futility and you'll end up paying an awful price. The way to handle your area of poverty is to say, "I need help."

## INTELLECTUAL POVERTY

When I attended Hope College in Holland, Michigan, I studied economics under Dr. Edward Dimnent. It was said that Dr. Dimnent was so bright and so knowledgeable that he was qualified to teach any undergraduate course in the catalog of Hope College. He could handle

You'll never
be licked
as long as
you know
what it is you've
lacked.

biology, chemistry, physics—any course in the sciences—
as well as the arts or humanities.

To top it all off, he was the architect of the college
chapel! Such expertise was feasible forty years ago. Today it's impossible. The simple reason is that the accumulated knowledge in this world is more than one mind can
comprehend. In addition, the rapid rate at which knowledge continues to be acquired through research precludes
the possibility of anybody's ever reaching a point at
which he or she can learn it all.

As a result, you might expect intellectual people to be
more humble today than they were twenty or thirty years
ago. It would seem logical that such an accumulation of
knowledge would mean the end of intellectual elitism and
academic arrogance. I'm not sure if that's happening. But
the point is: Everybody is ignorant about something. *Every person has his area of intellectual poverty.*

Let me share with you a personal illustration. I attended a tiny country high school in Iowa which did not
offer geometry. When I started my undergraduate studies
at Hope College, Michigan, I discovered that everyone
was required to take eight hours of science and that math
courses were applicable to that requirement.

Consequently, I found myself in a math course. The
first week the professor rattled off some statements
which referred to geometric principles. Because I had
never studied geometry, I didn't know what he was talking about. I noticed that the other students were nodding
as if they completely understood, so I did as they did,
thinking, "I'll pick it up later." The next week was the
same. I didn't have the foggiest notion what the teacher
was talking about, although I pretended I understood as
clearly as my fellow students did. But the truth of the
matter showed on my first test. I didn't get a good grade.

My professor approached me and kindly asked, "Are
you having problems, Bob?"

I said, "Oh, no, I'm doing fine."

That was a lie. If I had been honest, I would have admitted that I had an enormous gap and lack from my precollege work. But I didn't want to admit this fact because I didn't want the teacher to know how dumb I was. That was one of the biggest mistakes I ever made.

*Poverty? Can it be a positive possibility?* Yes, if it motivates me to a humble cry for help. Had I reacted honestly, openly, and admitted my impoverishment to my professor, I now believe he would have knocked himself out tutoring and helping me! After all, the deepest need of the human being is the need to be needed. An admission of my poverty could have turned into a positive possibility for real learning. I could have pulled an A instead of a D if I had learned this lesson: Success starts when I dare to admit I need help!

I've seen businesses restored, students graduated, and marriages healed through this humble and hopeful attitude. And I've even seen it help in parent-teen relationships.

John was sixteen years old. He resented the way his father and mother treated him and talked down to him. What could he do? He could split and run away fom home but things weren't that bad. So he pretended to ignore the problem by clamming up and refusing to discuss it.

John began to withdraw more and more into silence, sulking and pouting. Then his parents became angry. "Why don't you say something?" was their frustrated attempt to converse with John. But his only reply was a shrug of his shoulders.

"Something wrong?" his parents would ask.

John would mumble, "No."

"Did we do something?"

"No."

"Why don't you say something?"

"What do you want me to say?"

Their relationship was at a stalemate until John took this Beatitude seriously and realized it was much smarter

*What is this
pain?
It is the
birth pang
of a new
attitude
trying
to be born!*

to say, "Mom, Dad, I have a problem with the way you treat me." It was the beginning of an open and honest relationship with his parents.

Of course, parents also need this Beatitude. I would advise parents not to be afraid to be transparent with their children. Show them your weaknesses. Don't give them the impression you're perfect. Don't create shoes so large that your child will never be able to fill them. Be open, too. Share with them the predicament you find yourself in as a parent. Ask your teenager, "How would you handle this problem if you were the father or the mother?"

## EMOTIONAL POVERTY

Cherry Boone O'Neill, the daughter of my friend, Pat Boone, tells of her struggle against the disease, anorexia nervosa, in her book, *Starving for Attention.** When she learned to face up to her emotional poverty and to love and accept herself at the deepest level, Cherry was able to overcome a shocking disease more widespread than anyone could dream.

Anorexia, also known as the "self-starver's disease," is a psychosomatic disorder that really begins on the emotional and psychological level and works its way outward to the physical level. By the time it manifests itself physically, professional help is needed, because the external manifestation—severe weight loss—is just a symptom of what's really happening inside.

Cherry says, "I got down to eighty pounds. I was wasting away. I really was on a slow suicide trip, because I hated myself so badly. I didn't feel that God could possibly love me, considering what I was doing to myself and to the people that I loved. There was only a faint hope that God did exist and that there must be some way out

---

* New York: Continuum Publishing Co., 1982.

of my mess. There were times when I prayed to die, because I didn't feel that I could come out of it.

"But my parents stuck by me, as did my husband, who literally went through thick and thin with me. Finally, we received some professional psychotherapy from a Christian psychiatrist. My husband and I moved up to the Seattle area, and through the course of six months of intensive therapy, I became better.

"I believe, without a shadow of a doubt, that God led me to the right doctor at the right time. For within six months I had changed from wanting to die to wanting to live, and I had learned that there were things about me that were worth loving in spite of what I did and what I looked like.

"The Lord has blessed me so much. He brought me through something as traumatic and horrendous as anorexia. He has given me a beautiful little girl, and now that I am on the other side I can give hope to other people who are going through it. There are almost one million people in the United States who have anorexia. And these people, as well as obese people, share a common problem, for all eating disorders have very similar roots. A lot of it has to do with that low self-esteem."

"Blessed are the poor in spirit. . . ." So, blessed is Cherry Boone O'Neill. She dared to admit that she lacked self-esteem, she lacked the ability to lick the problem without help. So, today, she is happy with her family, her life, and—most of all—with herself.

Blessed are you when you face up to your emotional lack, admit your weakness. Blessed are you when you don't try to be an island and do it all by yourself.

### ADMIT YOUR NEED—IT'S NOT EASY, BUT IT *IS* ESSENTIAL!

In all areas of our lives, the principle is the same: *Happiness comes when you admit where you are lacking and where you have a need.*

I remember years ago, when E. Stanley Jones used to conduct "ashrams" as he called them. An ashram is a term from India. It means a time of spiritual growth and expansion. Dr. Jones always began his ashrams by passing out pieces of paper and saying, "No one will see what you are about to write on this paper. I want you to write what your need is today."

It happened at every ashram. While people were thinking and praying and writing, someone would say, "Brother Stanley, I don't have a need. What do you write down if you don't have a need?" And Brother Stanley would say, "If you think you don't have a need, then *that's* your need!"

If it is true that each of us is poor somewhere in our lives, then why are we so reluctant to admit it? Consciously, or sometimes subconsciously, we develop defense mechanisms against exposure. We try to shield ourselves—especially in areas where we're vulnerable.

We are reluctant to admit our needs because we're afraid that people might really reject us. We're afraid of public embarrassment. Actually the problem is even deeper than that; it's a fundamental lack of self-esteem. We fear the lack of dignity that may come with rejection or embarrassment.

What we need to realize is that we don't need to be afraid of embarrassment or rejection. *What we do need to fear is the result that comes from hiding our lack, our need, our poverty.*

You may remember a time several years ago when the popular singer Tony Orlando announced "I quit!" in the middle of a performance and left the stage—to the surprise of the audience, the press, even his associates, the singing group "Dawn."

Not long after that, our paths crossed, and Tony shared with me what happened that night:

"When I broke on that stage—and that's exactly what happened—I just simply could not stand physically anymore. I was saying things that didn't compliment my family. They didn't compliment my grandmother, who raised me, along with my mother, who so desperately tried to raise me with depth and character.

"Then I felt a silence. And this silence was so loud that it was godly. That silence was, in my opinion, conscience. And that conscience was the voice of the Lord that said, 'Tony, you must take care of yourself.' In my own heart I was saying, 'I've got to recuperate. I've got to reconstruct.'

"So I said to everyone, *'I quit!'* Actually, without realizing it, I really meant, *'I've got to begin again.'*

"The media, of course, dramatized my leaving the stage and embellished my words to make it sound as though I was saying, 'I quit show business.'

"In retrospect, however, I can honestly say I didn't really quit. I just stopped for a moment."

Then Tony referred to the Possibility Thinker's Creed:

> When faced with a mountain,
> I will not quit!
> I will keep on striving
> until I climb over,
> find a pass through,
> tunnel underneath,
> or simply stay and turn
> the mountain into a gold mine—
> with God's help!

He said, "I quit when Christ wasn't in my life. But I came back to this glorious life and this glorious business with the attitude that there is no way I can quit when I say, 'I am sorry for having offended You, O Lord. But I wasn't a friend of Yours then and didn't know You loved me as much as You do. I was wrong. Never again will I quit. I will keep on striving until I find a pass through, tunnel underneath, or simply stay and turn that mountain into a gold mine.

"To this day, I believe my career is more of a gold mine now than ever before."

## THE BEGINNING OF A NEW BEGINNING

"Blessed are the poor in spirit. . . ."

How can this Be-Happy Attitude change you and me? By inspiring us to learn the power of two miracle-working confessions: (1) "I need help!" and (2) "I am sorry!"

### "I Need Help!"

- "I've got a problem—can you help me?"
- "I don't understand—can you enlighten me?"
- "I can't agree with you—can we meet somewhere in the middle?"
- "I've got a problem accepting this—can you give a little from your position?"
- "I'm really at a loss—can you direct me?"
- "I'm ready to quit—what is your advice?"
- "I'm at my wits' end! I've had it!—Please tell me what you think I should do."

These forthright confessions are the beginning of a new beginning! Let's examine the miracle power available to us when we learn to say, "I need help."

If you feel trapped, lost, out-of-control, chained by difficulties, then I have good news for you. *Your chains can lead to a change* if you are willing to say these three words.

"Blessed are the poor in spirit." Happy is the one who knows where he or she is poor and is very open about it. Success comes to the person who is able to ask for help. The surprising thing is that admitting your need for help doesn't give your ego a blowout. On the contrary, it causes you to be a person of such emotional and

*If you're too proud
(or too afraid)
to admit
you are hurting...*

*Don't be surprised
if
nobody seems
to care.*

intellectual integrity that people will trust you. And they will go along with you. In the process you will gain tremendous self-esteem.

The alternative is to play games, put on a front, pretend to be something you're not, and hope that no one will ever catch you without your mask on, your hair fixed just right, your guard up. You're not going to get the help you need by putting on a false front, by pretending you don't have a problem, or by hoping it will go away.

The truth is that there is somebody right now who would find great joy in helping you with your lack if he or she only knew that you had it. But if you pretend that you've got it made, with no problems, there's no way that person can help you.

There's always somebody ready to help anybody. Alcoholics Anonymous has been teaching this for years. A person will only find healing when he or she finally dares to admit, "Hey, I'm poor, I've got a problem. I'm helpless." When we get to this point, then we are ready to let go and let God take over.

A prominent personality who overcame alcoholism after a long struggle is a poignant illustration. In her words: "I struggled with my drinking problem for years. I kept saying, 'I can handle my liquor.' I refused to accept the truth that I was an alcoholic. I procrastinated; I rationalized: 'Some day I will cut down. I can handle it.' It was not until I hit the bottom that I was able to admit defeat and then say the three hardest words I ever uttered in my entire life: 'I need help!' "

It really works. I speak from experience. I was raised in an Iowa family where we always had bread with lots of butter. There was always an abundance of pie and other desserts. Consequently, I was a fat butterball when I was a baby, and I had to struggle with a weight problem as I grew up. I tried diets. I counted calories. (I still do.) But the weight accumulated through the years. Finally I decided that I would eat only lean meats, vegetables, and fresh fruits for dessert.

Then one night, almost seven years ago, I was taken out to dinner. The bread was passed. My host said, "This is fantastic. Feel it." I felt it, it was soft and warm. The fellow next to me was already spreading the butter, which was melting into the warm, fragrant bread. My host continued to tempt me. He said, "You must try the steak with the Béarnaise sauce." I followed his advice. By the time it came to dessert, I was feeling a little guilty. I was coaxed again, this time with, "They make the best pie here; it has a chocolate crust. You can't pass it by. Go on a diet tomorrow." I took the pie.

When I walked out of there, I calculated that I'd had about three thousand calories. That night I went to bed greatly depressed and filled with remorse. I woke up at two or three in the morning. I was racked with guilt. There was a total sense of futility because, frankly, it was the one area in which possibility thinking totally failed me. I could build churches, towers—even a cathedral. I could write books, but I could not get rid of my fat. I could raise millions of dollars to do God's work, but I couldn't turn my back on a piece of chocolate pie.

Now, in this black of my night, I prayed one simple prayer: "Dear Jesus, I don't know if You're dead or alive. I don't know if You are even real! I have believed it! I preached it! But I can't prove it by my weight control. Jesus, if You are there, can You help me?"

Poor in spirit, I admitted my lack. And instantaneously, an image went through my mind. I saw the old Floyd River on our family farm in Iowa. It was flooded way up to the grassy slopes. There in the middle of the stream was a great, gallant, strong tree that had been uprooted. It was being carried away by the current. Somehow I knew my body was that tree.

The sloping hillside where the water lapped appeared very gentle. It didn't look wild; it didn't look rough. It seemed safe. But if I got too close to the water, the river could carry me away. That was what butter, ice cream, and cake were for me. I'd take one bite, thinking I could

*If your life*
*is*
*really in a mess...*
*remember this...*
*... stress*
*can be the start*
*of real success!*

stop after one simple little taste. But one bite always led to another . . . and another . . . and another. I was being destroyed by a seemingly harmless little bite. Then I heard the message. It was in the past perfect tense: "I have snatched you from destruction."

I had to refrain from tasting, from the nibbles that led to whole meals. I had an internal transformation. I knew then that I had been liberated from subconscious forces that kept me addicted to sweets. I still have my little ups and downs, but never have I reverted to what I was.

The Lord helped me once I admitted that I was unable to do it without Him. As long as I continued to believe that I could safely eat a little here and there and remain in control, I was doomed. But when I cried out for help, I was saved!

"Blessed are the poor in spirit, for theirs is the kingdom of heaven."

### "I'm Sorry!"

When you learn to make this confession, you'll find happiness, because you will discover the miracle-working power to be an honest person. You and I are free when we admit we've been wrong. Instead of an *ego* trip, we are on an *integrity* trip—the road to real happiness. For the integrity trip really feeds our self-esteem. We can be proud of ourselves for being open and honest and humble! By contrast, the ego trip is a constant threat and finally fatal to genuine self-respect!

On the integrity trip we're no longer slaves to perfectionism. So we aren't embarrassed when people catch us making mistakes. When we have done something wrong, we need only say, *"I'm sorry."* To the ones we've hurt we can say, "I'm a human being. The Lord has forgiven me. I've forgiven myself; I hope you will too."

I will never forget the morning I asked my oldest daughter, Sheila, to do the breakfast dishes before school. Not realizing that she was already running late and facing too many tardy notices, I was stunned by her reaction. She burst into profuse tears.

Again, misinterpreting the motive behind the outburst, assuming that she was merely trying to get out of an unpleasant chore, I demanded that she dry her eyes and get to work—*immediately.*

She reluctantly obeyed me, but I could hear her anger in the careless clanking of the dishes in the sink. On the way to school, she turned her back to me and stared sullenly out the window.

Usually, I took positive advantage of the uninterrupted time that I was able to spend with my children while driving them to school by teaching them poetry or Bible verses or just sharing together.

On that morning, however, there were no poems, no verses, no songs—only deathly, stubborn silence. I dropped Sheila off, mumbled a good-bye and left for my office. I tried to work, but I couldn't concentrate. All I could see was the scared, tear-stained face of my daughter as she hesistantly climbed out of the car to face her teacher and classmates.

I had begun to realize that my timing had been way off. I had no right to demand that she do the dishes without giving her some forewarning, some planning time. I realized that I had been wrong to upset her so close to the time when she was going to be facing peers, a time when she needed support.

The more I thought about it, the more remorseful I became. Finally, I decided that I had to do something. I had to say I was sorry, and my apology could not wait until suppertime. So, I called the school and I asked the counselor for permission to take her to lunch.

I shall never forget the look of surprise on her face when she saw me waiting for her in the office. I said, "Sheila, I've gotten permission to take you to lunch. They said that you could have an hour off. Let's go."

I led her by the arm down the empty school corridor.

As soon as the heavy doors slammed behind us, I turned to my daughter and I said, "Sheila, I'm sorry. I'm so very sorry! It's not that I shouldn't have asked you to help out at home, but I had no right to insist on it this morning without any previous warning. I upset you at a time when you most needed my love and support—just before you went to school. And I let you go without saying 'I love you.' I was wrong. Please forgive me."

Sheila put her arms around my neck and hugged me and said, "Oh, Dad, of course I forgive you. I love you, too."

Oh, the power of those restorative words, "I'm sorry!" They heal relationships—between ourselves and our friends and loved ones, and between ourselves and our Lord.

The psalmist wrote, "A broken and contrite heart, O God, thou wilt not despise" (Ps. 51:17).

He wrote for many. Throughout the Scriptures we see them—the broken and contrite:

- The penitent thief
- The prodigal son
- David, the adulterer
- Saul of Tarsus, a murderer of Christians
- Mary Magdalene, the prostitute

These scalawags—what do they all have in common? They all belong to God's Hall of Fame. In the corridors of heaven they all have positions of honor.

How did they acquire such noble recognition? All of them reached a point in their personal shortcomings, sin, and shame when they cried out, "O God, be merciful to me, a sinner!"

Yes, if your life is in a mess, stress can lead to real success—for after all, *real* success is being admitted to the Kingdom of heaven.

You and I need this humble attitude, to be poor in spirit, in our spiritual lives. You and I need it in our prayer lives. What if you have doubts? What do you do with them? Do you pretend they'll go away? Act as if they don't exist? Sing the songs, read the prayers? Act as if you really believe? No. Rather, go to God and say, "If you're there, God . . . to tell the truth, I don't even believe in You right now. I wish I could. If it's wrong to doubt, I hope you'll forgive me!"

Once you start being honest, in all of life and especially in your prayers, it's amazing what will break loose for you. Don't try kidding anybody, least of all yourself.

"Blessed are the poor in spirit, for theirs is the kingdom of heaven." If you have a need, God has an answer. He specializes in matching up answers to problems, healings to hurts, and solutions to perplexing situations.

### WHAT'S HOLDING YOU BACK?

Only when you and I reach those depths of despair are we then on the way to joy, because God particularly pours out His blessings upon those who know how much they need Him. The *promise* is joy. The *principle* is to ask God for help, admit we cannot do it alone. The *problem*, of course, that stands in the way of our crying out to God is the problem of an *unholy pride*.

There is such a thing as a holy pride—self-esteem and self-respect represent a healthy pride in ourselves as God's loved and redeemed creation. But arrogance and vanity result from an unholy pride that says, "Get out of my way, I want to do it myself"—like a stubborn small child refusing a loving parent's help.

"Blessed are the poor in spirit, for theirs is the kingdom of heaven." And so you and I come to a time when we stop playing games and putting on false fronts. We reach

*It takes guts...*
*... to leave the ruts!*

a point in life when we know that we are spiritually bankrupt. It is at this point that we kneel before our Lord and say, "God, I want to be born again. I want a new life. I want a joyful Christ to come and live in me. Oh God, I turn my life over to You."

A few years ago I received a letter that touched me deeply. Its impact had as much to do with who the writer was—her credentials and her professional integrity—as it had to do with *what* she said.

The letter was from Dr. Mary Ellen Bening, who works at the United States International University in San Diego. She has her Ph.D. in Social Sciences. Her job is to edit doctoral dissertations that are being produced at the university. This impressed me because it meant she would naturally be very up-to-date as to the latest research in human behavior.

Dear Dr. Schuller:
On the 26th of August my husband and I attended the 11:15 service at your son's church to hear your sermon. I shook your hand after the service but was unable to speak to you. What I had experienced during the service left me speechless.

My reason for coming that Sunday was that two weeks earlier I had listened for the first time to a televised service from the Crystal Cathedral. On other occasions when services were being aired I had turned to other channels in search of nonreligious programs; however, your sermon on life's contradictions captured my attention. . . . [In your sermon] you demonstrated that it is not a contradiction to be a deeply reflective, reasoning human being and an adamantly faithful Christian. . . . After hearing your sermon I could not stop thinking about its meanings and diverse applications. I also began to think about the alternative path which Christ offered, and for the first time I began not only to see but to feel the precious gift He gives. When I awakened on the 26th, I had the feeling that perhaps I was ready to receive that gift.

Your sermon that morning, entitled "Breaking Through: There's Hope for You" focused on faith, a capacity I most needed to understand, because my earlier inability to grasp the meaning of faith had prevented me from becoming a Christian. I had imagined that certain fortunate people experienced a calling from God, were mystically touched, felt a spiritual awakening, and hence received the faith. It never occurred to me that faith is an option!

My husband and I arrived early at the church on that special Sunday. And as the service began something wonderful happened. I felt myself being enveloped in peace, love, and strength. I would call it a spiritual renaissance except that I cannot remember feeling so alive before. I experienced a birth in the church that day, and I was amazed at how simple it really was! I had assumed that I would have to pass some monumental test before I would be qualified to take my rightful place in a church. Faith seemed like another degree, the most advanced of degrees, that one earns after unlocking the secrets of the universe.

*In reality, God asked so little and gave in return so much!*

Mary Ellen Bening

Here was a letter from an intellectual—a very learned, bright young woman. She had thought she had it altogether, never dreaming that she lacked anything or needed anything beyond her ability to think and learn and perceive. And yet, even Dr. Bening had been lacking. Spiritually she had been empty; spiritually she had been impoverished. Her soul had been dry and thirsty and craving for something—what it was, she hadn't known.

But then she saw her lack. She saw what it was she needed. She needed to believe in the loving, saving grace of Jesus Christ.

She became poor in spirit when she realized that in the process she didn't have to become poor in intellect. When she saw that she could be a believer in Jesus without sacrificing her intellectual integrity, she grappled Jesus to her side, embraced Him with her soul, and was born again.

When you discover the secret of the first Be-Happy Attitude, when you are able to say "I need help!" or "I'm sorry!" or "I have a lack!", then you will have taken the important first step toward being truly happy. For then you will have the attitude that can free you to move into the other Be-Happy Attitudes.

I strongly believe that there is a logical progression to the Beatitudes. Jesus gave them to us in the order He did for a very important reason: They are interdependent on each other, and one is a prerequisite for the next.

Think about it. Before Jesus can comfort us, before He can help us and heal us, we must have the attitude that we are *willing* to be helped! He cannot make us happy unless we *want* to be happy.

So are you willing to be helped? Do you want to be happy? Are there some areas in your life where you are lacking and need some help? Then Be-Happy. For you have the one essential ingredient you need to begin discovering the secret of the remaining Be-Happy Attitudes.

Be-Happy Attitude #2

# "I'm really hurting—but I'm going to bounce back!"

*"Blessed are those who mourn, for they
shall be comforted."*
Matthew 5:4

**D**R. SCHULLER, *why do bad things happen to good people?"* I can't tell you how often I've faced this question in the thirty-three years I have spent as a pastor.

I answer, "Part of the problem is that we ask the wrong questions. If we ask the wrong questions we're never going to come up with the right answers."

*"Why do bad things happen to good people?"* This is the wrong question, because it's the one question God never answers.

The Old Testament prophets lamented in times of trouble, *"Why, O Lord?"* Always He remained silent to that question. Even when Jesus Himself cried out from the cross, "My God, my God, *why?"* God didn't answer.

God never answers the *why,* because the person who asks "why" doesn't really want an explanation; he wants an argument! God refuses to be drawn into an argument. If God answered one "why," we would come with another. There would be no end to it.

If the wrong question is *"Why do bad things happen to good people?"* then what is the right question? It is *"What happens to good people when bad things happen to them?"*

Jesus answered that question in the Beatitudes. In the second Beatitude, which is the subject of this chapter, the reality of tough situations is confronted head-on. Jesus says, in essence, "When bad things happen to good people, they are blessed, for they are comforted."

Christianity isn't a Pollyanna religion. It doesn't claim that bad things won't happen to us. We are never told in the Old or New Testament that if we live a good life we'll never have any sickness or tragedy. However, we are promised in Isaiah 43: "Fear not, for I have redeemed you; I have called you by name, you are mine. When you pass through the waters . . . they shall not overwhelm you; when you walk through fire you shall not be burned, and the flame shall not consume you. For I am the Lord your God"(vv.1–3).

If God keeps His promises, then how does He comfort good people when bad things happen to them?

As a pastor, I am in the specialized work of dealing with the hurt, the lonely, the suffering, the sick, the dying. For thirty-five years I have been trudging the soft green lawns of cemeteries with my arms around young wives, husbands, fathers, mothers, relatives, and other loved ones. I have watched caskets lowered—hundreds of them: tiny ones, medium sized and large ones—draped in flowers and flags. I have seen people buried in graduation gowns, pulpit gowns, bridal dresses. Believe me, I am not blind to the reality of suffering. I have walked and wept my way through much human sorrow.

## NO TWO SORROWS ARE THE SAME

A vast number and variety of human emotional experiences come under the general label, "sorrow." Marie, a friend of mine and a member of my congregation, shared these intimate feelings with me upon the death of her husband: "No two sorrows are the same. I lost my son as a teenager; I lost my daughter in her twenties. Now my husband has passed away. Each grief has been painful, but each grief has been different."

Over and over I've seen sorrow, and over and over again I have witnessed this one fact: *God does comfort good people when bad things happen to them.* It *is* possible to be happy even in a world where sorrow casts its long, gray shadow.

Trouble never leaves us where it finds us; sorrow will change our tomorrow. But God inspires us to become better people, not bitter ones. He shows us the negative can be turned into a positive, a minus into a plus, and that's what the cross is all about.

How can we find relief from grief? How can we turn our mourning into a morning? (1) Realize what you can do for yourself! (2) Realize what God can do for you!

### "HERE'S WHAT YOU CAN DO!"

### Don't Blame God!

If you are going through a heartbreak and really having a difficult time, don't blame God! Human error is always the culprit: error of judgment, error of will, or error of purpose. Human selfishness, indifference, rebellion, folly, stupidity, brashness can always be found as the root cause of human misery and suffering.

Cancer and heart disease, along with other related illnesses, are the top killers in America today. No one will ever be able to place the blame for these diseases on God. In time, or in eternity, we shall see the truth: all disease is dis-ease, a lack of harmony between a human organism and its environment. Disease is too often caused by not eating right, not sleeping right, not exercising right, not breathing or breeding right; it is a question of man's not attaining a harmonious balance with his surroundings. If disease appears, man is doing something wrong; God is not to blame!

But, you say, can't we blame God for not showing us how certain deaths could be avoided or how certain illnesses could have been cured?

Think a moment. The real problem is not our ignorance, but our carelessness. Almost all disease, death, and sorrow is brought upon us not through lack of knowledge, but through lack of obedience to the light God has given us through several different channels:

(1) *God revealed the Ten Commandments.* He gave us these ten laws to protect us from an alluring, tempting path which would ultimately lead only to sickness, sin, and sorrow. Following the Ten Commandments will result in spiritual health, mental health, and physical health! Killing, lying, stealing, and adultery are bad for the health! (Consider the current epidemic of venereal diseases!) Under the banner of sophistication and liberation, many of us tell God to go to hell! In so doing, we only send ourselves there.

(2) *God revealed secrets of health.* He has given us throughout the Bible, as well as through medical science, guidelines for us to follow regarding our daily bodily habits of eating, drinking, sleeping, working, exercising. Yet, it is true: Some doctors still smoke and drink to excess. Some ministers eat improperly. Some athletes fail to exercise often enough, and generally overlook their physical well-being. Can we honestly and fairly accuse God for not giving us more insight into health when we blatantly disregard the knowledge He *has* revealed?

What happens
to
good people
when
bad things
happen
to them?

———

They become
. . .

better
people!

(3) *God disclosed secrets of salvation from sin.* We
know that sorrow, separation, sickness, and disease
are ultimately caused by sin. We know that much
physical illness is caused by mental tension, stress,
worry, anxiety, fear, and guilt. We also know that if
we accept salvation and yield our minds and our
hearts to the saving Spirit of Christ, our negative
sins and emotions will be drawn out and healing
of mind and body will begin. Yet, many of us are
still hesitant to give ourselves over completely to
Christ. We reject God's salvation.

Can we not then blame God for permitting people to be
so selfish? Doesn't God have the power to control every
person on earth, to force everyone to obey Him? Should
we not blame God for creating man with the capacity to
sin?

Consider for a minute the dilemmas that God faced at
the dawn of creation. When God created humankind, His
objective was to make a material form of life which
would be a reflection of His own nonmaterial Self. Thus,
He chose to make man "after His image," a decision-
making creature, capable of discernment, judgment,
evaluation, choice, and decision.

When God created such a person, He realized fully that
this creature would have the power to decide against
God. But let's look at the alternative. If He had designed a
man who could never make a wrong decision, this creature would never be able to make a personal decision of
his own. He would be nothing but a perfect, sinless, guilt-
less, error-free . . . person? NO! Machine? Yes! Computer?
Yes! Human being . . . NEVER! God decided to take the
greatest gamble of the ages—to make an opinion-form-
ing, idea-collecting, decision-making creature. What He
created was a potential sinner, but a potentially loving
person as well.

Don't blame God for permitting sin. Thank God that He has never, in spite of our sins, taken our freedom from us and with it our capability of becoming sincere, loving persons.

Don't blame God for the suffering in this world! Blame human beings for personally choosing the path leading to heartache and sorrow. Blame human beings for rejecting the divine truth when it was shown to them. Blame human beings for refusing God's salvation, even when offered in the name of Jesus! You have but to look at the cross and know that no human being can ever blame God for not going to the limit to save us.

## Don't Blame Yourself

Grief always seems to be associated with guilt. But self-condemnation will solve no problem and will change no circumstance. It is merely a negative, nonconstructive emotion which can wreak havoc in your life.

You probably remember reading about the tragic accident at the Hyatt Regency in Kansas City several years ago. If you recall, one hundred fourteen people were killed and many more injured when a concrete walkway encircling the atrium collapsed. A young friend of mine was there that night and witnessed the horror. As she said to me later, "Dr. Schuller, it was like being in a disaster movie. The only difference was that this was *real*! I wanted desperately for someone to take it back and fix it, put it back the way it was before."

Of course there was no way of undoing the damage. People all around my friend were dying. She wasn't trained in emergency procedures, so there was nothing that she could do. That feeling of helplessness, coupled with the horrific memories, nearly destroyed her.

She explained, "There was nothing I could do. I could get handkerchiefs all night, but it didn't bring people back. I went home that night and couldn't sleep. The guilt was overwhelming because I couldn't make them live. Hundreds were dying and there was nothing I could do.

"I've been a Christian all my life, so I prayed and prayed that people would live. They published in the paper a list of the names of the victims that were still hospitalized. Daily, I prayed for them. But I just couldn't seem to overcome the guilt that came with my sense of helplessness. So, I started to withdraw. I withdrew from friends that I'd made before, and I didn't try to make new ones. People who know me will tell you that such behavior is really against my character. I held everything inside. I wouldn't talk to anybody about it. I guess you could say that I just stopped living.

"I felt that *I* should have died in the disaster. Why was I alive when so many others were dead? No one can understand unless they have been through a disaster. No one can know how deep that hurt is. I just didn't want to hurt anymore. I determined to end my life. I intended to overdose on drugs. So, I arranged for one of my girlfriends to pick my children up, and I started taking the drug my doctor had prescribed for depression. I was about halfway through the bottle when I thought about how much I loved my family and how much my family loved me. I called the telephone hotline you have here at the Crystal Cathedral—NEW HOPE.

"The counselor at NEW HOPE asked me questions about myself. He said, 'It sounds like you've got a lot to live for.' He kept telling me that I had a lot of things I still needed to do and a lot of people that I could still help. Somehow, he instilled something in me that no one else had been able to do.

"Meanwhile he had called the police. The paramedics took me to the hospital, but by the time I arrived I was in a coma. I remained in a coma for three days. There was no brain activity whatsoever. I was pronounced clinically dead and my family was called to see me before they un-plugged the life-support systems.

"People had been praying for me and one of my uncles whom I'd been very close to all my life was standing there holding my hand and telling me that he loved me. My subconscious heard him, I guess, for I opened my eyes about three hours before they were going to unplug the machine.

"Everything that has happened since has been better than I could ever have dreamed. I wish I could tell every-one who's depressed, or anyone who's thought about dying or killing themselves, that it passes! It may not seem like it, but it does pass and it always gets better."

### DON'T FIX THE BLAME—FIX THE PROBLEM

A member of our church showed me a slogan used by the company where she works:

DON'T FIX THE BLAME, FIX THE PROBLEM!

What is your problem? First, recognize that the real problem is not the tragedy that has hit. The real problem is your reaction to it. If you do not take control of your reaction to your loss, you can and probably will eventu-ally be destroyed by it.

How do you "fix the problem"?

(1) *Decide not to go on for the rest of your life surren-dering to sorrow and tears.* To do this only disgraces your loved ones, your friends, and yourself. Moreover, contin-ued grief dishonors the God who wants only to be cred-ited with giving you a rebirth of joy! Decide that this nonconstructive sorrow mixed with self-pity has to STOP!

We can all take a lesson on handling our grief from Andre Thorton. Andre, a valuable hitter for the Cleveland Indians for nearly a decade, went through a tragedy that

*What is the cross?*
*It is a*
*minus*

———

*turned into a*
*plus!*

✝

would have devastated most of us. In 1977, Andre, his wife, and their two children were driving to Pennsylvania to take part in her sister's wedding. In that part of the country, the weather can turn bad even as early as October. As they started their journey that evening, it began to rain. Then it snowed. As they wound their way through the mountains of Pennsylvania, the winds became very strong, caught the back end of their van, and caused it to spin and turn over. They hit a guard rail. Andre was knocked unconscious.

When he woke up, he was lying in a hospital bed next to his son. A short time after he regained consciousness, a nurse came over and said, "Andre, I'm sorry to have to tell you this." She began to cry. Then she said simply, "The coroner is with your wife and daughter."

Andre told me, "It was a gut-wrenching time. I felt as though the insides of my body were being torn out. But even at that moment we can count on the Lord's Word. The Lord said in His Word, *"I will never fail you nor forsake you"* (Heb. 13:5).

"His Word was there. I'm so thankful that I was a Christian and had been for a number of years before that. So I was able to trust in that Word and to trust in my Lord at that particular time.

"I know that Christ was there with us in the midst of our most difficult moments. The Lord's strength upheld my son and me and allowed us to go on. I think the greatest thing I learned at that point is that our God is faithful."

I had to ask Andre, "But to lose your wife whom you loved and adored as well as your darling daughter—did you never doubt God's love?"

Andre's reply was wonderful. He said, "I think we all have periods when we wonder if we could have done something differently. I was no different from anyone else. But I'm thankful that God doesn't let us entertain those thoughts. Rather than entertaining those thoughts of doubt I could trust God and know that whatever He was working out, whatever plan He had set down, was a plan that was going to glorify Him. When I look back at the tragedy today I see the lives that were touched by what the Lord has done through our lives. And so I see no longer a tragedy, but a joy, as other lives are brought back out of a living death to abundant life!"

"You know, Andre," I said, "Psalm 23 says, 'Surely goodness and mercy shall follow me all the days of my life' [v. 6]. When you cannot see the goodness of God, you can experience His mercy. That's what you have experienced, Andre."

"Oh, there's no doubt about that!" he answered. "I am a child of God merely by the acceptance of His Son. As God's child, I know that He directs and guides my life. Proverbs 16:9 says, 'A man's heart chooses his way, but God directs his steps.' I chose the way of Christ as my Savior, and God directs my steps. I'm thankful for that because I don't have to wonder where I'm going."

"Where did you get this faith?" I asked.

"I grew up in a difficult time, when there was a lot of confusion in our country and a lot of questions on my mind. I saw my best friend stabbed to death at the age of seventeen. I grew up in the tremendous confusion of racial tension. The Vietnam War was at its height. People were saying God was dead. Naturally, it was a time when a young person like myself asked many questions. I was no different. I asked questions such as: 'Where are we going? What is life all about? Who's the justifier of life?'

"I can remember my mother saying to me, 'Andre, I can't answer all of those questions for you, but I can direct you to the One who can.'

"I was going away to Fort Dix, New Jersey, as part of the Pennsylvania National Guard. When I left, Mother gave me a Bible, and when I got to the barracks I began to read and study it. At that time I didn't believe there was no God; I just didn't know Him to the point where I could grab hold of Him and say, 'Father, help me!'

"After reading the Bible I realized that I was God's child, that the gap which separated me from Him had been bridged by the death and resurrection of His Son, Jesus. That joy and assurance was what I needed to see that there was a greater hope than what the world had to offer.

"So, you ask me where I got my faith? I'll tell you: I got it from my mother. I thank God that I had a mother who loved her son so much that she shared with him the most precious thing she could give him—the gift of her faith!"

Andre was not destroyed when he lost his wife and his daughter. God gave him the strength to go on with his life. Today Andre has married again and has a new baby. He carried on, he kept on going, and didn't stop living when his wife and daughter did!

(2) *Do not accept defeat.* Somehow we must learn to accept the reality of the bad things that happen to us without accepting emotional defeat. "The death thy death hath dealt to me is worse than the death thy death hath dealt to thee!" These words were spoken by a widow as she stood looking at the body of her dead husband. Do not quit! Tough times never last, but tough people do! Be brave! Fight back! Come back again. There is a world out there—hungry, hurting. Think of them—they are alive; they need you!

In the book, *Gone with the Wind,* we read about the Southern gentleman who broke down under the tragedies involved in the Civil War. Observing his collapse, another character in the novel philosophizes, "He could be licked from the inside. I mean to say that what the world could not do, his own heart could." Then the simple philosopher concluded, "There ain't anything from the outside that can lick any of us."

(3) *Bury your selfish griefs.* Grief which keeps you from thinking of and helping others is selfish. Around you is a world filled with living human beings who are hurting more than you are. There are lonely, heartbroken, dying

women . . . men . . . children out here! They need you. You
are stronger than they are. You can comfort them. The
secret of happiness that is reiterated throughout the Beatitudes can be summed up in two words: "I'm third." Are
you hurting? How do you come back alive again? Think
of God first, think of others second, and then put yourself
third.

(4) *Add up your joys; never count your sorrows.* Look
at what you have left in your life; never look at what you
have lost. At a time of sorrow you are so overwhelmed
and swamped by the shock, the pain, and the grief that
you are not even conscious of the joys that still are alive
deep under that blanket of grief. Determine to uncover
your smothered joys and let them breathe and flourish
again! There are many things that you are still thankful
for, even though you do not feel your gratitude. Begin by
reminiscing. Relive your happy memories. Treat yourself
to replays of that great collection of joyful experiences
that have occurred in your past. There are many wonderful things that have happened to you in life.

I have a friend who keeps an "Italian philosophy" poem
on his restaurant wall. The following are the words,
worth remembering:

> Count your garden by the flowers,
> Never by the leaves that fall.
> Count your days by golden hours,
> Don't remember clouds at all.
> Count your nights by stars, not shadows,
> Count your life with smiles, not tears.
> And with joy on every birthday,
> Count your age by friends, not years.

(5) *Turn your sorrow into a servant.* Once you have
buried your griefs, you are ready to turn your sorrow into
a helpful partner. Grief can be a demonic dictator if you
let it. It can turn you into a cynical, doubting, resentful,

*The good news is...*
*the bad news can be*
*turned into good news...*
*...when you change*
*your attitude!*

self-pitying recluse or drunkard. Or it can be your servant, helping you to feel more compassion for others who hurt, giving you visions for new avenues for ministry. Make the positive choice—let your sorrow become a servant that will serve God and your fellow man!

I recently received a letter from a New York viewer of my television program. I have read and re-read the letter so often that I know it almost by memory. Let me share it with you:

Dear Dr. Schuller:

I have never written a letter like this before in my life. This is the story of a bitter man . . . and the person who saved him. I am that bitter man. In 1961 I was married. I love my wife. Our love is the only thing that has kept me going. Shortly after our marriage we suffered a financial reverse. This really made me bitter.

Then we wanted children and discovered we could have none. This made me more bitter. After a while we adopted a child and for a brief time, we were very happy. Then we discovered that this adopted child, a little boy we had named Joey, was mentally retarded because of brain damage! That made me more bitter. But the bitterest day in my life was the day that Little Joey died. When we buried him, I was so bitter, I didn't believe in God, Christ, or anybody or anything.

For some months now my wife has been watching this religious television program on Sunday mornings. She begged me to watch with her, but I wouldn't. Six weeks ago, I happened to walk through the living room, when something you said caught my attention. I listened. I also listened the next week, and the next, and the next. I am writing to tell you that in six short weeks I am now a changed person. All my bitterness is gone.

I am thanking *you* because you introduced me to *Jesus Christ*. Because of this, my wife and I have decided to dedicate our lives to helping mentally retarded children. I can't tell you what a changed life I have because my thinking has changed through Christ!

I am joyfully yours, an "Hour of Power" listener.

Let your sorrow turn you into a better person and your sorrow will turn out to be a blessing!

(6) *Accept the comfort that God is trying to offer you.* At the beginning of this chapter, I said that God is not the source of sorrow. Man's sin brought sorrow and continues to bring sorrow into this world. God moves in immediately and forthrightly to bring comfort. He offers the comfort of His promises of love and eternal life.

"Blessed are those who mourn, for they shall be comforted." Yes, there's a condition attached, an "if" connected. You will be blessed, you will be comforted, *if* God is your friend, and *if* Christ is your savior. Accept this comfort that God offers to you.

### HERE'S WHAT GOD WILL DO!

God offers *real* comfort. Not neurotic pity. Not a sympathy that only weakens the hurting person. He offers a tough love that turns us into sweeter and stronger persons!

When our daughter, Carol, lost her leg in a motorcycle accident at the age of thirteen, my wife and I fell over ourselves trying to comfort her. We brought her favorite stuffed animals to the hospital, we called her friends and asked them to visit with her. We never left Carol's side; One of us was with her almost constantly.

Then one day we received a call from our friend, Dorothy DeBolt. As many of you know, Dorothy is the mother of fourteen adopted children. Those children are all very special. Some are blind, some are paraplegic. One is a quadruple amputee. All are physically or mentally challenged children.

Dorothy has done wonders with all of these children. Despite their handicaps, she has motivated them to do far more than anyone would ever have dreamed. They all dress themselves. There are no ramps in the house; they all know how to climb stairs so that they would never be barred anywhere by the absence of ramps.

When Dorothy heard about Carol's accident, she called to express her love and concern. Yes, she expressed *love*—she cared that Carol had experienced so much pain. And yes, she was *concerned.* She felt Arvella and I needed to be warned that there was a right way and a wrong way to help Carol.

She said simply, "Be careful how you comfort her."

How wise were her words. Carol needed comfort, not pity, and comfort came not by drying her tears, but by lifting her attention beyond the present pain to the future victories.

God comforts. He doesn't pity. He doesn't commiserate. He picks us up, dries our tears, soothes our fears, and lifts our thoughts beyond the hurt.

How does God comfort us so masterfully? Five ways: (1) He gives us courage; (2) He gives us a sense of calm; (3) He gives us companionship; (4) He gives us compassion; and (5) He gives us a new set of commitments.

## GOD GIVES US COURAGE

When we are in despair, God gives us the courage to go on, to live through our grief, to pick ourselves up to the point where we can face tomorrow. I'll never forget the time several years ago when I received a call from the family of Senator Hubert Humphrey, who by then was dying of cancer. His family asked me to visit them, hoping I could inspire him to go back to Washington, D.C., one more time. When I arrived at the little apartment in Minneapolis, he was waiting for me. He sat, gaunt, upright in a chair, completely dressed. His white shirt was about an inch and a half larger than his thin neck.

That was courage! It took a lot of courage to put on a shirt and tie—to put trousers on, shoes and socks, and to sit up in a chair. When you are that sick, that's a big step forward, believe it or not. Where does such courage to move ahead come from? It comes from God.

I said to this courageous man, "Hubert, when you have been really down, depressed, and discouraged, what brought you back up again?" I hoped the question would cause him to recall times when he'd been victorious over depressing circumstances.

He began to recall some Bible verses, slogans, and inspiring experiences. Suddenly, I saw a spark in his eye! So I said to him, "When are you going back to Washington?"

He looked at his wife, Muriel, and said, "Maybe I should—once more."

He did—and lived his last weeks out as he lived his life—bravely. I was honored to preach the funeral sermon only a few months later, with Billy Graham, Jesse Jackson, President Carter, and nearly every ranking Senator in the congregation. I am told nearly forty million Americans listened and watched over the television networks.

I chose for that message the topic, "Courage—The Big C." " 'The Big C'—that's what they call cancer," I said. "Hubert Humphrey knew that, but he knew a bigger 'C'—Courage!"

## GOD GIVES US A SENSE OF CALM

How does God comfort people when bad things happen to them? He gives them courage. He also gives them a sense of calm—in the most unexpected times and ways. As it is said in an old Christian hymn, "Sometimes the light surprises a Christian while he sings; it is the Lord who comes with healing on His wings."

I recall the sister of the late congressman, Clyde Doyle. She had two children, a son and a daughter. Both of them were killed when they were teenagers. Her husband also died at a fairly early age. She was completely alone. You

*Never look
at
what you
have lost*

—··—

*Look
at
what you
have left*

know, it's easy to go to someone and say, "Don't look at what you have lost, look at what you still have." But here was a woman who had no one left!

I asked, "Where did you find comfort? What gives you the strength to keep going?"

She said, "I live in Long Beach. I used to go to the beach every day. Often I just sat there numb. I could not think, I could not feel, but I could still see. And I watched the waves as they built into a curl of foam, as they washed up onto the sand and then retreated. I did that day after day, week after week, month after month, and year after year. One day, as I watched the wave curl, break, foam, and sweep across the sand, I was struck with a message from God. I heard a voice within me say, 'There is nothing but life!'"

And she said, "I knew then where my son was! I knew where my daughter was, and where my husband was!" For the first time, she was able to feel a sense of peace. And then she was able to start building her life again.

## GOD GIVES US COMPANIONSHIP

"Blessed are those who mourn, for they shall be comforted." They get courage . . . enough to make it through a funeral—or whatever they are facing. They are given a sense of calm. And they get another big "C"—companionship. In my thirty-three years as a pastor, I have heard the same comment over and over again from people who have had a devastating experience. They say, "Oh, we received so many telephone calls and letters. I heard from people I hadn't heard from in years. I was amazed at how many people care about me."

I'll never forget the funeral where no one came. The deceased man had three sons. All of them lived right there in this town. Yet none of them attended their father's funeral. Only the mortician and I were there.

I said, "What is wrong? Where is everybody?"

The mortician said, "He was a very, very selfish man. In his life he never had time for his family; little wonder they have no time for him now."

There's a condition to the promises I'm sharing with you today. The promise, "Blessed are those who mourn, for they shall be comforted" does not apply to any and all persons. Remember the question to which I'm speaking in this chapter is, "What happens to *good* people when bad things happen to them?"

When my daughter, Carol, had her accident and lost her leg, nothing meant more to her than the photo she received from John Wayne. He signed it, "Dear Carol: Be happy; you're loved."

I tell you, that one sentence made as deep an impression on me as it did on Carol. You can accept a great loss if you have somebody loving you through it. God will send you friends.

Keith Miller is a theologian, philosopher, and psychologist who, along with people like Bruce Larson, helped establish what has been called relational theology. His ministry through the years has been to interpret the teachings of Jesus Christ in a way that helps people become healthy. Over a million copies of his book, *The Taste of New Wine,* are now in print.

Keith enjoyed the success, the love, and the admiration that came to him as a result of his ministry. But then he went through the sorrow of a painful divorce. He felt like a failure and, regrettably, some Christians wrote him off, saying, "How could you be a Christian if you've had a divorce?" But then many, including people whom he'd helped, came to him and said, "How can we love you?" Through all their support he was able to feel and understand the reality of grace.

Now he has a whole new ministry to others who are hurting and are finding real power because they've given up on their own power. They're finding real love.

What happens to good people when they go through bad times? They can find companions who will love them and support them. A new love will come into their lives. They will find a sense of courage and a center of calm relief, hope, and peace that they never knew existed before.

## GOD GIVES US COMPASSION

Courage, calm, companionship . . . and compassion. Every good person who goes through bad times develops a greater sensitivity. There's a marvelous line I've quoted often: "In love's service, only broken hearts will do." Good people turn their scars into stars.

Dr. Benjy Brooks is a great woman. She has been the recipient of the Horatio Algier Award, and also has the distinction of being the first woman pediatric surgeon in the United States. She holds the position of Professor of Surgery at the University of Texas Medical School in Houston, Texas, and Special Assistant to the President in Ethics.

When Dr. Brooks was in the fifth grade, her teacher told her mother that she was mentally retarded. Benjy says today that she just marched to a different drummer. She said, "I didn't really fit into that sausage mill, to come out a little sausage like everybody else. Unfortunately, that's what our educational system does to children. At times, it takes away their creativeness and the fact that they are different."

But Benjy was determined to be a doctor. In fact, she was often found under the kitchen table "operating" on her sister's dolls with manicure scissors. And she was not about to let a teacher or an educational system stand in her way.

Then something happened that had a profound effect on Benjy and her medical practice. Her only brother, a test pilot in the Air Force, was killed at twenty-seven years of age.

And so she grieved. She says about her grief, "I don't think you get over it. You learn to live with it. And I learned to live with my brother's death. Later, in my medical practice, I saw him *at every age* as the little boys, then older boys, came through. I was able to love them and give to them instead of him."

## GOD GIVES US A NEW SET OF COMMITMENTS

How does God comfort good people when bad things happen to them? He gives them courage, companionship, and compassion. He also gives them a new set of commitments. One of the best examples of this is Art Linkletter.

I count it an honor to call Art a friend. His humor and delightful way of looking at American life has brought joy and laughter into all our lives. But when you look beyond Art's wit and optimism you see a man who has turned his cross into a commission—a commitment to reach the lives of young people who are ensnared in the deathtrap of drugs. All of this grew out of his daughter's tragic death as a result of drugs and his son's death in an automobile accident.

I asked him once, "Art, how do you turn a tragedy into a personal triumph?"

He answered me in his warm, wise, loving manner, "The most difficult thing is to admit the tragedy, to accept it. It is something in your life over which you had no control, and God's plan for us, as we all know, is more than we can fathom. It's part of the pattern of life—life and death.

"Having once admitted and accepted the deep, deep pain of the wound, then you begin to realize that you have expanded your own capability of loving and caring for others. Until you are hurt, you can never truly understand the hurts of others. Until you have failed, you cannot truly achieve success. In my own case, the pain in my life started me on a crusade against drug abuse—trying to help young people and families.

"Not everybody may be called to start a crusade as I was, but everybody can reflect love and caring. Every person's life touches some other life that needs love today."

I agree. "In love's service only broken hearts will do."

People facing tragedy suddenly take a new look at their whole life. Their whole perspective changes. Some of the things they had thought were so precious don't seem to mean much anymore. Some of the treasures they valued so highly don't seem as valuable. Their value system changes. And believe me, when your value system changes, your heart changes, your mood changes, your mind changes. Your life and your relationships change.

I remember calling on the home of a very rich woman who had suffered a great personal tragedy. This woman owned vases from China—from the Ming Dynasty—she had jewels and many other beautiful and valuable things. She greeted me and said, "Dr. Schuller, I heard you say once on television, 'Trouble never leaves you where it found you.' That is so true."

She said, "These things I own don't mean nearly as much to me now. Oh, I still love them; I'm not going to throw them away. But if there was a fire and I could save just one thing in the house, I wouldn't take that Ming vase now, as I would have before. Do you know what I'd take? I'd take the family pictures."

When tragedy hits, values change. Family becomes more important—husband, wife, parents, children. Relationships become more precious, and life itself more important than any day-to-day occupation or any material possession. When your values change, your life changes. And that's why the people that mourn are really comforted. Believe it or not, they're happy.

Be-Happy Attitude #3

# "I'm going to remain cool, calm, and corrected."

*"Blessed are the meek, for they shall inherit the earth."*
Matthew 5:5

B LESSED ARE THE MEEK, *for they shall inherit the earth.*" Doesn't that sound ridiculous? We live in a high-powered country called the United States of America. Don't we all know that it is the high-energy, powerful promoter—the big wheeler-dealer—who gets ahead?

"Blessed are the *meek*, for they shall inherit the *earth*." If Jesus had said, "Blessed are the meek, for theirs is the kingdom of heaven"—*that* we could understand. But to say that the meek shall inherit the *earth* sounds a little ridiculous to our ears, as finely tuned as they are to popular theories of success.

What was Jesus teaching when He said, "Blessed are the meek, for they shall inherit the earth"? Does this verse mean we are never to speak up and defend ourselves? Injustices do occur in our society. We live in a world where there are prejudices. How do you handle them? Does this verse mean we should allow ourselves to be doormats, letting people trample over us?

I am reminded of a story that my Catholic friend, Father Joseph Murphy, told me about some nuns who attended a baseball game. Behind the nuns sat some anti-Catholics. One anti-Catholic said very loud, for the benefit of the nuns, "Let's go to Texas; I hear there aren't many Catholics there."

His campanion replied, "Let's go to Oklahoma; there are even fewer Catholics there."

And the first one said, "Let's go to Alaska; there are almost no Catholics there."

At that point, the nun turned around and said, "Why don't you go to hell? There aren't *any* Catholics there."

"Blessed are the meek." Does this mean we must quietly accept insults and injustice with unlimited forbearance? Well, if we go back to the original Greek and examine the word that was originally translated as "meek," we see how misconception arises concerning this Bible verse.

The word *meek* is really not a good translation in terms of modern usage; it meant something different four hundred years ago in Old England, when the King James translation was done, than it does today. A better modern translation of the verse might be, "Blessed are the mighty, the emotionally stable, the educable, the kindhearted, for they shall inherit the earth." This is the person who will be successful and "inherit the earth."

"Meek"—what does it mean? The answer lies in the word itself:

- M—Mighty
- E—Emotionally stable
- E—Educable
- K—Kind

## BLESSED ARE THE MIGHTY

I can hear the protests now: "Wait a minute! Did you say, 'Blessed are the *mighty*'? How in the world can you substitute *mighty* for *meek*? You've gone too far this time, Schuller!"

Oh, but you *can* read this verse, "Blessed are the mighty." Think of it. What is real strength? What is real might? Who is the stronger—the young man who gives in to his rage and becomes physically or verbally abusive? Or the young man who remains calm, assured of his inner strength?

Who are the mighty? The powerful are mighty when they have learned to restrain their power. They know that real might lies in control and discipline, lest they rip out young plants along with weeds and tear out the tender shoots of human kindness and gentleness. They are those who remain gentle while they build strength, who are merciful while they are mighty. Blessed are they, for they shall not merely win a war; they shall win the hearts of a nation!

The weak are also mighty when they turn their problems into projects, their sorrows into servants, their difficulties into dividends, their obstacles into opportunities, their tragedies into triumphs, their stumbling blocks into stepping stones. They look upon an interruption as an interesting interlude. They harvest fruit from frustration. They convert enemies into friends! They look upon adversities as adventures.

I will never forget the 1982 New York City Marathon—not because of the winner, but because of the girl who came in last. Linda Down and her twin sister were born twenty-eight years ago with cerebral palsy. As a result of that condition, they were left with a lack of motor coordination and balance, as well as muscle spasticity. They can only walk with the assistance of special crutches. Yet Linda Down inspired me as well as all of America when she completed a marathon run—26.2 miles—on crutches!

For a disabled person to dream of running in the New York City Marathon may seem to be an unintelligent goal. But Linda's no dummy. In fact, she's a licensed social worker with a Master's degree. So I asked her,

"Whatever inspired you to try getting into a marathon?" She replied, "Well, I guess part of it was wanting to test myself and see if I could actually do it. I always thought I couldn't because I was disabled. Part of it was because I had been unemployed. I wanted to try and make some kind of a positive statement that would help people. I thought that if I could do this, then it would help people to feel that they would be able to do things in their life that they were afraid of trying, because they felt it was impossible.

"It took a whole year to prepare for the marathon, and there were times when I really thought I'd never make it. My longest training session on the street was seven hours. That gets very long after awhile—just running for seven hours. I'd think, 'I'm going to make an idiot of myself.' But I hung in there till the end and I did it! I made it! I ran the entire 26.2 miles.

"I guess I just wanted to do it very badly. And I figured that no one really expected me to get more than two feet, so however far I got would be a success for me. I didn't know at the beginning if I'd be able to make it all the way to the end but I made a promise that God could take me as far as He wanted me to go and I would keep going until I just couldn't stop. And we made it!

"It took me eleven hours and fifty-four seconds to finish the marathon. That's a record I don't think anybody's going to break for awhile!

"A number of people have approached me on the street since the marathon and have congratulated me. One woman in particular stands out in my mind. She told me she had been in a deep depression prior to seeing me run the marathon. But she said that ever since she saw me she had been unable to forget my face. And because of what I was able to do, she thought maybe she could start to come out of this depression she's been in."

Linda Down, a victim of cerebral palsy, ran an entire marathon, and she's inspired millions! She's found the secret of happiness. What is it? It's her attitude—her Be-Happy Attitude: "If I attempt the impossible in my condition, perhaps I can inspire others to be happy and successful too."

What is a Be-Happy Attitude? In part, it is being able to harness my handicap and use it to pull others out of the ditch of depression! It is this: "Blessed are the meek—blessed are those who are strong enough to turn their tragedies into triumphs!"

## BLESSED ARE THE EMOTIONALLY STABLE

Who are the emotionally stable? They are those who through discipline have developed a divine poise. They hold their negative impulses in check. They avoid and resist distractions and temptations which would excite and stimulate, but which drain their financial, moral, and physical resources.

People who *don't* control their emotions will permit themselves to fall into deep discouragement and depression. They'll quit and walk away from it all. Then they'll say later on, "I wish I could go back, but I can't. They won't have me back, because I walked away from it when it got difficult. They don't want that kind of person."

Blessed are the emotionally stable. They have their ups and downs, but they don't allow their down times to distract them from their goals. They don't quit when they hit their first snag, their first setback. They hang in there for the entire count, rather than throw in the towel after a low blow.

The meek are emotionally stable. They are those who have the strength to resist temptation, and it is only those who have this inner strength who will finally succeed. There are many, I'm afraid, who are too easily persuaded by the flashing star, the loud music, the bugle call to seek excitement. Too often, people lack restraint and get caught up in cultural fads. They waste their time chasing shooting stars.

Blessed are the honest, hardworking folks. They are more interested in substance than in style. They are more concerned about character building than about popularity rating. They are more dedicated to making solid achievements than to running after swift but synthetic happiness.

The emotionally stable stick to their objectives. They keep their eyes focused on their goals. And when they meet with problems, they patiently overcome those problems and work through their difficulties. More than one person has reached the top because he patiently endured difficult times. He might have been tempted to turn and run, or to lash out at the person who hurt him. But he didn't. More than one person has suffered through a time of stress in the company, in his marriage, with the children, and patience has paid off.

In the New Testament (Luke 18:15), Jesus tells a story to teach the people the value of patience and encourage them not to lose heart. A certain widow sought protection from her enemy. She went to the judge of her city time and again. At first the judge, who "did not fear God or respect man," turned a deaf ear to her pleas. However, she implored him over and over until he finally gave her the legal protection she needed.

The meek are patient. And the patient will inherit the earth. A modern-day example of patience and the reward it brings is a young lady whom I have grown to respect and admire. Her name is Lisa Welchel. Many of you know her as Blair, the snobby rich girl on the television series, *The Facts of Life.*

Many of you would say that Lisa has "inherited the earth." She is successful, famous, wealthy, beautiful, and talented. But most of all, she is respected and admired by her peers and her colleagues.

If you are familiar with the fictional character, Blair, you'd think, "Come on, Schuller, she may have inherited the earth, but Blair is anything but meek." True, Blair is not meek. But Lisa is. She embodies the original meaning of this Beatitude. For Lisa is "meek" in that *she knows where her strength and success comes from.*

Lisa got her start when she was seven years old. She read that auditions were being held for the Mickey Mouse Club, so she wrote and asked if she could audition. She was told that the auditions had already been held and the show had been cast. But Lisa didn't quit. She wrote lots and lots of letters. Her final letter said, "I'm a Christian, and I feel that Disney is the only place I can work right now because the context of other shows is not what I could represent. I would really appreciate a chance to audition. I would be willing to fly myself out there." Disney agreed to give Lisa a chance. They liked her and she got the part. From there, she got the part of Blair, who is really very different from Lisa.

Lisa is a charming, delightful girl who lives and works in Hollywood, which many would say is a difficult if not impossible place for a beautiful, young, single girl to retain old-fashioned values and Christian behavior. I asked Lisa about this, and here's what she said: "Well, you know, I feel that all the values the Lord has laid down for us are really for our own benefit. And if we think that we want to do something contrary to those values, well, that's fine, but we're only going to be hurting ourselves if we give in. God knows the future, and He knows why He set down certain rules. I feel that the Lord is just. Like He says, He's our Father and He's looking out for us. So long as I can remember that God's rules are only for my good and for my own happiness, and that He knows better than I do, then they are easy to adhere to."

Lisa knows the secret to happiness. And let me tell you something—a girl who keeps herself pure in private life has a warmth radiating from the eye that is just totally opposite from the hard look some people pick up. She is so bubbly, so enthusiastic. I asked her, "Lisa, where do you get your enthusiasm, your love for life?" Her answer

*Passionate persistence
without
impertinence
produces
progress!*

was psychologically and theologically sound. She said, "It's from knowing that I am loved no matter what, and that I don't have to perform and I don't have to be a good person. I don't even have to follow the Lord's laws to be loved. It's just total grace and it's all mercy. It's knowing that I'm loved just because He created me. So if I blow it, I blow it, but Jesus is still standing here with open arms. And if I do good He's standing there to commend me. When you know you're totally accepted for who you are, it's a lot easier to be yourself with others. If they accept me, that's great, but if they don't, that's okay, too, because then I'll just run home to Daddy—to Jesus, to my Heavenly Father."

"Blessed are the meek." Blessed are the emotionally stable—the patient, the persistent—for they shall inherit the earth. They shall make it. They shall see their God-given dreams come true.

There is a success principle that I call the laminated principle. It works like this: You make a promise—and deliver. You accept an assignment—and fulfill it. You attempt something "impossible"—and pull it off. Finally, year after year, maybe decade after decade, you have applied one accomplishment on top of another, one achievement over another—promises kept and commitments fulfilled. Your reputation is like a laminated beam that has durability and power. People believe in you. They take you at your word. They'll sign a contract with you because they know you're going to deliver. At that point you've "inherited the earth." Blessed are the patient people, blessed are the persistent. They shall ultimately win.

## BLESSED ARE THE EDUCABLE

If we were to examine the original Greek of the Beatitudes, we would see that when Jesus said "Blessed are the meek," He could have meant, "Blessed are the *educable* for they shall inherit the earth." Educable people—those who are teachable—don't suffer from a "know it all" attitude. They allow room in their life for growth. They listen. They're not defensive. They're not on an ego trip. Rather, they are on a success trip. If their way isn't the best, they'll switch. Blessed are the teachable, for they shall succeed.

Blessed are those who know what it is that they do not know, and who are eager to listen to others who are older, wiser, more experienced. Blessed indeed are they who, in true meekness, remember that a little learning is a dangerous thing. Blessed are those who never forget they are never too old to learn. They shall inherit great wisdom and, with it, success.

The educable are humble as well as teachable. Humility doesn't mean to put yourself down, to say, "I'm nobody. I can't do it." That's not humility. It may be an acquired, learned behavioral response imposed by a culture or a faith. It may be the projection of an inferiority complex. But real humility is not self-denigration. Real humility is the awareness that there are others who can help you. Real humility is also the capacity to say, "I was wrong; you were right."

Real humility is the ability to say, "I don't want my way if I'm wrong. I don't want my own way if it will prove to be a mistake."

Look at the alternative. How far does a cocky, know-it-all person really get? Not too far. And if he's able to somehow achieve his goals through thievery or manipulation, his ill-gotten gains will only feed his destructive attitude, and this is certain to produce unhappiness.

Jesus said it: "What shall it profit a man, if he shall gain the whole world, and lose his own soul?" (Mark 8:36, KJV).

Who are the meek? They are the people who begin by saying in true humility, "God has something for me. What is it?" Humility isn't thinking less of yourself; it is thinking more of God and of His dream for you. To be meek is to do God's work in His way, wherever you are.

I recently had the joy of speaking at Dunbar High School in Washington, D.C. This school happens to be in the inner-city of Washington. There are probably four hundred or five hundred young people in that school. I was thrilled to be there because Dunbar High School bears the name of a man who is one of my favorite poets, Paul Lawrence Dunbar. I said to these shining, eager faces, "Have you heard these lines written by that great black poet, Paul Lawrence Dunbar?"

> The Lord had a job for me,
>   But I had so much to do,
> I said, "You get somebody else,
>   Or wait til I get through."
> I don't know how the Lord came out,
>   But He seemed to get along.
> But I felt kind of sneakin' like—
>   Knowed I'd done God wrong.
>
> One day I needed the Lord—
>   Needed Him right away;
> But He never answered me at all,
>   I could hear Him say,
> Down in my accusin' heart:
>   "Brother, I'se got too much to do;
> You get somebody else,
>   Or wait til I get through."
>
> Now, when the Lord he have a job for me,
>   I never tries to shirk;
> I drops whatever I have on hand,
>   And does the good Lord's work.
> And my affairs can run along,
>   Or wait til I get through;
> Nobody else can do the work
>   That God marked out for you.

Be open. Be humble. Correctable. Educable. Then you will hear God's voice. You will see God's plan. Grab onto it, give it all you've got, and you will inherit the earth!

### BLESSED ARE THE KIND

This is the final key to understanding what Jesus meant when He said, "Blessed are the meek." Without kindness the mighty are ruthless. Without kindness the emotionally stable are emotionally cold and hard. Without kindness the educable become arrogant.

The truly meek person is mighty, emotionally stable, educable—*and* kind. Without kindness we have only M-E-E, which is significant, for without kindness we are self-centered and surely doomed to failure and unhappiness. The M-E-E attitude is an Un-Happy Attitude. The M-E-E-K attitude is a Be-Happy Attitude.

Who are the kind people? They are the *sensitive spirits*. Happy indeed is the heart which is sensitive to another's insecurity. Loving is he who offers reassurance to another's hostility, affection to another's loneliness, friendship to another's hurt, and apologies to all. Blessed are such sensitive souls, for they shall inherit the devotion and esteem of good people on this earth!

I met several of these sensitive spirits—about one hundred eighty-five of them—at a school in Long Beach, California. It is the Florence Nightingale School for the mentally retarded. Clyde Thompson, the principal at the time of my visit, and Larry Bruns, a member of the staff, were members of my congregation. They invited us to visit the school. It was an unforgettable experience.

The mentally retarded fall into three classifications. In the highest classification are the educable. They are only slightly retarded and have the mental capacity to actually earn a high-school diploma. They can go out into society and most people will never know that they are slightly retarded.

By contrast, in the lowest classification are those who are apparently incapable of any formal education—the hydrocephalic, the huge-headed children, and the microcephalic, the tiny-headed children.

In the middle category are the Down's Syndrome

*I'd rather change my mind...*
*and succeed !*
*Than have my own way...*
*and fail.*

children and many others. Many of these may learn to read or count, and almost all understand pictures.

Going through this school was a fantastic experience. While I was on my tour, at least twenty children stopped Mr. Thompson as Mrs. Schuller and I were walking with him. They would run up to him and say, "Mr. Thompson, look—I did it all by myself." Over and over we heard this same sentence. "Look, I did it all by myself."

Clyde Thompson and his staff are sensitive spirits. They have built upon the strengths in these children and helped them feel pride, self-esteem, achievement. And the students themselves are sensitive spirits. In the Florence Nightingale School they record no problems of violence, street fighting, knifing, or kicking. You do not see scribbling on the walls.

If somebody loses a pencil or a coin on the playground, the first child who finds it will run to the principal's office and say, "Here, I found this on the grass." There is no stealing.

Everyone in that school from the age of six through twenty-one years learns to do *something*—nobody fails. They are taught to be creative—to weave, to sew, to print, or to draw. When they finish school, there is a factory down the street where they are all hired and can work. I watched as some graduates of the school filled an order for a commercial firm which made garden hoses. They needed to put six washers in a little plastic bag. It was set up like an assembly line.

How do the administrators make sure that retarded children who can't count will put exactly six washers in each plastic bag? Simple! The educators have developed a little piece of wood which is about one inch high. The children are told to put enough washers on that wood to reach the top. When this happens, they empty the washers into the plastic bag. The peg holds just six washers. So they never make a miscount. They work a full day; they do not complain. They have the Be-Happy Attitude, and they are beautiful persons!

I left that school surrounded by a mental environment of love, good-will, creativity, and self-esteem: "I did it all by myself!"

"Blessed are the meek." And the meek are the kind people, the sensitive spirits. They build up those around them. They are also the *quiet* people. They do so much good for so many without fanfare, glory-seeking, or head-line-hunting. They shall inherit the trust, respect, and love of the truly beautiful people on this earth!

It's been nearly twenty-five years since I buried Rosie Gray in a simple ceremony in a cemetery in the little town of El Toro, California.

I had started my church in that town in a drive-in the-ater, for want of a better place. And on the first Sunday a California rancher lifted his paralyzed wife into his car to take her to this new "drive-in" church. Then came the day when he telephoned me and asked me to call on his wife in their home.

I will never forget Warren Gray, her husband, meeting me outside his little ranch house and saying, "Reverend Schuller, before you meet my wife I must tell you something about her. You might think she does not have her senses, but her mind is perfect, absolutely perfect. She has had a stroke, and she cannot raise her head. She cannot close her eyes and she cannot move them; they simply stare ahead. Her head just stays on her chest. She cannot walk; she cannot talk. She can cry a little and grunt a little, but that is all."

I went into the house. She sat slumped in an old over-stuffed chair, her head resting with her chin on her chest. Her eyes were open wide; they never blinked!

I knelt in front of her so my eyes could make contact with hers, and I asked her, "Rosie, do you love Jesus?" A tear formed and rolled down her cheek.

"Rosie, do you want to be baptized?"

A couple more tears rolled down and she grunted, "Uh, uh, uh."

The following Sunday Warren parked their car in the

*Blessed are those*
*whose*
*dreams*
*are shaped*
*by their*
*hopes ...*
*... not by their*
*hurts!*

front row of the drive-in. I attached a long drop cord to my microphone, walked over to her car, and, reaching through an open window, baptized her.

At that time our church was ready to move into a beautiful chapel that we had just built on two acres of land. What were we going to do now about Rosie Gray? The drive-in setting had been perfect for her needs.

The decision was made to have services at 9:30 in the new chapel. Then I would go back to the drive-in to preach to Rosie in her car. I would do that for her until she passed away. "That won't be long," we all thought. But she lived one year, two years, three years, four years, five years—she just would not die. Amazing!

Finally, God put into our minds His Dream for a most unusual church. Why not design a building where walls would open and people in their cars could join inside-the-church worshipers in prayer and praise?

So, we bought a larger piece of property and designed such a church. We had the groundbreaking ceremony on a Sunday. The local newspapers ran the story on Monday morning—the ground had been broken for what was called the world's first walk-in, drive-in church. On that same afternoon I had a funeral . . . for Rosie Gray.

Today the Crystal Cathedral where my congregation meets has walls that open to drive-in worshipers. And I shall always know that our unique church would not be the way it is had it not been for Rosie Gray! She was a quiet, meek soul, but she had a big impact on the direction of my ministry.

The kind people are the sensitive spirits. They are the quiet people, through whom God can do so much. They are also those who are *willing to be third.* Happy, indeed, are the people who are willing to put Jesus first, others second, and themselves third in line. Richly rewarded in this life are those who learn the lesson of our Lord that if any man would be master, he should learn to be a servant:

- "Whoever would be great among you must be your servant, and whoever would be first among you must be your slave" (Matt. 20:26, 27).
- "He who finds his life will lose it, and he who loses his life for my sake will find it" (Matt. 10:39).

The kind people are the sensitive spirits, they are the quiet people, and they are willing to be third. But most importantly, they are *God-shaped, Christ-molded* people.

I shall always treasure a marvelous picture that I received from Bishop Fulton Sheen when he was still alive. Inscribed on it are these words: "To my dear friend, Dr. Robert Schuller," and then this text:

> Some come in chariots,
> Some on horses,
> But we come in the name of the Lord.

Yes, blessed are those people who come not with a big splash and a lot of show, but humbly, honestly, carrying the Word of the Lord.

It begins to make sense, doesn't it?

"Blessed are the meek, for they shall inherit the earth."

Of course! Consider it by its contrast. Cursed are the cocky, the arrogant, the haughty and boastful, for they will have few friends! Unhappy are the elbowing, crowding, shoving, pushing, get-out-of-my-way, I'm-first bullies; they shall make many enemies! Headed for failure are the know-it-all Joes. Deaf to constructive criticism, careless of shrewd counsel, and indifferent to warnings, they are headed for a fall!

Doomed are the hot-heads! Unhappy are they who lose their cool and are too proud to say, "I'm sorry." They will never inherit the earth. They will not even hold their job, or perhaps their husband or wife. Hellbent on this earth are the impatient, restless, rootless, ruthless promoters. They may gain a crown and lose the kingdom! "What shall it profit a man, if he shall gain the world, and lose his own soul?"

"Blessed are the meek, for they shall inherit the earth." This Be-Happy Attitude is beginning to sound like the best advice ever offered.

Indeed, it is true. In the long pull those who win the world around them are those whom Jesus calls the "meek"—the controlled; the patient; the honest; the quiet; the forceful; the powerful-but-restrained, disciplined, poised people. The God-molded, Christ-shaped, Holy-Spirit-dominated lives are like a train that will make many a "happiness stop."

Look at the ultimate example of the truly "meek"— look at Jesus Christ:

He was controlled emotionally:
He was spat upon,
    insulted,
        stripped,
            ridiculed,
                despised.
He was led as a lamb to the slaughter.
  Yet he never struck back!

        FOOLISH?
        He inherited the earth,
        didn't He? There's not
        a land where He is
        not loved!

He demonstrated quiet determination:
  Steadfastly, He set His face to Jerusalem.
  He knew what He had to do. And He did it!

        RIDICULOUS? INSANE?
        He inherited the earth,
        didn't He? Men of every
        color and national origin
        kneel before Him!

He was gentle, kind, forgiving, loving—
even to those who killed Him.

STUPID! you say. WAS IT?
He could face God with a clear conscience
when He died!
"It is finished," He said. And today
the world loves Him!

His enemies? They are the truly dead. But Christ lives
on! Harry Kemp wrote:

I saw the Conquerors riding by
With cruel lip and faces wan:
Musing on kingdoms sacked and burned
There rode the Mongol Genghis Khan;

And Alexander, like a God,
Who sought to weld the world in one;
And Caesar with his laurel wreath;
And like a thing from hell—the Hun;

And leading, like a star the van,
Heedless of upstretched arm and groan,
Inscrutable Napoleon went
Dreaming of empire and alone. . . .

Then all perished from the earth
As fleeting shadows from a glass,
And, conquering down the centuries,
Came Christ, the Swordless, on an ass!

"Blessed are the meek, for they shall inherit the earth."
Until you understand this Beatitude, which is rooted in
being the same kind of person Jesus was, by accepting
Him as your Lord and Savior, you will never discover the
real secret of happiness. You will read this entire book

and wonder why you are still unhappy, still depressed, still searching for something more.

Are you meek?

- Are you *Mighty* enough to be controlled and disciplined?
- Are you *Emotionally Stable* enough to resist temptation?
- Are you *Educable* enough to realize you can't do it all by yourself?
- Are you *Kind* enough to be sensitive, quiet, unselfish—Christ-molded?

If you are, you will have mastered the third of the Be-Happy Attitudes. You'll come to the end of your life with pride behind you, love around you, and hope ahead of you. Who could ask for more?

Be-Happy Attitude #4

# "I really want to do the right thing!"

*"Blessed are those who hunger and thirst after righteousness, for they shall be satisfied."*
Matthew 5:6

**M**OST OF US IN AMERICA don't know what it is to be hungry or thirsty. Right?

My daughter, Sheila, recently had to have some x-rays taken. She was told that the night before she could have only clear jello, clear broth, and a few glasses of water— and nothing after midnight.

At first, Sheila didn't think it would be too difficult to comply with the instructions. When she went out to dinner with her husband the night before the x-rays were to be taken, she felt a few pangs of disappointment when she looked at her cup of broth and then at his plate brimming with delicious food. A couple of times she instinctively reached out and took a chip from the basket in the middle of the table, only to realize she couldn't have it. "At that point," she later recounted, "I felt pangs of disappointment, but not hunger—not yet."

The next morning Sheila went to the office. Her stomach was starting to growl by now. She desperately craved a Danish pastry and a hot steaming cup of coffee. She couldn't wait for her test to be over so she could have something to eat and drink again.

She tried to work. Her mind was fuzzy, and she was feeling weak. She consoled herself: "I only have to wait one more hour, then the test will be over and I can eat again."

She drove herself to the hospital for the test, bothered now by a slight headache. The test was grueling and long, and before it was over her headache had become a throbbing migraine. When they told her the test was finished and that she could go home, she felt wobbly. She was having difficulty focusing. Her depth perception was giving her problems.

So she called her husband: "Jim, quick. I need you to take me to lunch."

It was amazing what eating a good meal did for her. "My strength came back," she told me later. "My headache left. My vision cleared." She added, "Dad, I felt real hunger and thirst today for the first time! Now I understand what happens to us when we don't give our bodies the nourishment they need."

So most of us in America never know what it is like to be hungry and thirsty. Right? Wrong! Almost all of us suffer from some kind of emotional and spiritual hunger.

Mother Teresa observed during one of her early visits to America, "In India—people are dying of physical starvation. In America—people are dying of emotional starvation."

Why are so many of us constantly restless in a pursuit of "something more"? Something is missing, we vaguely but strongly suspect, even when things are going well for us.

How can we understand, analyze, interpret, or explain the emotional restlessness that relentlessly pressures us to reach further, climb higher, acquire more? The result? The clock never stands still. We fail to fully enjoy the present moment. Our emotions are projected into the activities and events of tomorrow. So busy are we in our planning the future that we never taste the pleasures of the present.

"Once I hoped that I'd be wealthy enough to own my own home," a person who must remain nameless confided to me. "When that happened, I immediately wanted something more—a vacation place. By the time I acquired that second residence I found myself traveling so much I seldom was at home to enjoy my primary residence. The more I got, the less I enjoyed everything I had."

Nothing leads to more despair and frustration than that gnawing feeling that something's missing from your life. It's like getting up in the middle of the night and going to the refrigerator. You open it, not really knowing what you want. So you nibble at this, you try that, but nothing tastes good. You finally close the door and go back to bed still hungry—unsatisfied. Many of us are similarly unfulfilled emotionally.

The trouble is that too many of us spend our lives the way I used to spend my days off. For me, Monday has always been my one day in seven for rest. When my church was smaller and my schedule was less hectic, my wife and I would spend Monday as our day away from the office and the home. On these totally free days we would ask each other, "So, what shall we do today?"

We would bounce around various ideas, but either they didn't strike our fancy, or they were too costly or too impractical. Finally, frustrated with our indecision, we often ended up getting in the car and just cruising. We had no particular destination in mind. We just set out, hoping we'd see something that looked interesting or fun. Often, however, by the time we decided what it was we wanted to do, the day was too far spent. We'd blown the whole day.

How can you be sure that you won't blow the one life you have to live? How can you satisfy your heart's deepest hungers? Where does genuine satisfaction come from?

- Does the answer lie in *fame*?
- Is *success* the answer?
- Does satisfaction come with *power*?
- Does *sexual gratification* bring real satisfaction?

Let's look at each of these and in the process maybe we will discover what it is that we are missing.

## DOES FAME SATISFY?

Jesus does not say, "Blessed are those who *seek after fame*, for they shall be satisfied."

I have a friend who is a household word in the entertainment business. He's still quite young, yet he was very famous early in life, when his television show enjoyed the highest ratings. He made a lot of money! He was in big demand. Then the ratings dropped, and as soon as they did, the network cancelled his show. He has no other career. He has no other business. He has nothing to fall back on.

This young man has been trying to find something to do, but nothing clicks. He's really going through a terribly rough time. And my friend is not unique in his experience. He is but one of many entertainers who have experienced fame only to have the public turn its back on them. Fame is fleeting. It does not satisfy!

I have another friend in the entertainment business, Hugh O'Brian, that famous actor who played the legendary lawman, Wyatt Earp, on television. Hugh was far more fortunate than my other friend. Hugh has a way of saying it that I love. He said, "I found out very early in my business that no matter who you are and no matter what business you're in, all of us go through five stages in life. Let me put it to you this way. The first stage is: *Who is Hugh O'Brian?* This is where you begin your journey— when you sow the seeds for success.

"The second is: *Get me Hugh O'Brian.* That's when you have your first taste of success.

"The third stage is: *Get me a Hugh O'Brian type.* That's when you're really successful—when you are at the top of the ladder, when they can't afford you but they want somebody *like* you.

"The fourth stage is: *Get me a young Hugh O'Brian.* We all grow old. We'll all go through the fourth stage. It all depends on how you handle it. Stay active and productive during this period. Maintain a purpose.

"The fifth stage is: *Who is Hugh O'Brian?*

"Now, no matter who we are, we all began at stage one and we're all going to wind up eventually at stage five, back where we came from. All the success and the money in the world won't buy you more tomorrows when your time has come.

"Consequently, it's what you do between stage one and stage five that makes a difference in your life. It's extremely important early on to develop projects, hobbies, and an avocation that keeps you active. That way, no matter what stage you're at—you can have a PURPOSE in life."

Hugh O'Brian's purpose—his magnificent obsession—is a program he founded called the Hugh O'Brian Youth Foundation. Its purpose is simply to seek out, recognize, and reward leadership potential in high school sophomores, and provide annual state and international leadership seminars for these future leaders. The idea for the program was inspired after Hugh spent nine days in 1958 with Dr. Albert Schweitzer in Lambarene, Africa. That profound experience deeply affected Hugh.

One of Dr. Schweitzer's statements especially struck home. Dr. Schweitzer said, "The most important thing in education is to make young people think for themselves." He also told Hugh, "Everybody has the ability to create his own Lambarene. Everybody has the ability to be a teacher of tomorrow—to teach young people about their potential and how to use it."

As a result of Dr. Schweitzer's influence, Hugh O'Brian developed his program aimed at motivating high school sophomores. The purpose of the program is to teach this age group not only how to dream, but how to bring their dreams to reality. As Hugh put it: "Most people are preoccupied in sending delinquents to camp. The great majority of our youth are positive, but we only hear about the negative minority. I figured it was time to pat the good guys and gals on the back and show them that there are rewards for being responsible members of the community.

I believe that our young people are the greatest natural resource that this country has. We have tremendous untapped leadership potential among the high school students of our great America. In this program, all we're trying to do is to give these young people an opportunity to ask their questions, to find out what the realities of life and business are all about. We want to equip them beyond teaching them ABCs. We want to help them dream.

"I love what I'm doing! I have a pretty realistic philosophy. I would like to share it with you as I have with thousands of young people who have participated in our seminars. It is called 'The Freedom to Choose':"

I do not believe that we are all created equal. Physical and emotional differences, parental guidance, varying environments, being in the right place at the right time all play a role in enhancing or limiting development. But I do believe every man or woman, if given the opportunity and encouragement to recognize his or her potential, regardless of background, has the freedom to choose in our world. Will an individual be a taker or a giver in life? Will he be satisfied merely to exist or will he seek a meaningful purpose?

I believe every person is created as the steward of his or her own destiny with great power for a specific purpose to share with others, through service, a reverence for life in a spirit of love.

*Sincere*
*self-forgetting,*
*sacrificial*
*service*
*to*
*searching and*
*suffering souls*
*satisfies*
*my self-esteem*
*more than*
*the stimulation*
*of a*
*celebrity status!*

Through his program, Hugh O'Brian and his volunteers have put their arms around more than a million young people. Hugh O'Brian is satisfied. (Well, maybe not—fortunately, he's still reaching for the sky!) But his satisfaction didn't come merely through fame. It came from having a purpose, from giving back to the country he loves, through doing something worthwhile and never counting the cost—for Hugh does not get paid for this work; he is the ultimate volunteer.*

## DOES SUCCESS SATISFY?

Fame doesn't satisfy. Neither does success. Tom Landry, the super-successful coach of the Dallas Cowboys, is successful. But more than that, he is *satisfied*. Surprisingly, he shared with me that his satisfaction doesn't come merely from winning football games, although he does feel it's important to try with all our might to be all that we can be.

In fact, Tom said that there is a slogan he keeps prominently displayed in the Cowboys' locker room: "The quality of a person's life is in direct proportion to his commitment to excellence." Tom went on to say, "I believe that very strongly. I believe that God gave us all talent to do whatever we want to do and He expects us to do the best we can. When you try to be the best you can, then success and winning take care of themselves.

"Confidence comes from knowledge. If you know your job well, then you'll have the confidence to do it well when you get out on the field. You've got to anticipate the positive element all the time, because once you start thinking about the negative possibilities—that you may miss the Super Bowl, or you may lose, you may be fired next week—such negative thinking drastically reduces

_____

* For information about the Hugh O'Brian Youth Foundation, write to: 10880 Wilshire Blvd., Room 1500, Los Angeles, CA 90024.

your chances of achieving your best. And so we try to think positively."

Tom Landry is a success. He says that anybody can be a winner if he wants it bad enough, strives for it hard enough, actively seeks it out by learning all he can and working with all his strength. Of course, positive anticipation, feeding on good, clear, positive attitudes is essential.

If we hunger and thirst after positive attitudes, hard work, knowledge, and excellence, the odds of our winning rise astronomically.

But that's not what this Beatitude says, is it? It's not, "Blessed are those who hunger and thirst after righteousness, for they shall be winners."

No, the Beatitude says, "Blessed are those who hunger and thirst for righteousness, for they shall be *satisified*."

My conversation with Tom Landry didn't end with talk about winning. He went on to explain how he had found real satisfaction.

"I wanted to be a good football coach, so my whole life was absorbed in that. As I went up the ladder all the way to becoming a professional football player and winning world championships with the New York Giants (that's where I was before I joined the Cowboys), I discovered that after the excitement of winning or being successful, there was always an emptiness and a restlessness that stayed with me afterwards.

"I didn't understand that. I thought that somewhere along the way you ought to win a victory that would sustain you for the rest of your life. But I never discovered that kind of satisfaction until one time a friend asked me to attend a Bible study that met at a hotel in Dallas on Wednesday morning. I thought he was crazy because I knew the Christmas story and the Easter story and I'd been to church every Sunday. But he was a good friend, so I went. I remember it so well. We were reading in the Sermon on the Mount in Matthew, where Jesus said, 'Do not be anxious about your life, what you shall eat or what you shall drink, nor about your body, what you shall put on. Is not life more than food, and the body more than clothing? . . . Seek first God's kingdom and His righteousness, and all these things shall be yours as well' (Matt. 6:25, 33).

"Well, that was my first real discovery of the Bible! It was the first time I'd ever studied it. I went on to learn what the gospel of Jesus Christ is all about. As a result I accepted Christ—one year before I took over the Dallas Cowboys. I learned what St. Augustine meant when he said, 'Our hearts are restless, O God, until they find their rest in thee.'

"I found that the emptiness and the restlessness left me. I really realized two things, Dr. Schuller. I realized that you can go to church all your life and not be a Christian. I had never known that. I think the other thing I discovered was that life is a matter of priorities. Up until that point, football was my first priority in life; my family and God took a back seat. But once I accepted Christ as my Lord and Savior, I discovered that God was first in my life. That made all the difference in the world and it's been that way in my life ever since."

## DOES POWER SATISFY?

Jesus didn't say, "Blessed are those who seek after fame," or "after success," or even "after power."

Chuck Colson, who was once one of the most powerful men in our country and then was imprisoned as a result of the Watergate scandal, is a living example of this: You cannot find happiness through power.

Chuck was not happy when he commanded great power influence. Instead, his power led to ruin and even imprisonment. But then Chuck Colson found Jesus and was born again. Today he has an active ministry going on in over three hundred sixty-five prisons in the United States and in twenty-one countries of the world. He has thirty thousand volunteers active in the United States, and some fifty-eight thousand inmates have graduated from his evangelistic and discipleship training programs inside the prisons. He says, "It is the greatest thrill in the world to be part of a movement of God's people raised up to bring the Good News that Jesus Christ can change lives in those dark dungeons we call prisons in America.

"I've been so close to those in the highest office in the world," he continues. "I've been in palaces; I've preached in great cathedrals around the globe but the greatest joy and fulfillment I've had is to be in prison on a grimy concrete floor with a burly convict who, in a flood of tears, gives his life to Jesus."

### DOES SEXUAL GRATIFICATION SATISFY?

How do you really satisfy that inner emotional hunger? Jesus didn't say, "Blessed are those who seek fame, success, or power." Likewise, Jesus didn't say, "Blessed are those who seek sexual gratification."

I disagree with Freud, who contended that the heart's deepest passion or need is pleasure. Man's ultimate need is for a healthy sense of self-esteem, self-worth, a sense of sanctified, Holy-Spirit-induced pride. It's the glorious feeling that Adam and Eve had before they fell into sin.

I once asked Dr. Joyce Brothers, the well-known psychologist, "Joyce, what are some of the most basic, deepest psychological needs that you see in human beings today?"

She replied, "I think that human beings need *love*. It doesn't have to be the love between a man and woman. It can be love of mankind. It can be love of God. William James said it so many years ago: 'The most important thing in life is to *live your life for something more important than your life*.' That's what happy people do.

"You know, we live in an age of miracle drugs," Dr. Brothers continued, "But the miracle that still does the most to lengthen life, to make it happy, is the oldest miracle we know. It is the miracle of love. And from a psychologist's point of view, I see that people who are good are happy. People who are happy are people who are good.

"Human beings are capable of so much. Again, psychologists have found that people use only ten percent of their ability. But there are some people who will not stop at that ten percent. They push the limits, to find out what they are capable of doing. Those are the happy people."

In my opinion, Dr. Joyce Brothers has a much better handle on man's needs than Freud did. What Dr. Brothers said to me reflected what I have always believed to be man's deepest need—love and a sense of self-esteem—not passion, not sexual gratification, not fame, and not power.

## THE SECRET OF SATISFACTION

Satisfaction, happiness, fulfillment—all are as elusive and fleeting as shadows, when we search for them through fame, success, power, or sexual gratification.

How then can we find satisfaction? Jesus said, "Blessed are those who hunger and thirst for *righteousness,* for they shall be *satisfied.*" In this powerful sentence, Jesus shows us how we can satisfy the heart's deepest hunger, its deepest longing.

Jesus says the way to satisfaction and happiness lies in seeking righteousness.

Question: What is righteousness?

Righteousness is not merely avoiding temptation successfully. It goes beyond that. Allow me to quote from my book, *Self-Esteem: The New Reformation:**

> We all know people who do not lie, kill, steal, commit adultery, yet they live a life of ease, comfort, and noninvolvement. They appear to be kind and gentle, and we are tempted to judge them to be "loving people." But real love is sacrificial commitment. Until these "good people" set God-glorifying goals, they are making no potentially creative and constructive commitments. If they take no dar-

---

* Waco, Texas: Word Books, 1982.

ing risk in mission, they're good—but good for what? (p. 112).

Righteousness is not absolute holiness or perfection, either. I don't believe Jesus is saying that a person who has an incurable compulsion to holy living will really be satisfied. If we had to live perfect, holy lives in order to be satisfied, we would be the most miserable of human beings, because we all make too many mistakes. We all commit sins. None of us is going to be perfect.

It is true that when we do make mistakes, when we do sin, we can ask for God's forgiveness. Is this the path to righteousness? Yes—if we understand the real meaning of true repentance. Allow me to quote again from my book, *Self-Esteem: The New Reformation:*

> Real repentance is a positive, dynamic and highly-motivated redirection of life . . . to a caring, risky trust which promises the hope of glory . . . through noble, human-need-filling achievements. . . . If the slate is washed clean of guilt, I am only half forgiven. I am not fully forgiven until I allow God to write his new dream for my life on the blackboard of my mind (pp. 103–104).

Negative repentance is an Un-Happy Attitude; it will drain you of your enthusiasm. It says, "I am nothing. I am worthless. I am bad." Righteousness will not evolve from such negativity.

Positive repentance, on the other hand, says:

- "I'm sorry I didn't believe in God's dreams. From now on I will."
- "I'm sorry for not loving myself as much as the Lord did when He died on the cross for me. From now on I'll remember God loves me—and I will try to love me, too."
- "I'm sorry I was so selfish that I surrendered to the fear of failure; I didn't want people to laugh at me. From now on I'll attempt to do something great for God."

• "I now commit myself to righteousness! I will do the right thing. I will respond to the dreams God gives me—even if they seem impossible."

Righteousness comes through *real* repentance. And repentance is a twofold process: (1) It is saying *"No"* to the negatives, the temptations to do and be less than our best. (2) It is saying *"Yes"* to the positives—the good, the healthy. It is saying *"Yes"* to God's dream for you and me.

## SAY *"NO!"* BY SAYING *"YES!"*

In order to be satisfied we need healthy nourishment. We need to be selective in what we feed our minds and our souls with. It's not easy in today's world when we're surrounded by "junk food" thoughts. By that I mean the negative attitudes, negative reactions, and negative responses that bombard us every day. We need to insulate ourselves against these negatives and diligently seek the positive, the good—righteous thoughts, righteous dreams, and righteous actions.

In such a negative-thinking world, we are constantly surrounded by negative vibrations. The most positive person you meet still has his negative attitudes. No person is one-hundred-percent positive. We are emotionally conditioned to negativity by the world in which we live. How do we break these hypnotizing, negative chains? How do we liberate ourselves from the imprisonment of negative thinking? How do we say "No" to the negatives, the temptations that will rob us of our happiness?

Say "No!" by saying "Yes!" Eliminate the negatives by sowing positives:

• A perfect farm, a profitable farm, a righteous farm is not a farm where there are no weeds growing. Rather, it is the farm that's planted with crops such as corn or pineapple and is bearing fruit.

- A perfect sheet of paper isn't a sheet of paper that has no mark on it, without scratch or flaw. No. The perfect paper is one that is filled with notes, thoughts, concepts, and ideas—a poem, an outline, or numbers that put together some creative possibility.
- A perfect communication between two people isn't the type of relationship in which there are no fights, no arguments, no cross words. Perfect communication is when both persons are able to open up and actually tell each other how they feel with respect and mutual esteem. Not silence, but creative, constructive, respectful conversation is righteousness in communication.

So, we cannot claim that we are striving after righteousness by making a list of "don'ts" and trying to abide with them. Hungering and thirsting after righteousness must mean more than that! It must mean desiring to live the positive kind of life that will bear fruit and do something beautiful for God.

The psalmist says that the *righteous* man shall be "like a tree planted by streams of water, that *yields its fruit in its season,* and its leaf does not wither. In all that he does, he prospers."

Many of you may have seen the wonderful movie, *The Karate Kid.* Remember the tough blond kid who fought against the hero in the climax of the movie?

Imagine my amazement when I learned that Billy Zabka, the young actor who played this terribly mean kid, was a Christian, and a very fine young man.

I met him and asked him, "Billy, how could you be so mean in *The Karate Kid?*"

"That was just acting," he explained. "I am a Christian first and an actor second. In fact, my career as an actor wasn't really going anywhere. I began to think that maybe God didn't want me to be an actor at all. He's called me so close to Him that I thought maybe He wanted me to go into youth ministries. I love kids and I

*Righteousness?*
*It is:*
*positive,*
*Faith-Producing*
*people*
*who are actively*
*pursuing*
*a God-given*
*dream!*

love camping. I'd rather be in the mountains than in a limousine!

"But on a summer camping trip with my church fellowship group, I shared with my friends that I wanted to be in a movie. I explained that it wasn't for me; it was for God. But I wasn't sure if that was what God really wanted.

"When I returned home, I found I was up for the role in *The Karate Kid*. I pulled up in front of Columbia Studios. Usually before these interviews I pray, 'God, I don't want to do this if there's going to be any sin. I don't want to do this if there's going to be any corruption on the set.'

"But this time, I prayed, 'Lord, I want to minister your Word and reach out to people and say you love them.'

"It was neat how when I gave up my dreams and said, 'I don't care about *my* dreams; I only care about *Your* dreams'—that's when He gave me the opportunity!

"The movie is successful and I don't go around trying to advertise Billy Zabka. I go around trying to show the love of God. Not preaching to them. Not telling them they're damned in hell. But just by being a Christian, just loving God."

Yes, Billy is a "righteous" man. I mean that in this sense of the word: He has said "No" to the temptations that would drag him down, including the temptation to shut himself off from those whose lifestyles were offensive to him. When Billy said "Yes," he would live for Jesus, including being a witness to others on the movie set, then he was able to bear fruit; he has the opportunity to be a light to millions who know him from his movie career.

Righteousness comes through positive affirmations:

- "I'm a child of God!"
- "I'm God's idea, and God only has good ideas!"
- "I *want* to do it! I *can* do it! I *will* do it!"
- "I'm going to take chances!"

When you say "Yes!" you will be living and trusting in
God's promises. When you attempt the impossible you
will discover that you will be filled with excitement! Enthusiasm! Energy! Youth! Happiness!

Righteousness is attempting to accomplish some beautiful possibility. Win or lose—the attempt will build your
self-esteem. Succeed or fail—you can be sure of this—you
will be able to live with yourself and not be ashamed,
which means you can be proud that you tried.

That's the joy! That's the deep satisfaction! That is the
great reward!

A dear friend of mine is Bill Dearden, chairman of the
board of Hershey Foods Corporation. Bill was just a
young boy back in the 1930s—an orphan. But he was fortunate to go to an orphan school started by Milton Hershey, the founder of the company.

Mr. Hershey had no children of his own, and he had
had a terrible time growing up himself. He only had a
fourth-grade education. He failed three times in business
ventures, but he had the courage to keep on trying. The
fourth time he started in business—a caramel company—
he was very successful.

He sold his caramel business for a million dollars and
started the chocolate company. Knowing that his wife
could never have any children, he decided to start an orphan school.

It was at this school that Bill Dearden received most of
his education. He went on to work in the company and
eventually became the chairman of the board. He tells me
that Mr. Hershey set the company up so that 51% is
owned by the school. So a lot of the money the company
makes goes back into the school.

I asked Bill, "How did you make it from being a little
orphan boy in the streets of Philadelphia to being the top
corporate chief and chairman of the board of one of
America's most respected corporations?"

He replied, "God has always had an important spot in
my life. I believe that through His love and direction all

things are possible. I think He helped me along the way—guided me, and directed me—and I think He will do that for everyone if they are willing to believe in Him."

Mr. Hershey had a burning desire to do something good with his life. So did Bill Dearden. And so the positive chain of real righteousness goes on.

If you live in Minnesota, you probably know who Joe Sensor is. For those of you who don't live in Minnesota, Joe plays tight end for the Minnesota Vikings football team. Joe is also a graduate of the Hershey School. He has recently become my friend, and I had the joy of baptizing his beautiful baby in the Crystal Cathedral.

Joe, whose father had died when he was very young, was offered an opportunity to go the Hershey School. He accepted the offer and found tremendous love and support there. Later, he was drafted by the Vikings and has had tremendous success in football. As a result of his success, he has been called to do about fifteen hundred speaking engagements in that last six years.

Joe Sensor has geared himself and dedicated himself to help as many children and young people as he can. As he once told me, "Professional athletes have the greatest opportunity because kids look up so much to professional athletes. The mother and father can tell them not to do drugs, and their words won't have much effect. But if a professional athlete tells them not to do drugs, they cling to that advice; it gets through to them. I am a servant of other people. I think that this is the most important thing that I can do with my life."

Bill Dearden, Joe Sensor. Who knows how many other young people in the last two generations have been changed because Milton Hershey hungered and thirsted to do something good with his life?

This is righteousness! This is how to find happiness!

But if righteousness is so great, why isn't everybody pursuing it? What holds people back? Why do people say "No" to the good things? Why do they say "No" to God?

There are three possible reasons:

(1) First, people say "No" to God because *they do not know any better.* There are still a lot of people who are hung up on the idea that if you really get religion, really get converted, really get saved and become a Christian, you may go off the deep end and become a little nutty or kooky or freaky. There are others who have been turned off by contact with religious hypocrites or fanatics or—worse—by joyless, negative Christians. So these people steer away from religion, never realizing what a happy life they can have when they commit their whole lives to Him.

Dwight Moody used to say, "People have just enough religion to make themselves miserable; they cannot be happy at a wild party and they are uncomfortable at a prayer meeting."

How true it is! Many people have just enough religion to be miserable, but not enough to enjoy it. And so often this is because they have no idea what Christian life is really like. Frankly, I do not blame those whose only impression of God is the negative witness some Christians give. No wonder they turn Him off! They just do not know any better.

(2) There is a second reason why some people say "No" to God: *They do not think they can say "Yes" to Him.* Lack of self-esteem holds them back. Their thinking is: "God is perfect and I surely know I am not; therefore, I do not think I should join up with Him." What these people don't realize is that God does not call us to be perfect; He just calls us to be willing! He doesn't expect us to be sinless, although He does expect us to say, "Lord, I am willing to try." It is far better to do something constructive imperfectly than to do nothing perfectly!

(3) The third reason some people say "No" to God is *they think they are not quite ready.* They have projects that they have not started, projects that are half finished, telephone calls to make, unanswered letters to write. When they get their desks cleared and have a chance to

think, probably then they will turn to God. But right now they are just too busy.

The trouble is, there may not be a "later on." Do it now! Do not let God wait. If you feel a positive, inspiring thought go through your mind today, there is only one way to answer it: "Yes, Lord."

Say it now. It is not going to hurt you. Right now, lay this book on your lap and say the words, "Yes, Lord." Repeat them out loud until they sound natural. "Yes, Lord! Yes, Lord! Yes, Lord!"

Do not be afraid of seeming overly dramatic or of being overly emotional; do not let any negative fear hold you back. Say it strongly, positively: "Yes, Lord." I predict that within an hour a positive thought will come into your mind. A positive mood will begin to creep over you. When that happens, do not say, "No." Say again, "Yes, Lord."

Perhaps you will receive an invitation to turn your life over to Christ. If you have never yet made a commitment of your life to Jesus Christ, accepting Him as your Savior and your Lord, your personal, living friend, I invite you to do so! If you have not committed your life to Christ, take this positive step today. Doing so will turn you into a better person, not a worse person.

"Blessed are those who hunger and thirst for righteousness, for they shall be satisfied."

Are you satisfied? Are you happy? Is life all that you hoped it would be? It can be—it *will* be—if you will say "Yes" to the dream that God has given you.

- Go for it! You might make it!
- Go for it! It might happen!
- Go for it! Somebody might be helped by it!
- Go for it! You might rise from poverty to prosperity!
- Go for it! If you prosper, you might be able to help the poor!
- Go for it! Someday, somebody will come to you and say, "Thank you!"

That's satisfaction. It comes when you know you are worthwhile, that you are a valuable person, that you have made a contribution, a difference.

Hunger and thirst mean "Go for it!"

"They shall be satisfied" means that they can have the assurance that they have helped someone, they have made a difference, their lives have counted for something—something GREAT!

Be-Happy Attitude #5

# "I'm going to treat others the way I want others to treat me."

*"Blessed are the merciful, for they
shall obtain mercy."*
Matthew 5:7

IN THIS BE-HAPPY ATTITUDE is a sure prescription for happiness. Learn to live by this refreshing happy attitude: "It's not what happens to me that matters most; it's how I react to what happens to me."

Be sure of this: If you have the attitude that you should forever be spared from all pain, hurt, and grief, you can be positive that someday you will be jolted with a depressing disillusionment. Sorrow, rejection, bereavement hit all of us at some point in our lives. To expect that somehow we are privileged persons and should be immune from hurt and hardship is unrealistic.

Some even feel, "Because I am a Christian, I should experience no pain and suffering. Because I'm a God-fearing person and a good person, I should experience no rejection or ridicule." If this is our attitude, we will react to adversity with self-pity. "It's not fair!" will be our immediate negative reaction. But the quicker we learn that life is *not* always fair, the sooner we can achieve emotional maturity.

We all have our share of suffering. And we all have two choices when we face a terrible experience. We can choose the Be-Happy Attitude, or we can choose the Un-Happy Attitude.

The Un-Happy Attitude is the way of anger and vengeance: "Revenge!" "I'll get even!" This negative attitude is a sure prescription for misery and unhappiness. People who are obsessed with fighting battles cannot be filled with joy. Their only satisfaction is having the bitter taste of frustration released through their spiteful, vengeful behavior.

Probably more times than we'll ever know, the unhappiness of those who choose the Un-Happy Attitude is multiplied through the breakdown of their physical health—high blood pressure, heart trouble, strokes, even cancer—produced by stress. This is the result of their choice of an Un-Happy Attitude toward unfortunate circumstances.

But there is an alternative attitude we can choose as we move through life. The positive attitude that will prove to be a Be-Happy Attitude is an option that is open to every person. It is the way of mercy and forgiveness—choosing to react positively and hopefully to whatever negative experiences that may befall us.

The good news I have for you is: God promises mercy adequate enough to meet any tragedy.

Jesus promised in the fifth Beatitude: "Blessed are the merciful, for they shall obtain mercy." This Beatitude holds three things—first, a *promise;* second, a *power principle* that has universal application; and third, a *prescription* for happy living.

### THE PROMISE

Many people in my congregation would testify to the truth of God's promise in this Beatitude. Their testimony is that when an unexpected tragedy hits, they have found the capacity to find happiness anyway. Now, that's not human nature. The natural tendency would be to get angry, bitter, and cynical—to say, "There is no God." When a person reacts positively to tragedy—that's a miracle. Psalm 23 concludes with the glorious line: "Surely goodness and mercy shall follow me all the days of my life." That's God's way of saying that life will often be filled with goodness, but that even when God's goodness cannot be seen, His mercy can be experienced! In the midst of tears, heartbreak, enormous loss, and terrible sorrow, suddenly a sweet mood, like a gentle kiss, will touch your wounded heart. That experience is called mercy. It comes as an expression of God's love.

Throughout the Scriptures God promises that He will be merciful to us:

- "His *mercy* is on those who fear [trust] him" (Luke 1:50).
- "God, who is rich in *mercy*, out of the great love with which he loved us . . . made us alive together with Christ" (Eph. 2:46).
- "He saved us, not because of deeds done by us in righteousness, but in virtue of his own *mercy*" (Titus 3:5).

The promise is there! It is for *you!* What wonderful news! What wonderful assurance! No matter where our road will lead, no matter what pain may hit, no matter what we do, God will be there with His mercy to forgive us, to hold us up, and carry us through the tough times. But this is only half of the Beatitude: ". . . for they shall obtain mercy." The other half is, "Blessed are the merciful . . ."

The question is: Which comes first? Do we need to be merciful before God will be merciful to us? Or does God need to be merciful to us before we can be merciful to others? What did Jesus mean when He said, "Blessed are the merciful, for they shall obtain mercy"?

*When God's goodness
cannot be seen...
...His mercy
can be experienced!*

I believe Jesus meant:

- God will be merciful to us.
- Then we will be merciful to others.
- Mercy will then come from a variety of sources.

The first step, then, is to accept God's mercy. All we need to do is *accept* the promise of the Beatitude. It is God's promise that if we treat people mercifully, God will be merciful to us.

I first heard the following story thirty-five years ago. Years later, a variation appeared and was made famous by my friend, Tony Orlando, in his song, "Tie a Yellow Ribbon 'Round the Old Oak Tree." I have been told it's a true story, and I believe it, because I believe in the power of mercy.

Three teenagers boarded a bus in New Jersey. Seated on the bus was a quiet, poorly dressed man who sat alone and silent. When the bus made its first stop, everybody got off except this one man, who remained aloof and alone. When the kids came back on the bus, one of them said something nice to him and he smiled shyly.

At the next bus stop, as everybody got off, the last teenager turned and said to the man, "Come on. Get off with us. At least stretch your legs."

So he got off. The teenagers invited him to have lunch with them. One of the young people said, "We are going to Florida for a weekend in the sun. It is nice in Florida, they say."

He said, "Yes, it is."

"Have you been there?"

"Oh, yes," he said, "I used to live there."

One said, "Well, do you still have a home and family?"

He hesitated. "I—I don't know," he said, finally.

"What do you mean, you don't know?" the teenager persisted.

Caught up by their warmth and their sincerity, he shared this story with them:

"Many years ago, I was sentenced to Federal prison. I had a beautiful wife and wonderful children. I said to her, 'Honey, don't write to me. I won't write to you. The kids should not know that their dad is in prison. If you want to, go ahead and find another man—somebody who will be a good father to those boys.'

"I don't know if she kept her part of the bargain. I kept mine. Last week when I knew for sure I was getting out, I wrote a letter to our old address; it's just outside of Jacksonville. I said to her, 'If you are still living there and get this letter, if you haven't found anyone else, and if there is a chance of you taking me back—here is how you can let me know. I will be on the bus as it comes through town. I want you to take a piece of white cloth and hang it in the old oak tree right outside of town."

When they got back on the bus and they were about ten miles from Jacksonville, all the teenagers moved to this man's side of the bus and pressed their faces against the windows. Just as they came to the outskirts of Jacksonville there was the big oak tree. The teenagers let out a yell and they jumped out of their seats. They hugged each other and danced in the center of the aisle. All they said was, "Look at it! Look at it!"

Not a single white cloth was tied to the tree. Instead, there was a white bedsheet, a white dress, a little boy's white trousers, and white pillow cases! The whole tree was covered with dozens of pieces of white cloth!

That is the way God treats you and me. It is a promise from God that He will forget the past and erase the record we have rolled up. It is a promise that He will throw away the black pages of our book and give us the kind of big welcome that the Prodigal Son received from his father, who said, "My son that was lost is found and is home again" (Luke 15:24, my paraphrase). This is the *promise* of this Beatitude.

## THE POWER PRINCIPLE

The Bible carries a promise—that God will be merciful to us. It also teaches a power principle which appears over and over in the Bible, stated different ways:

- "If you do not forgive men their trespasses, neither will your Father forgive your trespasses" (Matt. 6:15).
- "The measure you give will be the measure you get" (Matt. 7:2).
- "Cast your bread upon the waters, for you will find it after many days" (Eccles. 11:1).
- "Whatever a man sows, that will he also reap" (Gal. 6:7).

Give a little, you get a little back. Give a lot, you get a lot back. This is the *law of proportionate return* that Jesus is teaching in these verses—and this Beatitude. If you are critical, you can expect people to criticize you. If you gossip about people, you can be sure these same people are going to gossip about you. It is a law of life as real and unavoidable as the physical laws that control our world and our bodies.

Once, when I had laryngitis, I went to my throat doctor. The first thing he did was to get some gauze, wrap it around my tongue, pull my tongue out as far as he could, and stick a flat instrument far back in my throat. Inevitably, I gagged. He did it again. I gagged.

I said, "Done?"

To my dismay he said, "No, I have to do it again. I didn't get to see the vocal cords." Once more he prepared my tongue with another clean piece of gauze.

I said, "This time I'll practice positive thinking and I won't gag."

He said, "Dr. Schuller, that won't work."

"Won't work?" I was appalled! That was the first time

anybody had told me that possibility thinking wouldn't work.

The doctor quickly added, "Dr. Schuller, the gag is a reflex. Here, let me show you. Cross your legs." I crossed my legs. He hit my knee. My leg kicked up.

He said, "That's a reflex. The gag is also a reflex. Positive thinking cannot control reflexes, because reflexes come from the spinal cord. They don't pass through the brain."

Let me tell you something. In life there is a principle that you can compare with this biological reflex. If you act a certain way, you will get a certain response; there will be a guaranteed reflex action.

Here is a fundamental rule of life: If you want people to treat you nicely, treat them nicely. For every action, there is a reaction. For every positive action, there is a positive reaction. For every negative action, there is a negative reaction.

If you really want to get high on happiness, look at this Beatitude, and then live it. It really works. *It's impossible to give anything away. Whatever you give away will always come back to you.*

Let me illustrate with a simple object—a seed. It's impossible to throw away seeds. If you throw them on the ground, they sprout and grow.

As many of you know, I was born on an Iowa farm. Adjoining my family's farm was a river, which thrilled me because I loved to fish. I remember one time when a city kid came for a few weeks to visit the neighbors across the road. The city kid was our neighbor's nephew. His uncle had welcomed him but warned that he would have to help out with the work.

One day the city kid's Uncle John gave his nephew a can of beans to plant. He explained, "Just dig a little hole, put in a couple of beans, and stomp the dirt down on top of them. Do it all the way along the fence until you get to the end."

Unaware of the task that had been assigned to this city lad, I invited him to join me fishing. He replied, "Uncle John said I have to plant these beans. He said that I have to dig a little hole, put in three beans, and stomp it down."

I said, "Oh, that's too bad; I wish you could go fishing with me. Ever been fishing?"

"No, I'd like to go fishing with you, but I've got to finish these beans." From the looks of the full can, it appeared that he'd just started. Directly in from of him was a stump. Suddenly he had an idea! "Uncle John will never know," he said, as he dug a hole, dumped in all the beans, and covered them with dirt. He turned away from his task and said, "Let's go fishing!"

We had a grand time, and we caught a good number of fish. Coming home with all our catch, we ran into Uncle John.

He said "I see you've been fishin' . . . . did you get all the beans planted?"

His nephew said, "Sure did, Uncle John."

"That's great. Glad to hear it. And you still had time to fish?"

"M-m-m-, yeah."

"I'm surprised you were able to plant them so quickly."

He answered, "I work fast."

Uncle John seemed to accept his word for it. Soon it was time for the boy to return home. Months passed. The summer was drawing to a close. The city kid returned for a last visit before school started.

Uncle John said to him, "Hey, would you like to see those beans you planted?" They walked out behind the farmhouse. There was a neat row of beans for about fifty feet. Suddenly there was a stump of a tree covered with uncontrolled vines!

You can't fool nature, and you can't play with God. You can't tamper with natural laws. And this is a natural law: *If you treat people nicely, you will probably be treated nicely. The kinder you are to others, the more kindness you are likely to receive in life.* It is the law of proportionate return, and there's no way of getting around it.


## THE PRESCRIPTION

The *prescription* for joyful living is very simple: If you want to be happy, treat people right. If you carry somebody else's burdens, in the process you'll discover the secret of happiness.

Everybody wants to be happy. I've observed in the world today that there are those who are trying to reach happiness with selfishness, yet these people end up in a hell on earth. There are others who try to obtain joy by following the laws of Christ, by helping somebody else. If you live by the laws of Christ and choose to look for people who have burdens, you might be able to help them. But if you look for your own happiness, ignoring the needs of those around you, you will lose out altogether.

There is a story of a man who had a dream one night. He dreamed that he died and found himself immediately in a large room. In the room there was a huge banquet table filled with all sorts of delicious food. Around the banquet table were people seated on chairs, obviously hungry. But the chairs were five feet from the edge of the table and the people apparently could not get out of the chairs. Furthermore, their arms were not long enough to reach the food on the table.

In the dream there was one single large spoon, five feet long. Everyone was fighting, quarreling, pushing each other, trying to grab hold of that spoon. Finally, in an awful scene, one strong bully got hold of the spoon. He reached out, picked up some food, and turned it to feed himself, only to find that the spoon was so long that as he held it out he could not touch his mouth. The food fell off.

*God's care
will carry
you
so
you can carry
others!*

Immediately, someone else grabbed the spoon. Again, the person reached far enough to pick up the food, but he could not feed himself. The handle was too long.

In the dream, the man who was observing it all said to his guide, "This is hell—to have food and not be able to eat it."

The guide replied, "Where do you think you are? This is hell. But this is not your place. Come with me."

And they went into another room. In this room there was also a long table filled with food, exactly as in the other room. Everyone was seated in chairs, and for some reason they, too, seemed unable to get out of their chairs.

Like the others, they were unable to reach the food on the table. Yet they had a satisfied, pleasant look on their faces. Only then did the visitor see the reason why. Exactly as before, there was only one spoon. It, too, had a handle five feet long. Yet no one was fighting for it. In fact, one man, who held the handle, reached out, picked up the food, and put it into the mouth of someone else, who ate it and was satisfied.

That person then took the spoon by the handle, reached for the food from the table, and put it back to the mouth of the man who had just given him something to eat. And the guide said, "This is heaven."

"Blessed are the merciful, for they shall obtain mercy."

Another Bible verse says it in another way, "Bear one another's burdens, and so fulfil the law of Christ" (Gal. 6:2).

It is impossible to have thoughts of resentment and jealousy, anger and hate and ill-will—and be happy. You cannot sow these negative emotional seeds and expect to raise a harvest of smiles and laughter. Nobody can be happy and bitter at the same time. It is so incredibly simple.

The secret to the prescription then is to care. Caring becomes carrying.

I am sure you have heard of Mother Teresa of Calcutta.

She's been listed frequently in *Good Housekeeping* magazine's most-admired-women list. She is one of the most beautiful persons alive in the world today.

You probably know that Mother Teresa is about sixty years old and that she is an amazing person. But let me tell you more about her. Mother Teresa was the child of a peasant family in Yugoslavia. She was taken regularly to church, where she met Jesus Christ. As a teenager she felt a calling to go into full-time church work, and she became a Catholic sister. One day a missionary spoke to her home congregation about the great need to bring Christ to the people in India, so Teresa volunteered and was accepted for a teaching post in Calcutta.

At the convent in Calcutta, Teresa enjoyed very lovely quarters. She had beautiful accommodations that were surrounded by lovely gardens. She did her teaching in a very lovely and attractive classroom. But one day she had to make a trip to the dirtiest part of the town. When she walked the streets alone, through the back parts of Calcutta, she saw something she had never seen before. She saw human beings dying, and nobody was paying any attention to them. When she inquired, she found that this was very common. Nobody had time for the dying; there was no place for them to go. The young nun was haunted by this terrible situation. She felt that Jesus Christ was saying to her, "I am going to call you to serve the poorest of the poor. I am calling you to minister not to the living, but to the dying."

This was such a strong call that she asked the Church to release her from her vows. It took two years, but finally she was released. No longer a nun, she was sent out of the convent and into the streets of Calcutta. With only a few rupees, or pennies, in her pocket, she shuffled down the streets with no promise of a meal and no promise of clothing from the church. She was on her own, and she prayed, "Jesus, lead me to somebody who is dying all alone."

Two blocks away she saw an old lady lying in the gutter on the main street. The living body was being eaten by the rats that were running in the gutter. She picked up the woman and literally dragged her to the nearest hospital. She was refused admittance. "But," she exclaimed, "this woman is dying." She was told, "People die in the streets of Calcutta all the time. We cannot take her." Teresa refused to leave until they had taken the dying woman. She said, "If there is a God in heaven, and a Christ we love, nobody should die alone."

Shortly thereafter Teresa went to the city government and asked for an empty room—"a place where I can build a home for the dying." The civil authorities told her, "Well, we have this empty Hindu temple of Kali, if that would suit you." She said, "Beautiful. It would be beautiful for God. That is all I want to do in my life—something beautiful for God."

Two other sisters heard about Teresa's project, and they helped to drag the dying from the streets into this Hindu temple. Without medicine, without money, without an organization, without any backing, they did what they could, and nobody died in their place without at least a touch on the cheek and a kind word: "We love you." "Go in peace with God." They did not die alone.

Today, Teresa—or Mother Teresa, as she is widely known—is probably the closest thing to an authentic saint living on planet earth. She has created her own Sisterhood called the Sisters of Charity. It is a pontificate, which means it is now recognized directly below the Pope who, when he came to Calcutta to see what this strange ex-nun was doing, was so impressed that he gave her as a gift his own private, expensive white limousine. She took one look at this big, expensive car and said, "Oh, thank you."

The first thing she did was to announce a raffle. The money went for her house for the dying. Today, she has over ten thousand dying lepers in her colony. Her colonies have spread into twenty-eight cities, to Ceylon, to the Indian people who live in London, Rome, Venezuela, and Australia. She and all of those who are members of the Missionaries of Charity have taken the vow of total poverty. The only thing they may own is the cheapest cotton garment and a pair of sandals. Total surrender!

Malcolm Muggeridge, who interviewed Mother Teresa on the British Broadcasting Company and later visited her in Calcutta, said, "The thing I noticed about you and the hundreds of sisters who now form your team is that you all look so happy. Is it a put-on?" She said, "Oh no, not at all. Nothing makes you happier than when you really reach out in mercy to someone who is badly hurt."

"Blessed are the merciful, for they shall obtain mercy." Service is its own reward. A prescription for joyful living is: "Be good, be kind, be unselfish. Do unto others as you would have them do unto you."

If you want positive things to happen, you must be positive. If you want to be friendly with people and if you want people to be friendly toward you, be friendly to them. If you are surrounded by undesirable people, change them into good people.

How do you change them into good people? Bring the best out of them! How do you bring the best out of them? Call attention to the best that is within them! Until they begin to believe they are beautiful people, they will not treat you beautifully.

I'll never forget the young wife who came to see me. She complained, "My husband never compliments me. All he does is criticize! It doesn't matter what I do, how hard I work; I only hear how I could have done it better!"

I suggested, "You know that people who are highly critical often suffer from a low self-esteem. Is it possible that your husband has trouble in that regard?"

She thought for a moment. "Yes, I think that's possible."

"Well," I replied, "then it seems to me that the way to help him with his self-esteem and his critical remarks is for you to start complimenting him!"

*Selfishness
turns life
into a burden.
Unselfishness
turns
burdens
into life!*

"Oh! I never thought of that!" she cried. "But you're right! I can't remember the last time I complimented him. I've been so busy looking for compliments *from* him that I've completely neglected compliments *for* him."

If you want to change your world, change yourself. How do you change yourself? How do you become this kind of positive-thinking person? I know only one way. Education does not do it. Legislation does not do it. However, there is a living God—and a living Christ—who does. Christ can come into hearts that are filled with fear, anger, bitterness, and hurt, and He can liberate them with His mercy. It can happen to you. It happens when you meet Jesus Christ and ask Him to take over your life.

If you want to treat people mercifully, you have to begin by treating yourself mercifully. Accept yourself by knowing that Christ accepts you just as you are! However, if you lack a deep inner sense of self-esteem and self-worth, you will constantly have problems with other people. You won't treat them mercifully. You'll be unkind. You'll be critical or you'll gossip. You'll lash back until you've undermined the most important aspects of your life—and you find it collapsed around you.

Think about it. What is it that keeps us from treating people mercifully? It's resentment, jealousy, or the feeling that someone is a threat to you. If you can't handle resentment, jealousy, or "victimitis," then deep down in your own mind, heart, and soul you need to deal with your lack of a positive self-image. Your negative reactions are the result of hidden wounds that need to be healed.

## HEALING FOR THE HIDDEN WOUND

Do you have trouble with this Be-Happy Attitude? Do you have trouble being merciful? Are you critical of yourself as well as of others? If so, then you need to identify, isolate, and heal your hidden wounds. The first step toward healing is to realize that you are not alone. Everyone has been wounded at some time or another. Even Jesus, the Son of God, had wounds. Stop and count them; there were six:

(1) The ankles, where the nail went through.
(2) The palms of the hands, which were also pierced by nails.
(3) The brow, which was bloodied by the crown of thorns.
(4) The side, which was slashed by a spear.
(5) The back, which bore the stripes of a lashing.

Those are five of Christ's wounds. But the sixth wound was the hidden wound:

(6) The wound in His heart, placed there by the kiss of one of His own disciples. The hidden wound was the most painful of them all.

We all have them, don't we? We may disguise our wounds behind a smile and keep our guard up. But if we really searched our lives, exposed ourselves, we would find that every person has a secret pain, an intimate agony, a private hurt—a very isolated, unrevealed, unexposed wound.

Society inflicts hidden wounds on us. Some of you have been the victims of racial or ethnic prejudice, or of some other form of painful discrimination such as sexism or ageism. You know the discomfort of being laughed at, ignored, not being allowed to fulfill your vocational dreams, just because you are a certain race, sex, or age.

Sometimes those people closest to us inflict the deepest, most painful wounds. Some of you would weep right now, if I touched the tender memory, because of what a father or a mother, a spouse, child, lover, employer, or friend did to you.

Other hidden wounds we inflict on ourselves. We react too negatively to circumstances; we wound ourselves because we take them much too seriously. We read too much into other people's actions and exaggerate their rejection of us.

The hidden wounds you carry with you today—those private hurts that you can't talk about—what were the weapons that inflicted them on your heart? Look at the wounds of Jesus. The external wounds were inflicted by nails, a crown of thorns, a spear, a lash. But His hidden wound was caused by a kiss.

The weapons that wounded you are probably just as common as a kiss. They are words, looks, body language. Someone turned his or her back on you, didn't return your gesture of love and friendship, and that hurt. You were received with silence; maybe it was a snub. You were passed over. You never got the invitation. You were rebuffed. Words, looks, actions—these are the horrible weapons that inflict hidden wounds in human hearts.

Now the question is, *What do we do with these hidden wounds? How do we handle them?*

First of all, *don't nurse them.* There are many people who delight in nursing their hidden wounds. They still remember how their mother treated them. How their father treated them. How their first husband or first wife treated them. Thirty years later they are still obsessed with the wound. This is a neurotic, negative reaction.

*Don't curse them.* Don't let your wounds make you a bitter person. Don't allow anger at God or at the person who hurt you so deeply control your life. Don't curse your hurts, and *don't rehearse them.* Try to forget them. Remember, you can't forget your hurts if you keep talking about them *all the time.* One of the great men on the staff of the church for thirty years here was a minister named Dr. Henry Poppen. Dr. Henry Poppen had been a missionary in China and was held prisoner for many months in a little town in China when the Communists

took over. He was kept in solitary confinement, and the
treatment he received was abysmal. The experience was
tragic. It was horrific. It was awful. He escaped by a miracle; most of the other missionaries were killed on sight.
Well, when he came out he was an emotionally wounded
man. But he found healing for that wound through a doctor who said, "Don't talk about it any more. Just forget
it." In Dr. Poppen's case, these words of advice were just
what he needed. His memories were so ugly that to have
shared them over and over would have only made them
that much more a part of his life.

Don't nurse the wound. Don't curse the wound. Don't
keep rehearsing the wounding experience. What *do* you
do with your hidden wounds? *Immerse them.* Drown
them in a life of noble service.

I remember a time in the early years of my ministry
when I had a real personal problem with someone. Sometimes it hurt me so badly I didn't know how to handle it.
At these times my wife always had a solution. She'd say,
"I think you should go out and call on Rosie Gray." Or "I
think you ought to visit Marie; it was a year ago that her
husband died."

So I would go out to the hospitals and I would go calling on people. I would immerse myself as a pastor in the
hearts of people who were hurting. And in the process,
my little hidden wound was just drowned to death. It up
and died.

How do you handle your hidden wounds? Don't nurse
them. Don't curse them. Don't rehearse them. Do immerse them. And finally, *reverse them.* Turn the negative
into a positive. You do that when you allow your wound
to turn you into a more sensitive, compassionate, consid-
erate, thoughtful, merciful, gracious person.

If your wound is something that you can't share with
others without criticizing somebody else or tearing him or
her down, then you have to suffer in silence. If that's the
case, then trust God. Let Him heal your hidden wounds.

She is no longer with us—our dear Schug. Her name was Bernice Schug, but my children called her simply "Schug." Since both my wife's and my families lived in the Midwest, our children were unable to spend much time with their grandparents.

When we met Schug at church she was a widow. Her own grandchildren lived in northern California, so she was unable to see them as often as she liked. It was inevitable then that Schug would become our California grandmother. She lavished love and poppy-seed rolls on us and our children. She stayed over with the children when my wife had our last two children. She ate meals with us, she cared for our children, yet none of us knew how deep her hidden wound was.

One day Schug came to me and said, "Bob, I was reading in the church bulletin today that you are having a guest speaker next Sunday. I see you're having a Kamikaze pilot as your guest."

Oh! I remembered then that Schug's son had been killed in World War II by a Kamikaze pilot. "That's right, Schug. This particular pilot was trained as a Kamikaze and would have died as a Kamikaze had the war not ended when it did. But he has a tremendous story to tell of how he found Jesus."

"That may be. I don't think I will be in church that Sunday, though. I don't think I could handle it."

"I understand," I replied. "I don't think it will hurt if you miss one Sunday."

The next Sunday the Japanese pilot shared his story. His love and gratitude for Jesus shone from his black eyes. You could feel the love and release he had found.

People were moved by his testimony. And when the service was over, my associate pastor walked with him back down the aisle to the rear of the church.

Suddenly as they approached the last pew, an older woman stepped out. She stood firmly in front of the Kamikaze pilot and blocked his exit. She looked at him squarely and said, "My son was killed in the war by a Kamikaze!"

It was Schug. We all held our breath as she continued, "God has forgiven you for your sins, and tonight He has forgiven me of mine."

She threw her arms around this little Japanese pilot and hugged him and cried and cried as she released all the bitterness and anger that had been harbored for so many years.

Forgive a Kamikaze pilot, when a fellow pilot had killed a beloved son? Impossible! Yes, it is impossible for us, but not impossible for God!

After all, who is a better teacher on the subject of forgiveness than Jesus Christ? When He hung on the cross, brutally whipped, mocked with a crown of thorns, betrayed by His friend, and deserted by His disciples, what did He say to the people who watched Him die?

He said, *"forgive them;* for they know not what they do" (Luke 23:34).

Jesus is an expert on forgiveness. Let Him forgive you and heal you of your hidden wounds.

If you are merciful, people will treat you mercifully. If you are merciful, then God will release you from vengeful attitudes that will eat at you and destroy you. When you follow the example that Christ set, you will find, much to your surprise, that God will step in and bless you, too, with an Easter morning!

Be-Happy Attitude #6

# "I've got to let the faith flow free through me."

*"Blessed are the pure in heart,*
*for they shall see God."*
Matthew 5:8

**D**O YOU LONG TO KNOW GOD BETTER? Do you struggle with doubt? Do you ever wish you had more faith?

If so, you are not alone.

I have been in the ministry long enough to know that even people who have been Christians all their lives have to deal with doubt at one time or another. Many committed Christians go through "dry" times when God seems absent or far away. And there are countless people inside and outside the church—even some who claim to be agnostic or even atheist—who really *want* to believe, but who somehow have trouble developing a strong faith.

If this is your struggle—to have more faith, to conquer doubt, to know God in a real, personal, life-changing way—then this Be-Happy Attitude is for you: "Blessed are the pure in heart," Jesus said, "for they shall see God."

But what does it take to become "pure in heart"? I would like to suggest four steps that can really help: (1) Wise up. (2) Clean up. (3) Give up. (4) Take up.

### WISE UP!

If you could collect the smartest intellectuals from around the world, bring them together, and ask them one question, "How many of you believe in God?" several hands would go up. On the other hand, many hands would go up if you asked, "How many of you do *not* believe in God?"

If you divide the smartest, most educated minds of the world into believers and unbelievers, there would be quite a few in each group. That is because faith in God is not a matter of intelligence. Faith is not a result of intellect, any more than it is a result of ignorance.

Faith is not a matter of intelligence. It is a matter of instinct. Even science has recently confirmed the power of innate, inbred instinct. A notable example is the recent experiment by Dr. Maurice, a scholar and a student of the weaver bird of South Africa. This interesting little bird makes its nest out of reeds, lines it with silky grass, and does what no other bird does—he makes a hole in the bottom of his nest through which he makes his entrance.

Dr. Maurice, trying to test the strength of instinctive drives, took two eggs from a nest in South Africa, transported them out of the country, and incubated them until they hatched. He successfully raised the birds in cages through four and even five generations. None of these birds ever had any exposure to nests with a hole in the bottom of it.

Dr. Maurice took the fifth generation of weaver birds, brought them back to South Africa, and released them in their natural habitat. The birds found reeds, immediately lined their nests with silky grass, and then made holes in the bottom. Incredible!

There are mysteries in anthropology and natural science—mysteries that can only be described as instinctive. These instincts are powerful; they can propel swarms of bees, herds of whales, schools of salmon, flocks of geese thousands of miles. These instincts are also enduring; animals who are born with their peculiar instinctive modes of behavior have them as long as their species is in its native habitat.

Someone once said, "When God wants to make sure a truth is never abandoned or aborted, He will put it in the instinct." When God wanted to ensure that the need for religion would never die, He put it within the human breast. That is why humankind throughout history has been drawn to a belief in a God. Even the aborigines of Australia and the headhunters in New Guinea believe in a god or gods. They feel the instinctive urge within their souls to know and worship something greater than themselves.

Instinct. How else do you explain Bill Murray, son of the militant atheist, Madelyn Murray O'Hare? He was raised and indoctrinated in atheism, and he worked with his mother for years, but he still had a life-transforming experience that turned him into a believer in God.

If you are struggling with the idea of faith, wise up! Realize that God has planted faith within the instinct of every healthy human being. Just as a healthy bird instinctively takes to the trees, just as a healthy fish swims in the water, so the healthy human being is inclined to be religious. However, just as animals lose some of their innate drives when taken from their natural habitats, so man loses his innate ability to believe in a loving God when he is away too long from positive, faith-producing environments. That is why it is so important to carefully surround ourselves with positive, believing, healthy people.

Religion is a sign of health. Skepticism is a mark of illness. Unbelief is abnormal; belief is normal. For the normal human being will joyfully embrace faith and belief, but the cynical doubter cannot believe and will not believe until he can be healed of the negative memories that plague him and block him from his innate ability to see God.

Dr. Gerald Jampolsky, a noted psychiatrist and a dear friend of mine, was for twenty-five years a very strong agnostic. Then one day, without warning, his life totally changed, and he became a believer in God. I asked him once when we were together, "Dr. Jampolsky, in the years before you were converted, what did you think about people who went to church?"

He said, "For twenty-five years I thought people who went to church, prayed, and believed in God were not normal. I thought they were really kind of sick. Now I see that I was completely wrong. *They* were normal; I was not."

## CLEAN UP!

If the first step toward developing more faith is to wise up—to realize that belief is instinctive, normal, and healthy—then the second step is to clean up any negative emotions in your life that might be blocking your faith and keeping you from "seeing" God.

There was a time when my children were little that I was going through some torturing times with the development of my church. I had colossal burdens and pressures. And although I was going through the motions of being a pastor, a husband, and a father, my heart was not really in any of these. It was blocked by despair, depression, and fear.

Often during this time I would come home from the office, sit in a chair, pick up the paper, and read column after column without really being aware of anything I had read.

My little boy would come and talk to me. And I'd respond, "Yes, Bobbie." But I wouldn't really hear him.

One day my wife and I were walking through the garden. I remarked, "Honey, the roses are blooming." To my surprise, she replied, "They've been blooming for three months."

It was not until I cried out to God and asked Him to release me from my anxieties and worries that I was able once more to feel His presence. Like a finger pressing into my brain, He touched me, and I felt the fear and the despair drain out of me. In its place flowed peace, joy, and hope, despite the obstacles that still lay ahead.

When God touched me, my ears were opened. I could once again hear what my family was saying to me. My eyes were opened. I could once again see the beauty that God had created. I could even see possible solutions for the overwhelming problems I was facing.

Worry, anxiety, pressures, frustrations—all of these can cause us to be blinded to the real world all around us. When we take this one step further, you can see how easy it would be for some emotional blockage to keep us from being aware of the presence of God.

"Blessed are the pure in heart, for they shall see God." I believe Jesus is teaching that if we have emotional and spiritual health we will be able to "see" God, to believe in Him.

Dear Dr. Schuller:

I must write to tell you—when you spoke of the seed of grass that had been tossed from a vase and wedged uncomfortably in a crack in the sidewalk, to be trampled under the boots of men—well, that was my life, my early childhood.

My parents were well bred. Money and fame was their God. But I was never able to trust their love. Consequently, I was never able to believe in a loving father. However, I became aware that Christians were happy. I was not. I knew that my personality was disjointed and disconnected.

"In the presence of hope —
    faith is born.

In the presence of faith —
    love becomes a possibility!

In the presence of love —
    miracles happen!"

One day, after hearing your sermon when you said to put God first, others second, and yourself third, I offered God everything I had. I offered Him my money, my time, myself. I said, "God, I'm willing to be Yours if You'll help me."

The following Thursday happened to be Maundy Thursday. I noticed a little church with a sign saying, "Communion Today." I went in. I took the communion and, as I did, I asked God to make me into a mentally healthy person so that I would be able to be a believer. At that moment, it all happened. I felt cleansed of all the evil I had carried with me since childhood. I cannot tell you how happy and relieved I feel.

Then the writer of this letter added this very perceptive and analytically profound postscript: "P.S. It is a tremendous achievement for the emotionally disturbed person to trust God!"

How right she is! It *is* a difficult task for a person who has emotional difficulties to become a healthy believer in God. And so I ask you:

- Is it possible that somewhere in your subconscious there lurks hostility toward your father or your mother?
- Is it possible that you have within your subconscious some negative feeling toward your family, your friends, your business associates or competitors?
- Have you ever been hurt by someone who never came back to apologize to you?
- Do you have a secret that you have never shared with any other living human being—about something you have done, are doing, or are thinking about doing, which is either illegal or immoral?
- Have you suffered grief and heartache, and did your prayers seem unanswered?
- Do you feel inferior to others, and do you have trouble loving yourself?

There are countless questions I could ask. Let me just say that if you answered "yes" to any one of these questions, you are not totally free of negative emotions. And as long as you have negative emotions within yourself, then listen carefully: *Don't trust your doubt.* Doubt is a subconscious defense mechanism fabricated by an insecure, guilty, or troubled mind to keep us from believing in a God who might make demands upon us we're not prepared to meet.

Negative emotions block faith because they hinder us from confronting our need for God. It's like the overweight person who won't step on the bathroom scale or the person with overdue bills who won't look in the mailbox. When we most need help, negative emotions can keep us from turning to the One who could help us most; they block us from believing and seeing God's plan for our lives.

Now you know why Jesus was such a powerful believer! Jesus knew God. Jesus Christ had no emotional blockages! He had no selfish ambitions, no greed, no jealousies, no hatred, no self-pity, no selfish griefs. Emotionally, He was constantly positive. He was "pure in heart."

So if there is within your personality some resentment, some hostility, some guilt, some fear or worry, find it. Get rid of it. You will be surprised to find how much your faith will improve. How natural it will seem to you to be religious—as natural and normal as breathing.

I love a story I once heard about Leonardo da Vinci. According to the legend, some lads were visiting the famous artist. One of them knocked over a stack of canvases. This upset the artist because he was working very quietly and sensitively. He became angry, threw his brush, and hurled some harsh words to the hapless little fellow, who ran crying from the studio.

The artist was now alone again, and he tried to continue his work. He was trying to paint the face of Jesus, but he couldn't do it. His creativity had stopped.

Leonardo da Vinci put down his brush. He went out and walked the streets and the alleys until he found the little boy. He said, "I'm sorry, son; I shouldn't have spoken so harshly. Forgive me, even as Christ forgives. I have done something worse than you. You only knocked over the canvases. But I, by my anger, blocked the flow of God into my life. Will you come back with me?"

He took the boy back into the studio with him. They smiled as the face of Jesus came quite naturally from the master's brush. That face has been an inspiration to millions ever since.

If there is a negative emotion within you that is blocking you in your relationship with God, *clean up!* "Blessed are the pure in heart, for they shall see God." Here are some exercises to help you:

(1) Think of some hidden hurt in your past and pray a forgiving prayer for the person who was the cause of your hurt. C. S. Lewis said it: "We all agree that forgiveness is a beautiful idea until we have to practice it!"

(2) Think of someone of whom you are jealous, and pray for that person's continued prosperity.

(3) Think of someone you've hurt, cheated, insulted, slighted, snubbed, or criticized. Call him or her. Invite this person to have dinner or lunch with you. Confess to him or her your un-Christian attitude, and ask for forgiveness.

(4) Think of some neglected cause, project, or person. Surprise yourself with a streak of generosity! Really give a lot—of yourself and of your substance.

(5) Pray a totally honest prayer to Christ. You doubt God? Tell Him so. He'll still love you, even if you don't believe in Him! (God specializes in loving sinners!)

Perhaps you read the amazing story of the young Air Force man who is alive today because of the complete change of blood in his body. He had hepatitis and his liver was nearly useless. Doctors drained every cell of blood from this man's body and substituted a saline solution. They lowered his body temperature to eighty-five degrees. For eight or ten minutes he was, for all practical purposes, physically dead. The doctors then flushed the saline solution out and filled his veins and arteries with new, healthy blood. A medical miracle had occurred—a human life had been saved. Amazing!

Jesus said that if you want to see God, you have to be born again. Another way of saying this is that you need a spiritual "blood" transfusion. The old negative blood is drawn out. Then the new spirit of Jesus Christ, like new blood, flows through your entire nervous and emotional system, and you become a new person! "If any man is in Christ, he is a new creature." Through the Holy Spirit, you receive "new spiritual blood" in every cell. If doctors could give new life to an Air Force man, just imagine what God could do inside your mind!

Do you want a life-changing experience with God? Clean up—wash your mistakes away through Christ's grace. Accept the forgiveness of Jesus. Let Him clear up the negative, emotional blockages.

### GIVE UP!

Do you want a life-changing experience with God? If so, wise up! Realize it's instinctive and normal to be religious. Clean up! Wash your mistakes and negative emotions away through Christ's grace. And the third step is: Give up—anything that may be hindering you. Perhaps there is something in your life that you will have to relinquish, with God's help. If it is something that is blocking the birth of real faith, then you may have to give it up. If it is a choice between living and a bad habit—choose life.

Many years ago I officiated in the marriage ceremony of a Hollywood actor, Glenn Ford. Waiting for the ceremony to begin, we chatted in a back room of his home. Gathered in that room were Glenn Ford; his best man, Bill Holden; Frank Sinatra; Jimmy Stewart; and John Wayne.

"You know, you should quit smoking, Francis," John Wayne said to Sinatra, who smiled.

Before he could answer, Jimmy Stewart asked Wayne, "When did *you* give up smoking, Duke?"

I'll never forget his answer: "When I decided it was more important to live than to smoke."

We can find the strength to give something up when it threatens something that is precious to us—such as life.

Dr. Kenneth Cooper, bestselling author and founder of a world-famous fitness center in Dallas, Texas, is an authority on health and fitness, the man who first made *aerobics* a household word. In my opinion, Dr. Cooper is responsible more than any other single person for contributing to the physical fitness movement that is going on in the United States and around the world. Several years ago I interviewed him on *The Hour of Power,* and before my national television audience the following dialogue took place concerning negative habits and how to give them up:

K.C.: "There are at least fifty million overweight Americans with a total of one billion pounds above their ideal weight. I hope we don't sink off the face of the earth with statistics like that. It was an indictment of an overweight society when they renovated Yankee Stadium a few years ago. They had to reduce the seating capacity by nine thousand seats, because they couldn't change the overall dimensions of the stadium but they had to increase the width of each seat from nineteen to twenty-two inches—to accommodate the modern American's posterior! We have a lot of obesity in America."

R.S.: "So, are you saying that we need to exercise and cut back on our eating?"

K.C.:   "Absolutely. Obesity is rampant in our country, and obesity is accompanied by everything from high blood pressure to diabetes to heart disease and even depression."

R.S.:   [I felt that I had to toot my own horn just a little.] "You know, a few years ago I cut out white bread, cookies, and sugar. I only take fresh fruit for dessert."

K.C.:   "Bob, without question, you're doing yourself a lot of good. We recommend restricting cholesterol, cutting down on sweets, and concentrating on natural foods—on fresh vegetables, fruit, and lean meat. That's what we as American people need to do. In our Aerobics Center we encourage people to check with their physician first; to have their blood analyzed to find out what their cholesterol level is, what their triglycerides are, what their fasting blood sugar level is. From that they can be given specific guidelines as to what they should do to change their diets to improve their statistics."

R.S.:   "You also have strong feelings about tobacco and smoking?"

K.C.:   "Most definitely! The worst health hazard that we have in America today is cigarette smoking. Let me cite some quick statistics: If you smoke more than one pack of cigarettes a day, you're three times more likely to die of a heart attack than the nonsmoker or the former cigarette smoker. But the exciting thing is that when the cigarette smokers stop smoking, in as short a period of time as six months he or she can drop back into the low-risk category for heart disease. That's why I strongly believe that the dramatic improvement in the health of our people in the past fifteen to twenty years has been due to the fact that thirty million have quit smoking cigarettes since 1964."

R.S.: "Cigarettes are, as they say, 'nails in the coffin'?"

K.C.: "They really are. And remember, too, recent studies show that for every cigarette you smoke, you increase the likelihood of lung cancer by that much. For example, if you smoke *five* cigarettes a day, you are *five* times more likely to die of lung cancer. If you smoke *thirty* cigarettes a day, you're thirty times more likely to die of lung cancer than the nonsmoker. The statistics just go up and up."

R.S.: "But how can people give up smoking? How can they lose weight?"

K.C.: "I recommend first of all that they start an exercise program. For some reason, that gives them a discipline they didn't have before. All is possible through God. Some will be successful on their own, but many others will succeed only when they ask for God's help."

"Blessed are the pure in heart." It is always wise to give up anything that you think might be blocking you from a clear relationship with God.

I witness to you that the times I felt closest to God were the times when I gave up something I desired very much. My experience proves the words of our Lord, who said, "If any man would come after me, let him deny himself and take up the cross and follow me."

Recently, with my doctor's enthusiastic approval, I went on a fast. For six days I had no solid foods. During this time, I sometimes felt hungry, but I also felt especially close to Jesus Christ.

I remember the first time I began tithing, giving God ten percent of my earnings. Boy, was it tough. I had to give up something, but I did feel closer to God.

Years ago, I smoked. You must understand that there were no cultural biases against smoking in the community where I grew up. In my childhood church, all good

Dutch preachers smoked cigars or pipes. However, I became convinced that, for me, smoking was not right, and I gave the habit up. It was difficult, but once I had quit, I felt great.

You see, fasting and tithing and giving up smoking were all part of the principle of doing something difficult with God's help and making it a success. It was an adventure of walking by faith which gave God a chance to prove Himself to me. And He did!

Now, please understand that I am not saying you have to quit smoking or lose weight before you can "see God." But I am suggesting that becoming "pure in heart" may mean you have to give up something you like very much. It may be money. It may be smoking. It may be overeating. It may be alcohol or other habit-forming drugs. It may be extramarital sex. I do not know what it is that is blocking you from a close relationship with God. I don't *want* to know what it is; that is between you and Him. But make it a spiritual adventure and you will have an experience with God. Many people have a low faith level simply because they are scared to stick their necks out with God. Try it!

## TAKE UP!

Dr. Cooper suggested taking up an exercise program as the first step on the road to better health. The same principle applies to our spiritual walk. To be pure in heart, we need to take up something:

- a dream . . .
  - a project . . .
    - God's call to do something great!

After all, what does "pure in heart" mean? Does it mean that we are sinless? Of course not. If that's what it

You
can live
without
something
---
if
you have
someone
to live
for!

meant, Jesus would have been giving all of us an assignment that was doomed to fail. I'm not sinless. You are not
sinless. None of us are entirely sinless.

If Jesus is not requiring us to be sinless, then, what
*does* He mean when He says, "Blessed are the pure in
heart"?

As I mentioned in an earlier chapter, a *pure* field is not
one that has merely been plowed so that it's free of
weeds. No, a pure field is a productive one—where corn,
pineapples, or oranges are being grown.

The same is true in our lives. We can believe in God, we
can see Him, we can catch His vision for our lives, we can
feel His spirit moving in our lives when we:

- wise up,
  - clean up,
    - give up, and finally
      - take up God's call to do something
        great for Him.

There is one consuming cause that I can offer you—the
cause of Christ in our world today. God is alive, and
Christ is alive, and there are millions who are finding
Him. If you have not found Him, you have the greatest
experience of your life still coming! I offer to you Jesus
Christ as your cause.

Take up a "cause," and it's easy to give up "things."

A young married couple living in a cheap little apartment are happy. Why? Because they have a cause—their
new married love.

An artist lives in a musty attic—ill-fed, ill-clothed. But
he is happy! Why? Because he has a cause to live for . . .
his art. He does not need many material things.

A research scientist who comes to his classroom in
baggy pants, with an unshaven face and no tie, isn't interested in expensive suits. He is lost in a cause—that of
research and study.

You can get by without a lot of things if you have something great to live for. Jesus said, "Seek first his kingdom and his righteousness, and all these things shall be added unto you" (Matt. 6:33).

Do you want to have a real experience with God? Wise up. Clean up. Give up. And take up the cross of Jesus Christ. God is offering to you a cause—Christ's cause. Jesus needs you.

Christ has no hands but our hands to do His work today.
He has no feet, but our feet to lead men on the way.
He has no tongues but our tongues to tell men how He died.
He has no help but our help to draw men to His side.

It is that simple. Have you given your heart to Him? Maybe you are a Christian and have accepted Christ, but God is not real enough to you. Maybe there is something in your heart that needs cleansing. Maybe you have to give up something, or take up something.

I told you in the previous chapter about Mother Teresa. Mother Teresa left the shelter and the security of the convent with only a few rupees in her pocket. She went out into the poorest section in the vast city of Calcutta. She found a woman being eaten by rats while still alive, and she dragged this woman to a hospital. That is how she began her life work. Today, she is dedicated to helping the poorest of the poor. Those who have met her say she has a radiant, God-filled face. No wonder . . . listen to her!

She writes: "Joy. Joy is prayer. Joy is strength. Joy is love. God loves a cheerful giver. She gives most who gives joy. The best way to show my gratitude to God is to accept everything, even my problems, with joy. A joyful heart is a normal result of a heart that is burning with love. Never let anything so fill you with sorrow as to make you forget for one moment the joy of Christ risen."

She goes on: "We all long for heaven, where God is. But we have it in our power to be in heaven with God right now, at this very moment. But to be at home with God now means loving the unlovely as He does, helping the helpless as He does, giving to those in need as He gives, serving the lonely as He serves, rescuing the perishing as He rescues. This is my Christ. This is the way I live."

God is so real. He will be real to you, too, if you take Christ into your heart. Adopt Mother Teresa's goal to "do something beautiful for God." Look around you now to help someone who is hurting. Do it for Christ's sake.

If you want a life-changing experience with God, a dynamic faith, here's how you can get it. Ask God to take your life, to heal the subconscious memories. Ask Jesus Christ to forgive you for your secret sins. Then ask Him to take your life and show you how you can be a part of something beautiful for God! For faith combined with good works makes God come alive within you.

Take a look at a fountain pen. The ink flows through it to form words—communication. If you simply give your life to Him today, He can flow through you. He can make your heart right. He can clear the rubbish from your life and replace it with a holy dream! And you'll come to realize that the burning desire, the consuming dream, the strong sense of destiny—yes, all of this inner drive—is the very life of God surging in your soul! Your dream is God within you!

It is a decision! To become a believer! And decide that a positive mental attitude—a Be-Happy Attitude—requires that you let the faith flow free.

## Be-Happy Attitude #7

# "I'm going to be a bridge builder."

*"Blessed are the peacemakers, for they shall be called children of God."*
Matthew 5:9

HOW WOULD YOU LIKE to be remembered? What kind of reputation do you covet? What kind of image do you desire? What words would you wish to be carved on your tombstone?

Do you care? Many would say, "I don't care what people say."

Others might say, "I think it is dangerous to ask questions like these. I might become too self-centered in the process."

But consider: These questions can be very positive and motivational if our objective is to become a truly beautiful human being. For I believe that one thing Jesus is saying in the seventh Beatitude is that happiness comes when we care about our reputation for the right reasons—when we strive to live so that we might be known as "children of God."

"Blessed are the peacemakers, for they shall be *called* the children of God." Now here's a sacred sentence that holds out a *hope*—and a *"how to."*

167

### THE HOPE

The hope in this seventh Beatitude is that we might achieve a reputation which will feed our need for self-respect, self-esteem, and self-worth. What is the essence of self-esteem? It's knowing that I have done my best and I am recognized and honored as a child of God!

What do people think of me? How we handle this human question is extremely important. So many of us think of it in terms of being "popular":

- Young people handle this question when they strive to be popular by "going along with the crowd."
- Adults attempt to be popular through their accumulation of material prizes—"keeping up with the Joneses," joining the right clubs, dressing in clothes they believe will win social applause—and through many more social manifestations too many and complex to name.

But I am not really thinking about popularity here—or at least, not *that* kind of popularity. Unless you can maintain an honorable reputation you will not have the kind of popularity that will leave you with a wholesome and healthy sense of self-esteem! The young person who resists the temptation to do drugs feels victorious. He has been a winner! He has been the strongest! He feels good about himself. And such a person will eventually build a positive reputation.

The goal is not just to be popular—but to be popularly recognized as a beautiful human being—a child of God!

- Our attitude shouldn't be: "I don't care what people say."
- Our attitude shouldn't be: "I want to be popular at any price."
- Our attitude—our Be-Happy Attitude—should be: "I will strive so to live that I shall build a reputation as a beautiful child of God!"

## THE "HOW TO"

How do we build a reputation as beautiful children of God?

The seventh Beatitude tells us one way: "Blessed are the peacemakers, for they shall be called children of God."

On the morning of my ordination as a minister, I opened my Bible for my devotions. It fell open to this passage: "You shall be called the repairer of the breach, the restorer of paths to dwell in" (Isa. 58:12, KJV). And I adopted this Bible verse as a direction from my Lord to try to promote a peaceful resolution to any conflict I see. Peacemaking has been one of the important goals of my ministry.

I believe that all of us are called to try to be peacemakers. And being a peacemaker can be extremely rewarding. Helping bring peace where there is tension and conflict and strife brings about a healthy sense of satisfaction, self-esteem, self-worth.

Yet being a peacemaker can be dangerous, too. Playing the role of mediator can be quite costly. We have in my church a few police officers. They've often told me that the most difficult call is a domestic quarrel—one in which a husband and wife are fighting. In such a situation, it's not unusual for the mediator to get shot!

Peacemaking can be a tough role to play. And yet it is absolutely crucial. Ambassador Max Kampelman, who has been instrumental in recent arms negotiations, once quoted Senator Hubert Humphrey on the subject: "Negotiating between conflicting parties is like crossing a river by walking on slippery rocks. . . . It's risky, but it's the only way to get across."

Being a peacemaker *is* dangerous. It *is* slippery. You can fall and break your neck. You can drown. But it's the only way to get *to the other side.* Playing the role of mediator is risky, but it's necessary if breaches are to be repaired.

## BREACHES?

We see breaches all around us. In families. Between labor and management. Between nations. Between political parties.

People have said to me, "Schuller, why do you never take stands on controversial political issues?"

I certainly do not feel it is wrong to take a political stand! But I have always felt my special call in political situations is to try to be a repairer of breaches and a restorer of paths. I try to help people get together and resolve their conflicts.

Of course, there are many different ways to solve conflict. I like the story of Helga and Henry, a Swedish couple. They were married for sixty years, and they fought like cats and dogs every day of their married lives. Finally, their sixtieth anniversary arrived. Helga and Henry began the morning with a terrible spat. They argued all day long.

At the end of the day, Helga said to her husband, "Henry, tonight I tink ven ve pray, ve better pray for peace. Ve been fighting each other for sixty years, Henry. May the Lord give us peace. So tonight, I tink I'll pray that the Lord vill take you home and I'll go live with my sister, Olga."

Obviously, that's not the way I would recommend handling a situation of conflict. Most conflicts will be resolved one way or the other. But let us hope and pray that they can be resolved positively and constructively.

*When God sees a breach, He builds a bridge.* And He calls us to help in the process by being peacemakers.

My friend Hubert Humphrey was a peacemaker. He was a repairer of the breach. He continually inspired me, even in the last few weeks of his life, when he was so very ill.

That is why I hurried to Senator Humphrey's side when his family called me and asked me to come to Minneapolis and encourage him to go back to Washington for a last hurrah.

We conversed a little, then the Lord gave me an idea. I said, "Hubert, when you were really down and depressed in life, how did you get back up?"

I was hoping that in the process of recalling victorious experiences, he would regenerate and recapture the emotion from the reservoirs of his memories, and that this would help him bounce back.

He began recalling several experiences. After a while, I said, "It must have been really difficult for you when you were narrowly defeated by Richard Nixon for the presidency."

He said, "That was probably my toughest time."

"How did you recover emotionally from that?"

I could see the memory reinforcing him and renewing him. Then, when the spark flashed in his eye, I said, "Hubert, when are you going back to Washington again?"

I had caught him off guard, and before he had time to think it through, he said, "Yes, maybe I ought to go back once more."

Muriel Humphrey smiled and said, "That's wonderful. I'll call the President."

Well, I had prayer with him, he walked me to the car, and I went back to the airport and returned home. The next morning I heard on the news that Air Force One, with President Carter, had stopped in Minneapolis, Minnesota, to pick up Hubert Humphrey and take him back to Washington.

He called me later to thank me.

I said, "Hubert, I don't suppose there is any American today who is being applauded more than you."

He said, "That may be true."

"The irony of it is that twenty miles from me sits a man in almost total exile. His name is Richard Nixon. You now are honored. But because of the Watergate scandal, he is suffering the opposite fate. What's your opinion? Should he stay that way all his life? Should he be forgiven? Could there be a healing?"

We discussed it and I said, "I don't think Nixon can make it back without a lot of help: (1) He would have to be invited to a prestigious public event. (2) He would have to be invited to come out by someone all of America respects. (3) He would have to be invited by somebody who is not running for political office, because the opponent would really use this against him."

Senator Humphrey hesitated. Then he said, "It sounds like I'm the man. I'm surely not running for office."

He thought a while and then he said, "Yes, I'll let it be known that he can come to my funeral. I think that will be an event. And since it's being sponsored by a liberal democrat, I don't think they could fault it."

Well, that's exactly what happened. When Senator Humphrey's body lay in its casket under the Capitol rotunda, there sat Muriel Humphrey. And next to Muriel sat Richard Nixon.

Someone said, "How could they invite Nixon to Humphrey's funeral?" Another person sitting near us answered, "If you knew Hubert Humphrey, you wouldn't have asked that question."

"You shall be called a repairer of the breach. And a restorer of paths to dwell in."


## BUILD BRIDGES

*When God sees a breach, He builds a bridge.*

For years this has been my driving spirit. And the spirit behind the drive is what has often been called possibility thinking. In my recent book, *The Power of Being Debt Free,* in chapter four, I put it this way: Never reject an idea because it will create conflict. Never reject an idea

* Coauthored with Paul David Dunn (Nashville: Thomas Nelson Publishers, 1985).

When God sees a
breach...
He builds a
bridge!

When He sees a
scar...
He creates a
star!

because you have to change your mind or way of doing things. Never reject an idea because it's going to create problems or it's dangerous or risky.

Possibility thinking says, "Yes!" to an idea if it's going to help people who are in pain. It says "Yes!" to an idea if it holds the prospect of contributing to peace, prosperity, and pride in the human family.

Let me paraphrase again from *The Power of Being Debt Free:* In a world marred by war, poverty, and humiliation in the human family, let there be no offhanded, impulsive rejection of sincere proposals that, however implausible and unrealistic they may seem, do hold some promise of moving the human family closer to prosperity which can eliminate poverty, peace which can eliminate war, and pride which can eliminate human shame.

I really feel we are called by God to be repairers of the breach, restorers of paths to dwell in. Where a relationship has been ripped, torn apart, we are called to bring about reconciliation—where there's a rupture create a rapture. Where there is a scar, create a star; healing where there was only hurt.

### WHERE DO WE GET THE POWER FOR PEACE?

The only place you can get that kind of driving spirit, that kind of attitude, is from the Lord. That's why I don't see how proposals for peace can ever happen without divine intervention. For God can provide when all others fail. The power for peace will come when we are reunited with God.

I have in my hand a beautiful book—and a very rare book. It is called *Eighty: An American Souvenir,* and it is by an artist named Eric Sloane, of whom *Reader's Digest* once said, "No man greens the memories of our yesterday with a more bittersweet brush."

I met Eric Sloane one week when I was in New York City, making television appearances. I had an hour between appointments and I said to my driver, "How far is it to the Armand Hammer Galleries?"

"Oh," he said, "not far." So we stopped in the galleries. In one area was a one-man show by Eric Sloane. The walls were covered with beautiful paintings of sky and covered American bridges.

One customer was looking at a beautiful painting. He looked at me, and whispered to his wife. I knew what they were saying, so I walked over and said hello.

They said, "Oh, Dr. Schuller. We watch you every week." Then they turned to the paintings on the wall. "Isn't his work gorgeous?"

"Yes!"

They said, "It's too bad you weren't here last night, at the opening, because Eric Sloane himself was here."

Just then the door opened. How providential could it be? The couple I had been talking to said, "Oh, here he comes."

I watched a man walk in—ramrod straight, silver-haired. I spotted dimples and twinkles in the eye, a beautiful blue bow tie, a white shirt, and a double-breasted wool overcoat.

He greeted the customer, who led him over to me. As Mr. Sloane came close, he said, "Dr. Schuller, you look just like you do on television."

He was a friend. He said, "I'll tell you why I've loved your ministry, Dr. Schuller." Then he told me this story:

"I was a very young man when I inherited a million dollars in cash from my father. You wouldn't believe how quickly I spent it all! I woke up one Sunday morning and realized I did not have one dollar left. I was terribly depressed. My inheritance was gone, my father was dead, and I had nothing. I went into a little church—although I was not really very religious—and I heard the minister say, 'God's providence is your inheritance.'

"He didn't know about me.

"But the minister continued, 'God will provide, no matter how bankrupt you are. But you have to trust Him and turn your whole life over to Him.'

"At that time I was just a sign painter. But I took my brush, and underneath my easel I wrote the words, *God's providence is my inheritance*. Once I put that on my easel, my whole life changed."

He continued, "I couldn't be more successful than I am today."

I said, "Would you like to be my guest on *The Hour of Power* some Sunday?"

He enthusiastically replied, "I'd love to be."

Before I left, Sloane held up a book. He said, "Dr. Schuller, this is my autobiography. Most of the copies are still on the boat coming from Italy—that's the only place I trusted to have the printing done."

He added, "I have only six with me, but I want you to have one." And so Eric Sloane autographed one of his books for me for the Schuller library—with a bridge and the date.

That was on Monday. Imagine my shock when I heard three days later that Eric Sloane had died in the streets of New York! So I probably have one of the only autographed copies of his autobiography.

Eric Sloane. In this autobiography he reprinted an etching of a tombstone that could have been his choice for his own tombstone. On it were inscribed these words: "God knows I tried."

What do you want on your tombstone? How do you want to be remembered?

"God's providence is my inheritance." Sloane claimed it. And the same inheritance is waiting for you and me. All we have to do is claim it.

## PEACEMAKERS—WHO ARE THEY?

Do you feel bankrupt? Is our country—is our world—bankrupt for power? For peace? God's providence is our inheritance.

How do you want to be remembered? As a child of God? As a peacemaker?

Peacemakers. Who are they? Are they only politicians and world leaders? Or are they also people like you and me?

Everyone can be a peacemaker. The mother who resolves the toy tug-of-war between her toddlers is a peacemaker. The student who helps settle disputes in her dormitory is a peacemaker. The umpire who remains calm in the midst of verbal onslaughts from distraught managers is a peacemaker.

Every one of us can be a peacemaker—no matter who we are and what we do.

I shall never forget when S. Truett Cathy was my guest on the *Hour of Power*. Mr. Cathy is the founder and president of a very successful chain of fast-food restaurants called Chick-Fil-A. On the program, he shared the story of how he had launched this successful business:

"In the early stages of Chick-Fil-A, we were anxious to advertise our product. One day an idea dawned on me. There were competing newspapers in town, and the editors of these papers wouldn't walk on the same side of the street with each other! Since everyone knew about their feud, I invited the two editors to meet with me. I asked each one individually if he'd come down to discuss a full-page ad. Neither one knew I had called the other. When they got there and found themselves face to face with each other, they knew something was up.

"I said, 'If you'll do one thing for me, I'll give both of you a full-page ad. All I want you to do is sit over there in that booth and eat a chicken sandwich together. When you get through, shake hands. Then we'll add the caption, "We disagree on many things, but there's one thing we both agree on: This is the best chicken sandwich we've ever eaten!" ' "

"Blessed are the peacemakers." In S. Truett Cathy's humorous anecdote, of course, the two editors were just peace *talkers*! What we want to learn to be today is true peace *makers*, like the group of young people I met in Squaw Valley, California.

At that beautiful, snow-covered mountain resort I met the greatest collection of peacemakers I've ever met any- where—including high-level meetings in Washington D.C., and around the world. This was not a summit meet- ing on world peace made up of international delegates. These were young people—hundreds of them—who had gathered to compete in the twelfth annual National Handicapped Ski Championships. They had chosen Squaw Valley for the site of their competition because it had been the 1960 home of the International Winter Olympics.

I had carefully planned my week to include a trip to the Handicapped Nationals because my daughter, Carol, was skiing in them. As I mentioned in an earlier chapter, Carol lost a leg in a motorcycle accident some years ago. Soon afterward, she became acquainted with the handi- capped ski program and decided to become involved. She trained hard for the twelve regional contests in Amer- ica—all contestants must qualify in the Regionals before they can compete in the Nationals.

I was especially excited about attending the competi- tion because I had never seen Carol ski before. She was scheduled to ski her first race on Thursday, and I was slated to speak in Louisville at the Southern Baptist Con- vention on Wednesday, so I made plans to fly from Louis- ville to Squaw Valley in time for the first race on Thursday. However, when the weatherman announced a blizzard was on its way, they moved up the first race to Wednesday, and I missed it. I was terribly disappointed, especially because Carol won the Gold Medal first prize— for the Junior Division in the Downhill. I was very proud of her.

On Friday, the second races were to begin, and my wife and I were there for those. I had never seen so many one- legged people in one place in my life! There were even triple amputees, with two legs and one arm missing. And there were also races for the blind—even a sightless giant slalom. The course all the competitors follow is as long as the one that Olympians ski. No favoritism is shown because the competitors are handicapped. There are forty-seven gates through which they have to manuever coming down that mile-long, steep hill.

On Friday the blind were the first to ski. I'd never seen such a race before. The competitors are followed or led down the hill by a sighted person, who shouts directions such as, "Turn to the right. Now to the left. Straight ahead. Quick, quick, to the right!" This is the way they ski and race. It's an amazing sight.

Then there were the three-trackers. Carol is a three-tracker. The three-trackers ski without a prosthesis, with a ski on their one good leg. They are aided by outriggers—poles with miniature skis on them.

There are also skiers who are below-the-knee amputees, who have complete function of their knee and ski with their prosthesis like normal two-legged skiers. One of those skiers was racing through the course. Carol later related to us, "A funny thing happened yesterday. When the one-legged men skiers were coming down, one of the guys fell and his leg became detached—not from the ski but from his knee. That leg and ski came all the way down the hill and crossed the finish line! The judges didn't know whether they should award the leg or the body up on the hill!" These people have a fantastic sense of humor! They are great peacemakers.

### MAKE PEACE—WITH YOURSELF

Why do I call the young people I met at Squaw Valley peacemakers?

When I was a little boy, Adolph Hitler was starting to move through Europe, and people were beginning to talk about the possibility of war. I remember asking my simple, uneducated father, "Dad, what causes wars?"

I never forgot his answer. He said, "Well, somebody gets mad at somebody. It could be themselves—or even God. They take it out on others. Soon there's a fight. Their friends join in, and before you know it everybody's fighting."

There's a lot of wisdom to that. Years later, when I had the opportunity to study psychology and other advanced disciplines my father never had the benefit of, I saw how right he was. Most wars *do* start because somebody is mad at somebody, and often this angry person is someone who has not accepted himself or his condition. When you can't live with yourself, you will project your inner tension onto others!

The athletes I met at Squaw Valley are peacemakers because they have made peace with themselves and with God. I'm talking about people who have lost legs, arms, sight, mobility. They have every right to be bitter and angry at the world, but they aren't. They look in the mirror, they see what they are, and they accept it. They don't accuse God or anybody else. They are not fixing the blame; they are fixing the problem.

I can't think of many people who have been more of an inspiration to me, in fixing their problem and fixing their world, then Jeff Keith. You may have seen this young man, who lost a leg to cancer. The media covered his phenomenal accomplishment when he finished his historical run across the United States for the American Cancer Society. It took him about two hundred forty days, thirty-six pairs of shoes, and three prosthetic legs, but he made it!

I was with Jeff when his cross-country run was launched at Fennell Hall in Boston, Massachusetts. Both of us spoke at a kick-off prayer breakfast. Teddy Kennedy, Jr., also an amputee, was another speaker. I was very impressed with Jeff's message. He said, "Some people want to move mountains. I've already done that. Now all I want to do is move a country—inspire people to believe they can overcome their problems, too!" That's being a real peacemaker, for in the process of inspiring others to overcome their problems he settles the war going on in the hidden depths of a wounded soul!

Along his three-thousand-mile route, Jeff stopped at several hospitals to visit with depressed and discouraged cancer victims. Time and again young men and women, unable to see beyond their loss, were inspired by Jeff. Several got out of their beds for the first time since their surgery.

But cancer victims weren't the only ones who were helped by Jeff. He also stopped and visited prisoners at Sing Sing. Cell by cell, he talked to them all—this handsome young man with the artificial leg. And the hardcore, maximum-security prisoners were so impressed with him that they held a fund-raising dinner within the prison, with all proceeds going to the American Cancer Society.

I could go on and on about Jeff. He is changing his world for the better. He is fixing the problem. He is a true peacemaker.

### LOVE REPAIRS THE BREACH

Peacemakers. They are at peace with themselves, and therefore they can live at peace with others. But as I said before, peacemaking is not always easy. There are times when our own inner conflicts and insecurities hold us back from being "repairers of the breach and restorers of the path."

What helps us then? The restoring power of love.

Burl Ives, the legendary singer, is a happy man—a peacemaker. His secret? He has a big heart full of love. In fact, he's on the President's Committee for the handicapped. Yet, at one time, he found handicapped people challenging and difficult to relate to. Then, about four years ago, something very interesting happened to him that changed his attitude completely. One night at dinner in his Santa Barbara home, Burl explained it to me this way:

"Even though I had worked for many, many years in Washington with the handicapped, if I would see a cerebral palsy victim or maybe a blind person coming down the street—as much as I hate to admit it—I would avoid him or her. Face-to-face encounters with the handicapped frightened me. It was all right to sing and entertain, but when it came down to one-to-one, I managed to slip off to the side.

"But one day, when I was in Santa Barbara walking down to the docks, I noticed a group of children with a teacher some distance away. I paid no attention. I was walking along when all at once one of the little boys broke away from the teacher and ran to me. He clasped me around the knees and began to embrace me. There was this little boy, who obviously suffered from muscular spasms, and here we were face to face. I knelt down and I saw through to the boy. I saw his eyes and his soul, and there I encountered love—love for me. It had a great effect on me. Since then, I don't pass on the other side of the road."

What was it that kept Burl Ives from making peace with the handicapped? He was afraid of them. And as Gerald Jampolsky has said, "The opposite of love is not hate. The opposite of love is fear." So the opposite of peace is deeper than just conflict—the opposite of peace is insecurity.

Burl Ives was afraid that he wouldn't be able to handle these handicapped kids or his feelings about them, and so he was held back from being a peacemaker. Yet he discovered, through the love of a child, that there was nothing to fear.

"God Loves
You
--
And
So Do I "

... a prescription
for peacemaking

If we are to create peace in this world, we must understand what the issue really is. It's not love versus hate, or war versus peace. It's love versus fear and insecurity!

Willard Scott, the humorist and weatherman for the NBC *Today* show, the original Ronald McDonald and Bozo the clown, is a walking, talking definition of the word *happiness*. He says, "When I was a clown, I found that everybody loves a clown, no matter who the clown is. If you're a Democrat or a Republican, if you're Catholic, Protestant, or Jewish, it doesn't matter if you're a clown. It dawned on me that one of the things about being a clown is that you have no labels. There are no preconceived ideas about what this clown is, what he thinks about, or what he's related to.

"I have found that I can have a lay ministry on television just by trying to convey positive thoughts—love, really. I was raised in a Southern Baptist church and I remember our old preacher, Dr. Campbell. The thing I loved about him most was that he radiated love. His sermons were good, sometimes. Sometimes they were not the greatest. But you could always count on him whenever you needed someone to care for you. When someone died or someone got sick, Dr. Campbell was always there.

"And I remember when I was a little child of four or five years, after church all the kids would come out of the church. Dr. Campbell was six-foot-five—a big man—and wore a cutaway Prince Albert. He would sweep us little kids up in his arms and hug and love us. I believe that that kind of personal love and personal care and consideration had a tremendous influence on my life—as, of course, did my own mother and father, who adored and loved me and gave me everything that I could ever ask for. I do believe that no matter what our problems are, we can all love each other. We can share each other's lives. We can make our world better by being positive, and that's what I try to do."

## A SONG OF PEACE

You may say, "That doesn't work on the international level." But let me tell you a true story—the story of Roland Hayes.

Some of you young people may not realize that his was undoubtedly one of the great voices of the twentieth century; he was a tremendous concert soloist. And he had all the odds against him. He said once, "My mother is the person who taught me how to think positively, and I owe all of my success to her."

Roland Hayes was one of three children born to a Black family on a fifteen-acre cotton farm in Tennessee. When Roland was five years old, his father was caught under a branch while felling a tree and was killed. The mother tried as best she could to train and raise her three boys on their small plot of land. One day she called the boys together and said, "Boys, you just have to get an education. I have a plan. We are going to hitch up the wagon, go to Chattanooga, get a job, and see to it that you boys get an education."

The next day they hitched up their one horse to the wagon and Roland's mother rode in it. The three boys walked barefoot the sixty-two miles to Chattanooga, Tennessee.

While the family was living in Chattanooga, they sang in a church choir there. And one day the choir director, Mr. Calhoun, played for them a recording of Caruso and of Melba, two of the great singers of the day. Roland Hayes was so moved by the music that he said, "I believe that God has called me to sing a message of peace and brotherhood around the world." With that inspiration he went on to get a job and then enrolled at Fisk University.

While traveling with the college concert singers a few years later in Boston, Roland had a sudden impulse which, to his dying day, he said was from God—to drop

out and try to get established in Boston. Constantly recurring in his memory were the words of his mother, "Roland, you can do it if you believe you can and if you give
your life to God." He got a job as a hotel porter, earned
seven dollars a week, brought his mother up to Boston,
and rented a little apartment which cost him almost his
whole week's pay. He used orange crates for furniture.

Roland reasoned that he would never get anyplace unless he made a name for himself, so he decided to give a
concert—all on his own—in the biggest and the best
place, the main auditorium in Boston.

As he said years later, "I found out nobody ever did
anything for me unless I really stuck my neck out and
tried to help myself." He tried to find people to sponsor
him, but no one would do it because he was a nobody. He
thought and thought and he prayed.

Suddenly the bright idea came. He wrote a letter to all
the richest people in Boston introducing himself as Roland Hayes, one of the great concert artists of the future,
and inviting them to his first public American concert on
such and such a date—tickets, $1.50.

The impossible happened: Roland Hayes singlehand-
edly sold out every seat in the auditorium. The concert
was a great success. He personally made two thousand
dollars cash. In addition, someone in the audience from
Santa Monica, California, invited him to the West Coast
to give a concert. He gratefully accepted.

After the Santa Monica performance a music critic approached the young singer and said, "Mr. Hayes, when
you sang, you stirred me, as do all of the great concert
artists. But you had something more, and I cannot put my
finger on it."

That night in his hotel room Roland was haunted by
the man's comment. What did he have that others didn't
have? Could it be his blood? He remembered his old uncle
saying to him as they picked cotton, "Roland, your father
and me came from Africa, from a line of chiefs. Don't you

ever forget that. You got chief's blood in your veins." (It takes a strong self-image—positive self-esteem—to dare to be a peacemaker.)

As Roland Hayes prayed that night in Santa Monica, he had a revelation that he would leave the United States and go to East Africa to try to find the tribe from which he came and discover what made him unique. He spent the last of his money from the Boston concert to get to London, England, on his way to Africa. In England, however, his money ran out.

A friend of the pastor of the Royal Chapel inquired, "Roland, how would you like to sing for my pastor friend on Sunday?"

Roland accepted quickly. In the Royal Chapel that Sunday he sang the spiritual, "And He Never Spoke a Mumbling Word."

Three days later Roland got a telephone call from a friend, who asked, "Have you heard the news?"

"No. What?"

"Well, you sang in the Royal Chapel Sunday, and do you know who was there?" Roland remained silent. "The King and the Queen of England! And they are requesting a command performance at Buckingham Palace."

Roland couldn't believe his ears. Two days later he sang for the King and Queen, and in the audience were both Caruso and Melba, whose recordings had first inspired him to pursue a singing career.

Roland Hayes became an overnight success. That year—1924—looked wonderful for him. He was even booked for a concert at the Beethoven Concert Hall in Berlin. This concert would undoubtedly establish him as a concert soloist on the continent of Europe. En route to Germany, Roland stopped in Prague. He was called into the American consul's office. "Mr. Hayes," the consul said, "I have bad news for you. You are going to have to cancel your concert in Germany. The French have taken over the Rhineland and they are holding it with troops made up of Negroes brought from America. The Germans are furious. No black-skinned person will be able to sing in Germany at this time."

"Thank you for telling me this, Mr. Consul," Roland said, "I will surely pray about it." The days passed and he could not bring himself to cancel the concert.

On the night of the concert, Roland and his black accompanist carefully made their way to the auditorium and slipped in through a back door. Once inside, they peered through the curtains and saw that the place was packed to overflowing. Now Roland realized he was an internationally controversial case.

When the curtain went up, Roland Hayes stood in the curve of the baby grand piano, his accompanist seated at the piano beside him. He quietly folded his hands, looked upward, and spoke a private prayer to God: "God, make me a horn for the Omnipotent to sound through."

As he stood silently praying, suddenly he heard hissing, then stomping, and then the catcalls and boos. Somebody shouted, "Don't disgrace the Beethoven Concert Hall with plantation songs about black men from America."

Hate seemed to fill that auditorium. His accompanist said, "Mr. Hayes, we better get out of here."

Objects began to fly onto the stage, narrowly missing the soloist. Roland Hayes later recalled the incident and remarked, "I just stood there with my hands folded and prayed, 'God, what will I do?' "

A bright idea entered his mind. To the accompanist he said, without taking his eyes off the audience, "Let's begin with Beethoven's 'This Is My Peace.' " The accompanist picked out the music for this God-inspired first number, and slowly, softly the fingers began to roll across the piano. A surprised murmur ran through the hall as the German concertgoers heard the music of their favorite, Beethoven.

Roland Hayes opened his mouth and began to sing "This Is My Peace." His mighty voice rolled through the

auditorium, and the audience quieted down. By the time
he finished, there was absolute attention. He went on to
sing several classical numbers and ended the concert with
Negro spirituals, the plantation songs. At the close of the
concert, some members of the audience jumped up on the
stage, hoisted Roland on their shoulders, and paraded him
around the auditorium. He was the hero of the continent,
and he was an inspiration in settling the dispute between
France and Germany.

### THE PRINCE OF PEACE

"Blessed are the peacemakers, for they shall be called
children of God."

Who are the peacemakers? They are not necessarily the
people who are *talking* about peace all the time. Peacemakers are those who are *doing* something, creating
something, building something—bridges, mostly!

Maybe peacemakers are people like you and me who, in
our own ways, are trying to bring Jesus Christ into human hearts.

Do you want peace in your family? Do you want peace
in your community? Do you want peace with other races
and other cultures? There will not be peace anywhere as
long as there is a war going on in your heart and in your
soul.

So how do you make peace with yourself? You make
peace with yourself by meeting the greatest peacemaker
of all time, Jesus Christ. He was called "the Prince of
Peace." He lived, He died on a Friday we call Good Friday,
and He rose again on Easter. He's alive today. He is my
closest personal friend.

"Blessed are the peacemakers, for they shall be called
children of God." You can be a peacemaker once you
have your life together, once you've let Jesus become
your friend. When Jesus is your friend, you have an

internalized positive self-image. You become a possibility thinker and you begin to say, "I can do all things because I am somebody. I am a friend of Jesus Christ."

That's a great way to live. And that's why most Christians are relaxed persons. They're not uptight. And they don't carry around a bundle of emotional garbage that shows itself in the form of anxiety, fear, tension, or insecurity. They are not angry people who feel they're victims of the world's injustices.

I made a trip to Mainland China a few years ago, and my son led a tour of people who were invited to be a part of that mission. One night in Shanghai, I tapped on my son's door. It was rather late, but Bob was not in his room. Someone said, "He went out for a walk."

I immediately went out into the street to see if I could spot him. I saw a crowd—almost a mob—gathered on a nearby bridge. I cautiously approached the large group of Chinese and saw, in the midst of them, a six-foot-four-inch American. It was my son. Bob was talking to two of the leaders of this great crowd. I could see that he was excitedly sharing Christ with these two.

Afraid of intruding, I quietly retreated to the hotel. Later that night he told me what happened. He had been standing on the bridge (more important, he was about to build a bridge), and two bright young students had come up to him. They were university students who spoke English.

"Who are you?" the students asked my son. "Where are you from? What are you doing here?"

Bob said, "I'm a Christian. Have you ever heard about Jesus Christ?"

They said, "What's a Christian? Who is Jesus Christ?"

He told them, and he led them through some basic spiritual truths. He explained that Christianity teaches that God wants us all to be beautiful persons. It's a law of life that we all have our sins, our internal tensions. We all need salvation. And then he said, "Jesus came to save us."

He asked them if they'd like to accept Jesus as their friend. To his amazement, they said, "Yes."

So Bob prayed with them. There on the bridge in Shanghai, Bob and the young Chinese students prayed together. Bob told them about the Bible and, in response to their request, he later sent them Bibles and continued corresponding with them. What Bob was doing was a special kind of peacemaking.

Yes, all of us can be peacemakers—wherever we are. There may be a tension inside of you, in your home, or in your place of business. But you can resolve this tension if you give it all you've got. Tackling the problem of tension is no different than tackling any other problem. You can make peace in much the same way that you solve other problems. The people who ultimately win at what they go after are the people who give it all they've got.

Let me share with you one of the most inspiring sights that I've ever seen. It happened on the slopes of Squaw Valley. The handicapped skier's name was Kim Caulfield. She was about eighteen and blind. Kim was being led down the giant slalom. She made it through forty-four gates, and she was lined up straight with the finish line. Her guide behind her said, "Straight ahead Kim; go for it!"

Kim dug in and was flying over the snow when she hit a rut. The poles flew out of her hands. She fell flat on her stomach. She knew she'd have to get her body across the finish line or be disqualified. She looked beaten, but she didn't stop. She reached out for her poles. When she couldn't find them, she started swimming over the snow, straight ahead, until she crossed the finish line.

"Kim, you made it!" the judge called out. But she didn't hear him. She just kept swimming over the snow flat on her stomach for another five—ten—fifteen feet.

The judge kept shouting, "You made it, Kim; you can stop!" She still didn't hear. Finally a second voice, then another, then all of us who were spectators shouted, "You made it, Kim!"

Kim stopped, still flat on her belly. Then she heard the applause. She jumped up to her feet and danced for joy.

You can do it, too! You can be a peacemaker if you choose to believe in yourself and in Christ.

Be-Happy Attitude #8

# "I can choose to be happy— anyway!"

*"Blessed are those who are persecuted for righteousness' sake, for theirs is the kingdom of heaven."*
Matthew 5:10

THE LAST BE-HAPPY ATTITUDE. The final lesson. Jesus saves His toughest teaching for last. Only those who have gone through all the previous classes are qualified for admittance to this final lesson: "Blessed are those who are persecuted for righteousness' sake."

## HOW TO BE HAPPY

Be-Happy Attitude #1 was: *"I need help—I can't do it alone!"* In order to be truly happy, I must learn to admit those areas in which I am weak and to welcome constructive help and advice.

Be-Happy Attitude #2: *"I'm really hurting—but I'm going to bounce back!"* In the face of failure or loss, I must have the attitude that I'm going to grow from my experience and move on.

Be-Happy Attitude #3: *"I'm going to remain cool, calm, and corrected."* I must maintain a steady, stable, teachable attitude through the good times and the bad times before I will ultimately find true satisfaction.

Be-Happy Attitude #4: *"I really want to do the right thing!"* My attitude must be to achieve, maintain, and live by integrity, for honesty and righteousness attract good friends and great people who will help me. Here is the sensible secret of sane and safe ego control.

Be-Happy Attitude #5: *"I'm going to treat others the way I want others to treat me."* I will have a positive attitude, keeping in mind that there is a law of proportionate return. So when I am abused or mistreated, I shall choose to be merciful and forgiving, knowing that this will come back to me in kind and I will be blessed.

Be-Happy Attitude #6: *"I've got to let the faith flow free through me."* I must constantly scrutinize my motives, my methods, and my manners, being humble enough to know that I can get on the wrong track in a hurry. So, I shall maintain a positive, soul-searching attitude toward myself at all times, lest I get off the track and miss getting on the best track of all.

Be-Happy Attitude #7: *"I'm going to be a bridge builder."* To be truly happy, I shall maintain the attitude that an enemy can become a valuable friend. I shall strive as much as I can to live in respect and harmony and peace with all people. But this will mean making peace with myself first!

This brings us to the last Be-Happy Attitude—#8: *"I can choose to be happy—anyway!"* If, after applying all of these positive attitudes to the best of my ability, I still find myself the abused victim in human relationships—personal, social, or professional—I shall choose to believe that God can settle the score in His way and in His time. I shall be blessed by knowing that my hurts, borne quietly, patiently, and positively, can be turned into halos.

## STICKS AND STONES CAN BREAK YOUR BONES—
## BUT WORDS HURT, TOO!

Persecution is something all of us have faced or will face. For some—especially in certain countries—persecution takes the form of physical torture. Through the years it has been everything from the rack to bamboo under the fingernails to cigarette burns and electric shock. With terrorism on the march today, this subject becomes painfully relevant.

And persecution wears many faces! It is true that we in the free countries are not constantly shadowed by the threat of physical persecution for our beliefs. But at one time or another we can all expect to face some kind of harassment, snubs, rejection, or discrimination. Emotional persecution that attacks a person's self-esteem can be devastating! The calculated insult, the contrived putdown are weapons wielded even by religious people against their own kind.

Yes, persecution occurs at various levels in life and strikes from a variety of sources. Our supporters can inexplicably turn on us. (Judas was Christ's treasurer.)

Society can snub and turn its back on us.

When we fail to live up to our expectations, we often persecute ourselves. Regrets, guilt, remorse can torture the soul! Is any form of persecution more prevalent and widespread than self-recrimination?

Persecution attacks losers and winners, too! Even the achiever has enemies, people who are jealous and would "persecute." Excellence takes it on the chin today. Positive thinkers have always been persecuted. They said of Norman Vincent Peale, "Peale is appalling, but Paul is appealing." Clever, cute, but very un-Christian! Negative thinkers persecute positive thinkers. Rich people are persecuted, too, by suspicious, cynical "have nots" who assume that anyone who is wealthy must be a crook or a swindler. Super-successful people are often viewed with suspicion; persecution at that level is very prevalent in society.

Peer pressure can be a powerful persecution. The truth is: No social unit, no racial or religious community, and no age grouping is free from the sometimes blatant and more-often subtle stabs of persecution. Young people are often led into drugs and immoral conduct under the fear of persecuting taunts from their classmates. Social pressures in junior high, high school, and college are often applied to those who live by high ideals. The square and straight person can expect to be laughed at and scorned. Insulting epithets, chilly ridicule, and demeaning labels become weapons of emotional torture.

Do you feel persecuted? Then be of good cheer! You can choose to be happy—anyway. This Be-Happy Attitude is for you. Yes! *You* can be happy, too, even if you are the innocent victim of authentic injustice, insult, injury, discrimination, or oppression.

How can you be happy when you are facing persecution? Is this Be-Happy Attitude really practical? Is it possible? Oh, yes. There are several people I know who have gone through tremendous suffering, and they have emerged from the fire not unscathed, but stronger.

Follow with me and you will see how they did it, and how you, too, can turn your scars into stars. These people who have mastered this final Be-Happy Attitude were able to be victorious because they:

(1) *Remained POSITIVE!* They took a positive attitude—they chose to rejoice in spite of their circumstances.
(2) *Were PREPARED!* They had equipped themselves with a spiritual and emotional support system that became an invisible shield.
(3) *PERSEVERED in doing what is right.* They kept on

keeping on, and would not let others get the better of them.

(4) *PARDONED those who hurt them!* They forgave those who did the persecuting.

(5) *PERSISTED in trusting God,* even when He seemed far away! They kept in mind that God is the ruler yet, that He will have the last word and it will be good.

(6) *PRAYED for understanding and strength!* They accepted the help God offers to those that are suffering. They understood that they were not the only ones who had ever been persecuted, and so they resisted the temptation to fall victim to the persecution complex and martyr syndrome.

(7) *PASSED triumphantly through the necessary PHASES* that we must all go through when we face tragedy!

## STAY POSITIVE

Dr. Viktor Frankl, an eminent psychiatrist and author of the famous book, *Man's Search for Meaning,* is a living example of this Be-Happy Attitude.

Dr. Frankl, who is a Jew, was imprisoned by the Nazis in the Second World War. His wife, his children, and his parents were all killed in the holocaust.

The Gestapo took Viktor and made him strip. He stood there totally naked. But they noticed that he still had on his wedding band. As they removed even that from him, he said to himself, "You can take away my wife, you can take away my children, you can strip me of my clothes and my freedom, but there is one thing no person can *ever* take away from me—and that is my freedom to choose how I will react to what happens to me!"

That was the birth of an idea that years later he would develop into "logotherapy," a form of therapy that has helped countless thousands deal with what life hands them. And that basic lesson in positive reactionism remains the keystone in the whole arch of possibility thinking. My philosophy has been greatly shaped and influenced by Dr. Frankl's lectures, writings, and private meetings with him.

We are free to choose our attitude in any given situation—to maintain a positive attitude no matter how negative the situation. What a life-changing idea! Dr. Smiley Blanton, another great psychiatrist, once told of listening to a patient who was depressed. After several sessions he interrupted this suffering soul: " 'If only'— that's your problem!" He explained, "You keep repeating those words, 'If only I had . . .' 'If only I hadn't . . .' My prescription for you is to strike those words from your life! Replace them with the words, 'next time.' Do not deny the reality of mistakes made or sins committed, but learn to forgive yourself. You can do that by facing the torturing memories with a positive attitude, affirming, 'next time things are going to be different.' " Great advice to a victim of self-persecution!

Here then is a Be-Happy Attitude that we can all use: "Blessed are those who are persecuted for righteousness' sake, for theirs is the kingdom of heaven. Blessed are you when men revile you and persecute you and utter all kinds of evil against you falsely on my account. Rejoice and be glad, for your reward is great in heaven" (Matt. 5:10–11).

Jesus was saying much the same thing Viktor Frankl said: You can choose to take a positive attitude toward your persecution. And if you can do this, you will eventually triumph. This lesson in dealing with persecution is a lesson every Christian must learn, because everyone is going to face a time when he has to stand up for what he believes and run the risk of rejection or ridicule. If we learn this lesson well, we'll be able to tolerate rejection and *our self-esteem will be enhanced in the process.*

That's a Be-Happy Attitude! If we don't have a positive attitude, rejection will devastate our dignity. And it's impossible to be happy without a strong self-respect!

## BE PREPARED

We make a grave mistake if we assume that we will never face persecution simply because we live in a free country. There is a strong probability that *all* of us will face some kind of persecution at one time or another in our lives. And it is vitally important to spiritually arm ourselves with inner emergency equipment *before* the crises hit.

Most of us have emergency equipment in our homes and offices—a first-aid kit, a flashlight, perhaps a fire extinguisher, at least a telephone with which to call an emergency unit. We prepare for emergencies before they hit, for we never know when they will come and what they will do to us.

As we need to be prepared with physical equipment, we also need to be prepared spiritually *before* times of persecution arrive. We do that by spending time daily—or, at the very least, weekly—in positive praying, positive Bible study, and worshiping regularly at a positive-thinking church. We saturate our subconscious minds with positive Bible verses, positive hymns, and examples of people who made it through trials successfully, with their faith intact.

Before we can pass the test and graduate from the school of discipleship and commence living out the Christian faith in a secular and sinful society, we have to pass this final exam: We must be spiritually and psychologically conditioned for ridicule, rejection, and persecution. Only those who have learned that they can expect persecution and are prepared to maintain a positive attitude through hard or horrific times will prove to be star ambassadors of Jesus Christ in the world.

So, study the rest of this chapter carefully. It is a first-aid kit for unexpected crises. In it you will find positive Bible verses, positive hymns, and stories of people who have triumphed in the face of enormous persecution.

### PERSEVERE IN DOING WHAT IS RIGHT

Today, the social and moral pressures in our pluralistic society threaten the Christian as never before! The temptations to "become like" the nonreligious persons around us can be terribly intimidating! The temptation to adopt the value system of a secular society becomes a deadly serious form of insidious persecution. To my Christian reader: A warning! Compromise and abandon your principles, and you will literally lose your soul; you'll no longer be the person you were before. You will have lost your identity as a distinctive, independent person.

For when you give in, for fear of ridicule, to the pressure to be like everyone else, you'll have allowed yourself to be absorbed in the total collective society. Run with the foxes, dash with the hounds, and become just another part of the mass of humanity. You'll be a nothing! A no one! Yes, a non-individual! Only a blob absorbed in a mass! For a little bit of you dies every time you surrender a cherished ideal, abandon a noble value, or discard a moral principle.

So then, how do we stand up against social persecution? Once there was a politician who did the best job he could. But, being human, he made mistakes and was criticized, and reporters repeated errors of fact about him in the paper. Well, he became so upset that he drove out into the country to visit his dear friend, a farmer. "What am I going to do?" the politician cried. "I've tried so hard.

Nobody has tried harder than I have to do more good for more people—and look how they criticize me!"

But the old farmer could hardly hear the complaint of his persecuted politician friend because his hound dog was barking at the full moon. The farmer rebuked his dog, but the dog kept barking. Finally the farmer said to the politician, "Do you want to know how you should handle your unfair critics? Here's how. Listen to that dog. Now, look at that moon. And remember that people will keep yelling at you—they'll nip at your heels, and they'll criticize you. But here's the lesson: *The dog keeps howling, but the moon keeps shining!"*

Let people persecute you—but don't stop doing all the good you've been doing.

Think of the great names: Joan of Arc, Martin Luther King, Stephen, Paul. These names remind us of the final, ultimate Be-Happy Attitude. For these people were really blessed. Even in the face of persecution, they were blessed, because they stood fast for what they believed. They persevered in doing right.

How were these great men and women able to "keep shining" in the face of persecution? They were given the most precious gift of all—the assurance that no matter what happens—even death—nothing can come between us and God's love. "Neither death, nor life, nor angels, nor principalities, nor things present, nor things to come, nor powers, nor height, nor depth, nor anything else in all creation, will be able to separate us from the love of God in Christ Jesus. . . . We are *more than conquerors* through him who loved us" (Rom. 8:39, 38).

What does this mean to us? What could top being a conqueror? What is better than winning? Why, it is converting your opponent to your side. It is turning an adversary into an ally. It is turning an enemy into a friend. That is being *more than a conqueror!*

Jesus did this. When He was persecuted by the Roman

*If you think you're a total failure,*
*remember this :*


*Your*
*greatest successes...*
*will forever remain...*
*...God's secret !*

centurion, He did not lash back at him, nor did He threaten him. Instead, He won him over with forgiving love. Even as Jesus died, the centurion exclaimed, "Truly this was the Son of God" (Matt. 27:54).

There is something nobler than winning. There is something more rewarding than conquering. It is possible to be *more* than a conqueror. You may not live to see it, but you had better believe that when you maintain a positive attitude in the face of persecution and persevere in doing what is right, you will be blessed.

### PARDON THOSE WHO HAVE HURT YOU

"Not easy," you say. And you are right. One of the most difficult things to do is to forgive someone who has hurt you. Again, we take a lesson from Jesus in dealing positively with our persecution.

When he was on the cross, stripped of his dignity, Jesus cried out, "Father, forgive them, for they know not what they do!"

Sometimes it is *humanly* impossible to forgive. When that happens, we need to call upon divine intervention. We ask God to forgive those who hurt us and to work on our hearts so that we can eventually see our hurt from their perspective.

Frequently, more often than not, people who hurt others through their words or their actions are unaware that they've injured anybody. They "know not what they do."

Other times, they are incapable of being held accountable for their actions. "They know not what they do" in terms of being so mixed up, so troubled, so spiteful, or so insecure that they act purely out of gut instinct. They are incapable of thinking about others' feelings or others' lives.

Have you been hurt? Are you still carrying that pain

within? Is it impossible to forgive and forget? Then start by saying the prayer Christ prayed: "Father, forgive them, for they know not what they do."

## PERSIST IN TRUSTING GOD

When we are suffering, it is tempting to lash out at everyone around us—including God. And it is hard to keep on trusting Him when we are being rejected or ridiculed. But if we are to be victorious in the face of persecution, it is vital to maintain our trust in Him.

The Book of Job has been hailed by students of literature as one of the greatest epic poems ever written. But it is far more than a beautiful piece of literature. Job is a story of triumphal trust—for surely nobody has ever faced more persecution than Job.

"When he has tried me, I shall come forth as gold" (Job 23:10).

"Though he slay me, yet will I trust in him" (Job 13:15, KJV).

Both of these statements made by Job *after* he faced persecution are testimonial to the fact that he successfully endured his persecution. Job illustrates a faith that will not lose its grip, a faith that never lets go.

Let's examine Job's trials. He was very rich. He had three thousand camels, which would be like having a few hundred Rolls-Royces today. He had seven sons and three daughters. His fame was worldwide. He was what you could call super-rich, super-successful. At the age of thirty-nine, he had it made. And on top of everything, he had a reputation for being religious.

One day, according to the book of Job, the devil appeared to the Almighty and said, "So, you think Job's such a good guy? Let me tell you—it is easy to have faith when you're rich like that. The truth is that Job only comes across with a smiling, happy faith because life is easy for him. He's rich. But if he were poor and suffering, then we'd see what kind of faith Job really has."

In this epic poem God agrees that the devil can try Job. The first thing that happens to him is financial ruin. He loses all of his property. The next thing that happens is that his house collapses and all of his children are killed. Then once the money is gone, Job's opportunistic friends go. He's lost his money, his family, and his power; the community just doesn't respond to him anymore. Finally one day he sits in the ashes, naked. And he says, "Naked I came from my mother's womb, and naked shall I return; the Lord gave, and the Lord has taken away; blessed be the name of the Lord"(Job 1:21).

Then he adds this inspiring pledge: "When he has tried me, I shall come forth as gold!" (Job 23:10). It is the same faith that I describe in the Possibility Thinker's Creed: "When faced with a mountain, I will not quit! I will keep on striving until I climb over, find a pass through, tunnel underneath, or simply stay and turn the mountain into a gold mine with God's help."

This is the kind of faith we used to sing about in a hymn:

> Oh, for a faith that will not shrink,
>   though pressed by every foe—
> That will not stumble on the brink
>   of any earthly woe;
> A faith that shines forth bright and clear
>   when troubles rage about;
> A faith that in the darkest time
>   will know no doubt.*

Such was the faith that Job had: "Though God slay me, yet will I trust him."

This faith is sensational! Fantastic! Awesome! And it's

* William Bathurst

exciting to study it in depth because it puts us squarely face to face with three questions concerning persecution.

The first is, "How do human beings react to persecution?"

The second question is, "What is the nature of this trust that Job sustained?"

And the final question is, "Is it possible for you to acquire that same positive mental trust?"

Consider the first question: "How do human beings react to persecution?" The answer is threefold: (a) The most common negative reaction is simply to give up—and accept defeat. I call people who react like this CINDERS.

(b) The second common reaction is equally negative. Consider the SINNERS. What is a sinner? A sinner is somebody who deliberately chooses to abandon all faith. A sinner is somebody who by an act of choice takes the negative reaction. The ultimate sin—what is it? It's choosing to be a cynic, choosing not to believe.

(c) One reaction is seen in the *cinders*—the *burned-out* people. The second reaction is seen in the sinners—they're the *burned-up* people; they become angry at God and everybody else. Finally, there are the SENDERS. They don't get burned out. The don't get burned up. They just burn brighter—and shine like gold!

That's the way it was with Job when he was tested and tried. He did indeed glow with the golden light of inspiring faith.

The senders. They burn bright and send out a light in the darkness that says, "Watch me, world! I may be tested! Tried! Persecuted! But I still trust God." They send out a message to the world that you can believe in God even when He is silent. The amazing thing is this: The darker the suffering, the brighter the message that the sender shares with everyone.

The principle is best illustrated by a sight I witnessed while flying over the Pacific Ocean. I thought I'd seen the

*Three Reactions to Suffering:*

*1. Some are CINDERS...*
*   ...They get burned-OUT!*
*2. Some are SINNERS...*
*   ...They get burned-UP!*
*3. Some are SENDERS...*
*   ...They just burn BRIGHTER!*

wake of every possible boat or ship. I've seen the gorgeous wakes of luxury cruiseliners, and I've seen the lovely little wake of a canoe on a quiet stream in Canada. I've watched my children ski behind a motorboat in glassy wakes on an early morning mountain lake.

Long or short, narrow or wide—it's always been a thrilling sight to me to look back and see the wake that's left behind. But flying over the ocean I saw a wake such as I've never seen before. I saw it from the window of a commercial jet. At first I thought the marks on the water were hidden reefs. But my companion said, "It looks like the wake of a vessel, but those lines are too far apart to be that!"

As we flew on, we could see that the lines were in fact moving closer together, the way a wake would look. And finally we saw the vessel that created the wake. What had made this mammoth wake? Was it an aircraft carrier? No. It was just a very slim, slender, black, short line in the water with a periscope piercing the surface.

I said, "It's a submarine!"

My companion said, "It is, at that."

It had just surfaced. And a submarine, when it surfaces after plowing through the depths, leaves a wake that is remarkable.

I tell you today: People who go through the deep waters of suffering leave a wide wake if they choose (and it is a choice) to trust and forgive. In spite of their suffering, they send a huge message of hope to the world.

What are the reactions you can choose in the face of suffering? You can burn out, burn up, or burn bright! You can be a *cinder,* a *sinner,* or a *sender.* Your reaction must be to trust God—anyway! Your reaction must be to forgive—anyway! When the suffering is horrific, then *trust and forgiveness are your only positive options. All of the other possible choices are negative.* Don't be a cinder. Don't be a sinner. Do be a sender!

The first question I've already asked and answered is:

"How do people react to suffering?" The second question is: "What is this trust, really?" It's really quite simple: Trust is the belief that God is alive *anyway!*

I've said it before, but it bears repeating. Scrawled in the basement of a German home was a Star of David next to these words:

> I believe in the sun even when it is not shining.
> I believe in love even when I do not feel it.
> I believe in God even when He is silent.

*God is alive. Even though you may not be hearing Him or feeling Him—do not discard Him.*

The truth of this statement came through to me with renewed power in an amusing incident that happened to me several years ago. That week, I lectured on Tuesday at the University of Berkeley, and I was scheduled to speak on Wednesday to the Lutherans in Arizona on the five-hundredth anniversary of Martin Luther's birth. On Thursday I was to be at Northwestern College in Iowa, and on Friday I had to be at Johns Hopkins in Baltimore. As you can see, it was really a tightly scheduled week. Everything was carefully timed and planned. If I missed a connection, I would really be in trouble.

Everything went smoothly until I got to Phoenix to catch my eastbound plane. I was first at the check-in desk, to make sure that I would not be late. Soon there was a line of about thirty or forty people behind me with all their suitcases, waiting to check in. The plane was scheduled to leave in thirty minutes. Eventually the lady came to start the check-in. She look harassed. Trying to be understanding, I said, "You look as though you have troubles."

She didn't even look up to see my face. She just mumbled, "Boy, have I got troubles!" She said, "I suppose you're here to check in on this flight to Denver."

I said, "Yes."

She said, "Well, I just got word that that flight's going to be cancelled, and I suppose you are now going to want me to help you, which I'm obligated to do, but I don't know what I'm going to do!" Then she looked up and said, "Oh! Dr. Schuller!" And she took hold of my hands and added, "Say a little prayer for me; I'm in trouble. I don't know what I'm going to do. Let me talk to the computer for a minute."

She began to type on the keyboard, then she stopped and looked at the screen. Her face registered dismay and frustration. Frantic, she picked up the phone, "Ben! Help! The computer's dead! Nothing! It's just looking at me. You say we have a line problem? I don't care if it is a line problem. Make it come alive, *please!*"

The point is this: Some of you complain when God is silent, and doubt His existence. However, you don't stop believing in computers when one is silent because there's a line problem. Don't stop believing in God because you're not hearing from Him at the moment.

What was this trust that Job had? Job trusted that God was still alive, even though He seemed silent in the face of his persecution. But there's a second element to this trust. The second element is that God will have the last word. What you are facing now will not last forever. It is merely a phase in your life. It's not the end of the story.

Oral Roberts went through a horrific tragedy a few years ago when his son was found dead. I sent him a telegram, which said, "Dear Oral, first let me quote you: *God knows a lot more about this than we do.* And now, Oral, may I add my own line, *God will have the last word, and it will be GOOD!*"

Don't blame God, don't lash out in bitterness at Him. Even though He may have allowed your suffering, He never *caused* it. He can help you turn it into something beautiful if you will remember that God is not finished with you—yet. Know that God will have the last word,

*Possibility thinking can
turn persecution
into opportunities:
... for healing
... for forgiveness
... for compassion!*

that this suffering you are going through is not the last word. It is a passage, not a dead end.

What is the best possible reaction to persecution? The answer is: Trust is the only sensible response.

And what is this trust? This trust is that God is alive, even if He's silent. It is the trust that God will come back "on the line" and His last word will be good.

Now we come to the third question: "How can we trust God in times of suffering?"

Let me give you two positive thoughts. The first positive thought is this: Can you trust the banker if he has all his own money in the bank? Of course. And the same is true with God. God has a lot more to lose than you do. Really, it wasn't Job alone who was on trial. God was also on trial.

Every time you face suffering, remember that you are on trial, but so is the Almighty. He must come forth as gold too. His honor is at stake. At worst, all you could lose is your life or soul. But God could lose His honor. After all, He has made Promises. His Word is filled with them.

There is a second positive thought to keep in mind in the tough times that test our faith. What kept Job's trust going? He was an upright, honorable man. If your heart is right, your faith will burn bright. You can trust Him if you know you've done—and are doing—the best you could—or can.

## PRAY FOR UNDERSTANDING AND STRENGTH

Persecuted? Facing enormous adversity? Then don't lash out. Don't reject the help God offers. Grasp His helping hand and fall to your knees in prayer. Thank God for the help that He is giving you and will continue to give you. Ask Him to send companions who can help. Ask Him for a supernatural strength to believe and to rejoice anyway!

Many of you know who Corrie ten Boom was. Either

you read the book or you saw the movie of her life, *The Hiding Place.*

Corrie ten Boom participated in an underground railroad in the Netherlands during World War II. Untold numbers of Jews, who were hounded and hunted by the Gestapo, found escape in her house, where they were hidden in a remote, specially constructed room. Corrie, her sister Betsy, and her father hid numbers of Jews who are alive today, but would have been killed in concentration camps. But eventually the Gestapo caught up with the Ten Booms. They were sentenced to prison and hence to months of persecution.

I was so impressed with Corrie's story that I made a long-distance call to the Netherlands, which is where Corrie lived when I first met her. She came and spoke in our church. She was eighty years old at the time. I recently reread her unpublished sermon. It deserves a wider audience that I hope this book will offer. Here, then, is her testimony:

"Once I met a parachutist, and I asked him, 'When you jumped for the first time from an airplane to the earth, what did you think?'

"He said, 'I thought only one thing, and that was, "It works! It works!" '

"I am going to tell you that it works when you go with Jesus. Some people think that it does not work, and I hope that we will persuade them that they can never trust the Lord too much. The Lord said, 'In the world ye shall have tribulation: but be of good cheer; I have overcome the world' (John 16:33, KJV).

"Years ago my grandfather started a prayer meeting for the Jews. Every week he came together with his friends in an old watchmaker's shop. There he prayed for the peace of Jerusalem and the salvation of the Jews. That practice was so unusual that I remember the year when they started—1844. Today it is not unusual when Christians pray for the Jews.

"A hundred years later, in the very same house where

my grandfather prayed for the Jews, his son—my father—four of my grandfather's grandchildren, and a great grandson were all arrested because they saved Jewish people in Holland during World War II. Four of them had to die in prisons. I came out alive. I cannot understand it, but that does not matter. We have to be ready for tribulation.

"I can tell you that I never had experienced such a realization of Jesus being with me as during the time when I was in the concentration camp. Ravensbruck, located north of Berlin in what is now East Germany, is far away from my home in Holland. The barracks where we lived, my sister Betsy and I, was in the shadow of a crematorium. Every day about six hundred bodies were burned there. When I saw smoke go up, I asked myself, 'When will it be my time to be killed?' I did not know beforehand that I should be set free by a miracle of God, and a blunder of man, one week before they killed all the women of my age.

"I have looked death in the eyes, not once but often. When you see death in people's eyes, you wake up to reality. What a joy it was that Jesus was with me, that I knew He had died on the cross for the sins of the whole world and also for my sins. I was not afraid. I knew that when they killed me I would go to the house of the Father with many mansions. I would go into the world of the living. What a joy! I knew the best was yet to be. How can we know how strong and rich we are in Jesus Christ and in His presence? By looking at the cross.

> At the cross, at the cross
> Where I first saw the light,
> And the burden of my sins rolled away.
> It was there, by faith, I received my sight.
> And now I am happy all the day.*

"Sometimes in that terrible concentration camp we had

* Isaac Watts.

to stand naked; they stripped us of all our clothes. Seven times I went through that ordeal. The first time was the worst; I could hardly bear it. I never felt so miserable, so cold, so humble. I said to Betsy, 'I cannot bear this.' Then suddenly, it was if I saw Jesus at the cross. The Bible tells us they took His garments. He hung there naked. By my own suffering I could understand a fraction of the suffering of Jesus, and I was so thankful I could feel as He had felt. 'Love so amazing, so divine, demands my life, my soul, my all' [John Newton]. We must not forget we follow a scarred captain. Should we not have scars?

Under His faultless orders, we follow through the street.
Lest we forget, Lord, when we meet.
Show us your hands and feet.

"Jesus was with us, with Betsy and me, at the camp. In the morning we had to stand roll call very early. The chief of our barracks was so cruel that she sent us out a whole hour early. Betsy and I did not go to the square where we would have to stand for hours during roll call; we walked around the tent. Everything was black. The ground was made black with coal. The barracks were painted black. The only light we had was from the stars and the moon. But Jesus was with us; He talked with us and He walked with us. Betsy said something, then He said something. How? I don't know, but we both understood what Jesus said. There was a little bit of heaven in the midst of hell.

"Once Betsy woke me in the middle of the night. 'Corrie, God has spoken to me. When we are set free we must do only one thing. We must bring the gospel over the whole world. We can tell so much experience, and that is why people will listen. We can tell them that here we have had real experience that Jesus' light is stronger than the deepest darkness. When we meet people who are in darkness, we can tell them that when they go with Jesus they cannot go too deep. Always deeper are His everlasting arms.' One week later, Betsy died. Two weeks later, I was set free.

"Christian, are you afraid of tribulation? Don't be afraid. Do you know that Paul once said, in 2 Thessalonians 1:45, 'We ourselves glory in you . . . for your patience and faith in all your persecutions and tribulations that ye endure: . . . Ye may be counted worthy of the kingdom of God, for which ye also suffer' (KJV)? Don't be afraid, for God did not give us a spirit of fear, but a spirit of love, and of power, coupled with a sound mind.

"I remember when I was a little girl. I once said to my father, 'Daddy, I am afraid that I will never be strong enough to be a martyr for Jesus.' Daddy replied, 'Corrie, when you plan to take a train trip, when do I give you the money for the train? Three weeks in advance?' 'No, Daddy, the day I leave.' Father then said, 'That is what God does. Today you do not need the power and the strength to suffer for Jesus, but the moment He gives you the honor of suffering for Him, He will also give you all the strength.' I was happy with his answer and went back to play with my dolls. In the books I have written, I have told how the Lord gave me the strength and all the grace when I was persecuted and suffered so terribly.

"Not long ago, when it was still possible but already dangerous to enter China, a missionary was asked, 'Are you not afraid?' She replied, 'I am afraid of one thing, that I shall become a grain of wheat not willing to die.' That is good. I hope that you will feel this way, too. I know the Lord has all the power and the strength available for you. Yes, also for you young Christians.

"Are you thinking that maybe it does not work when Jesus is with you? Do you know why you are thinking this? Because you have never tried working with Jesus. Try it. Give yourself to Jesus. Open your heart to Him. In His words, 'Behold, I stand at the door, and knock: if any man hear my voice, and open the door, I will come in' (Rev. 3:20, KJV).

"Did you hear His voice this morning? When will you say, 'Yes, Lord, come in'? He will come in. He will not let you down. If you must go through dangerous and difficult times, don't be afraid, for Jesus is victor; Jesus is victor and Jesus will be victor forevermore. He is willing to make you and me more than conquerors!"

### PASS TRIUMPHANTLY THROUGH THE PHASES

Now, to keep a positive, Be-Happy Attitude in painful times, remember: "This, too, shall pass away." Persecution is never eternal. To recover from persecution, be prepared to pass through three phases. The first phase is *collision.* This is the phase that occurs when the consciousness of the awful reality of the situation really hits you. Your peace suddenly clashes with conflict. This is the phase when you realize this horrible thing that is happening is not a dream. It's really happening—to *you!*

The second phase is *withdrawal.* When you talk about fear, guilt, hatred, or anger, all of these emotions are expressions of the tendency to retreat, recoil, withdraw from accepting the horrible reality.

Collision is the first stage. Withdrawal is the second. Phase three is *adjustment.* In this third phase, you finally learn how to accommodate yourself to the loss. The only way you can reach this phase is to realize where you came from, who gave you what you have.

"The Lord gave . . ." Everything you have is from God. Your very life is from God. But not as a gift—mind you. For life is not a gift from God; it is a sacred trust!

The story was in the papers—the tragedy of little David Rothenberg, who was set on fire by his troubled father. David suffered third-degree burns on much of his body, including his head and his face. He lost most of the fingers on his hands. But he is alive—and that is a miracle!

I count it an honor to have David and his remarkable

mother, Marie, as dear friends. I know of no one who has faced more persecution than David. But when I met him I could see the sparkle in his eye. I could hear the humor in his voice. In spite of the physical deformities that David will have to live with all his life, as well as the emotional scars that he will always carry, he is a shining example of courage.

Of course, a great deal of credit goes to his mother. I shall never forget when she told me: "Dr. Schuller, it wasn't until the third day after the fire that I was able to turn Davy over to God. That's because those three days I was battling back and forth as to whether Davy should live or die. I didn't know if it was fair for him to live a life with such severe injuries. But when I gave it over to God and placed Davy in God's hands, then I knew I could accept God's will—whatever He decided would be best for Davy. Today, of course, I am very glad that David has lived. I feel that he's been a tremendous inspiration to millions of people throughout the country. He's been an example of courage, an example of faith. In fact he has given *me* more faith in God. Because of Davy I know that God never gives us any more than we can handle."

Marie also shared with me how much it meant to David when her friend, Judy Curtis, read to David the parts in the New Testament that described the suffering of Jesus. David said to Judy, "They did that to Jesus—and He didn't do anything wrong!" David could relate to Jesus. And so he loves Jesus.

I was thrilled to be able to give David the Scars into Stars award that my church has given previously to Art Linkletter and Della Reese. It was the third time in the history of our ministry that I have given that award away. The award is a silver plate. For David we had inscribed on it these words:

"The Scars into Stars award presented to David Rothenberg in the Crystal Cathedral, Sunday, November 4, 1984, because you are turning your tragedy into a triumphant miracle by teaching millions of people the meaning of bravery in the face of incredible pain and suffering, the meaning of forgiveness in the face of unbelievable provocation, and how to turn a scar into a star by accepting Jesus Christ as Lord and Savior."

It is possible! No matter how great, how deep, how bitter the suffering—when we turn our trials over to Jesus, He can turn them into triumphs! He can do the impossible. He can work miracles. And He can carry us through the phases of collision and withdrawal into the healing phase of acceptance, if we but let Him.

I was first introduced to Rita Nightingale, a lovely young Englishwoman, through her book, *Freed for Life.** Her story is gripping. Compelling. And unbelievable.

Rita's story began in Bangkok, Thailand. She was ready to board her plane to Paris when she was suddenly called aside by an officer. She wasn't worried. She had nothing to hide—or so she thought. They took her to a room full of soldiers with machine guns and all kinds of weapons. They emptied all of her luggage. She still was not worried. Then they started to tear out the linings of the bag that her boyfriend had given her in Hong Kong, and they pulled out several small packets. They told her it was heroin.

From that moment on, no one told Rita anything. She was shocked and afraid because suddenly no one would speak English to her; everything that was said was uttered in a language foreign to her. The next thing she knew she was in a police cell.

Rita admits that she had been living a rather wild life, looking for adventure, yet she had never dreamed she would one day find herself in a prison cell. She had gone from being a glamor girl from Hong Kong to a cell in Thailand.

Glamor was one thing. Drugs were another. Rita had

---

* Wheaton: Tyndale House, 1983.

never been involved with hard drugs. The heroin was a shock to her. She had not put it there, so it must have been planted by someone.

Trying to convince the police in Thailand that she was innocent was an impossibility. The courts believed the police. She had been found with heroin in her possession, and that's all they cared about.

Rita was sentenced to twenty years in prison. The prison conditions were primitive—thirty women to a cell nine feet by fifteen feet. They slept feet to feet on the wooden floor with the mice and the cockroaches.

You can imagine the rage and the bitterness Rita began to feel when it dawned on her what had actually happened. She had been used by a boyfriend who she had thought cared about her. The prospect that she would lose the next twenty years of her life was real. Her rage soon spread toward the whole world, even to the lawyers and embassy officials who were trying to help her.

When a lady came to visit her in prison and told her that God loved her, Rita was furious.

"How could God let this happen to me if He is so loving! If He loved me, I wouldn't be here!"

Then Rita had another visitor. She was an old lady—in her seventies—from Rita's hometown. Rita couldn't believe that this sweet little old lady would come all the way from England to Bangkok to talk to her.

When Rita heard her Lancashire accent, she started to cry. This was something for Rita, who had grown hard in the past months.

After the lady left, Rita asked herself over and over again, "Why?"

The little old lady had left a book with her. It was called, *The Reason Why.* In it Rita read the words of Jesus again. Although she had heard the story of Jesus before, it had never meant much to her in a personal way before. Through reading the book, she thought again about all she had wanted before—the excitement, the night life, the casinos. She had had it all, but there was still something missing.

It took prison for God to open Rita Nightingale's eyes. She suddenly knew that Jesus was who He claimed to be, so she asked Him into her life.

Overwhelmed by the flood of emotions that came when she gave her life to Christ, Rita fled to the one and only private place in the prison—under the hospital hut. The buildings were all built on stilts, but no one ever went under them because of the snakes. It was there, under the hut with the snakes, that Rita's eyes were opened to the reality of eternal life. There, huddled in the darkness under the floor, she prayed and accepted Jesus Christ as her personal friend—her Lord, her God, her Savior.

It wasn't long before Rita noticed that her attitude was completely different. God didn't change the circumstances around her for a long time, but He began to change Rita and her attitude toward them.

Suddenly, one day, she was notified that she had been granted a pardon. No reason was given; the pardon came out of the blue. Rita attributes it to the fact that Christians around the world were praying for her.

She heard about her pardon through the news. That made it official. The news also said that the situation was very unique. Never before had a convicted drug smuggler been granted a royal pardon by the king of Thailand.

The day after Rita received the news of her pardon, the gates were opened and she was free. Today, Rita is a beautiful, born-again Christian. She is working in England for Chuck Colson in his prison ministries.

### THE BEATITUDES—THE BE-HAPPY ATTITUDES

They were taught by one Man.

They were lived out by one Man. He remains himself the best example of how to deal with persecution.

God
will
have the
last word
and
it will be...
GOOD!

He lived through persecution. He died by persecution. He rose again after the persecution. If you want to find happiness—real, deep, forever happiness—then wrap up your lessons on the Be-Happy Attitudes by learning more about this man who wrote them and lived them: Jesus Christ. I have referred to him as *the greatest possibility thinker who ever lived.*

Jesus should have been the world's greatest *im*possibility thinker. He had *nothing* going for Him.

Jesus was a member of a despised minority, a citizen of an occupied country, a nobody as far as the Romans were concerned, a joke to the occupying power, a nuisance to His fellow Jews.

Jesus lived among an oppressed, cynical, and embittered people!

Taxes were oppressive.

Freedom was unknown.

Survival was uncertain.

Religion was restrictive, negative, and joyless.

Yet, Jesus never made a politically inflammatory speech, never organized a guerrilla force, and never led a march on Jerusalem or Rome.

Jesus was from Nazareth, a city reputed to be culturally deprived and morally corrupt. "Can anything good come out of Nazareth?" was a common expression.

Jesus was not highly educated. Whatever His schooling was, it was simple. The only account of His writing was a note He scribbled in the sand.

Jesus had no organization. His followers were men with broken speech, rough hands, and cracked fingernails. They were unpolished, uncultured, unlettered, ignorant failures. In many ways, and in critical times, they proved to be unstable, uncertain, undependable, and disappointing.

Yes, Jesus knew ingratitude, rejection, misunderstanding, and betrayal.

By all the psychological laws of human development,

Jesus should have died a judgmental, frustrated, critical, angry, unbelieving, cynical, rebellious, violence-prone, emotionally deprived, radically militant revolutionary!

Jesus remained unmarried, a single adult all His life. So He spent His years without the encouragement, comfort, or companionship of a wife or children. In a society where children were a man's greatest treasure, He died never having fathered a single son or daughter.

Think of His death.

Jesus was only thirty-three years old! He was so young. He died before His mother! He was not given even a half-century, or more, to make His mark, write His books, build His empire, and conquer the world.

This—at least and at last—should have made Him a cynical impossibility thinker, crying out through tight lips, and bitter tears:

"It isn't fair!"

"I'm too young to die!"

"Oh God—give me more time!"

Jesus—where was His Heavenly Father when Jesus needed Him most?

Jesus—all His life He was good, kind, loving and very religious. Every Sabbath He was in the synagogue. The Holy Scriptures—how He loved to read them. Prayer? His life was a prayer for all seasons!

Jesus.

How He loved His Heavenly Father.

How He trusted His Heavenly Father.

How He served His Heavenly Father.

Jesus. When He was on the cross, when He needed His God most—God seemed to have abandoned Him.

Jesus was persecuted—He was whipped, He was scorned, He was rejected, He was crucified—yet Jesus never once showed bitterness. . . . When He was on the cross He said, "Forgive them, for they know not what they do."

To Jesus every problem was a possibility in disguise.

Sickness was an opportunity for healing.

Sin was an opportunity for forgiveness.

Sorrow was an opportunity for compassion.

Personal abuse was an opportunity to leave a good impression and show the world how possibility thinkers react!

To Jesus every person was a gold mine of undiscovered, hidden possibilities!

Peter? A tough-talking fisherman. But—he could make a great leader of a great new church.

Mary Magdalene? A common prostitute. But—she could become a sensitive, sweet soul. She could one day anoint His body for burial.

Matthew? A vulgar materialist. But—he had possibilities to become a great writer! Even write a gospel!

To Jesus the important fact about you and me is not that we are sinners, but that we can be saints. So Jesus proclaimed the greatest possibility: The immeasurable MERCY of GOD.

To Jesus the whole world was jammed, pregnant, loaded, bulging with untapped, undiscovered, undetected POSSIBILITIES! Jesus really believed in the supreme possibilities!

Man *can* be born again!

Character *can* be changed!

You *can* become a new person!

Life *can* be beautiful!

There *is* a solution to every problem!

There *is* a light behind every shadow!

Yes! Jesus had an unshakable faith in these ultimate possibilities:

God exists!

Life goes on beyond death!

Heaven is for real!

Jesus was prepared to prove it. By dying—and rising again!

Jesus was impressed by what the world could become—never depressed by what the world was.

He truly believed that common people can become uncommonly powerful. He knew without a shadow of a doubt that ordinary persons could become extraordinary persons if they could become possibility thinkers.

So, Jesus made it His aim to give self-confidence to inferiority-complexed people. He made it possible for guilt-infected, failure-plagued, problem-swamped persons to start loving themselves and stop hating themselves!

He also gave hope to the hopeless, comfort to the comfortless, mercy to those whose hearts and lives were breaking all around them. He gave them the gift of abundant life and the secret of happy living through the Beatitudes:

"Blessed are the poor in spirit, for theirs is the kingdom of heaven."

"Blessed are those who mourn, for they shall be comforted."

"Blessed are the meek, for they shall inherit the earth."

"Blessed are those who hunger and thirst for righteousness, for they shall be satisfied."

"Blessed are the merciful, for they shall obtain mercy."

"Blessed are the pure in heart, for they shall see God."

"Blessed are the peacemakers, for they shall be called children of God."

"Blessed are those who are persecuted for righteousness' sake, for theirs is the kingdom of heaven. Blessed are you when men revile you and persecute you and say all kinds of evil against you falsely on my account. Rejoice and be glad, for your reward is great in heaven."

When Jesus spoke those words, was He thinking about His own persecution that lay ahead? Oh, yes, for surely no one has endured more persecution than Jesus. Surely we follow a scarred captain. He leads us nowhere that He has not walked Himself.

Jesus endured the physical persecution of the whippings, the crown of thorns, the nails in the hands and feet.

He died by one of the most painful of deaths—crucifixion. He also endured emotional persecution: He was taunted by the Romans who put a mock robe around His thrashed shoulders; a sign jeered down at him from the top of the cross—"The King of the Jews." When He asked for something to drink, they ridiculed Him even more by proffering up to him a sponge dipped in vinegar, and then laughed at His gasps and sputterings.

All the while, He endured the persecution of loneliness. He walked His "lonesome valley" all by Himself. The night before his arrest, Jesus prayed in the Garden of Gethsemane. None of His disciples, not even one out of twelve, stayed awake to pray with Him and comfort Him in His time of direst need. And when He was arrested, betrayed by the kiss of Judas, whom He loved and accepted into His inner circle of closest friends, the other disciples fled and even denied that they ever knew Him.

Jesus was arrested, placed on trial, and accused of blasphemy. Did He not claim to be the promised Messiah? At least, did He not allow people to get the impression that He was the Son of God? In His public trial He was challenged to deny His deity, to withdraw His blasphemous statements, and clear up the confused minds of the simple people who believed Him to be God visiting earth in human form.

But He could not tell a lie, so He remained silent. The verdict was predictable: death by crucifixion! A crowd gathered to see how a possibility thinker dies. How did He die? He died seeing and seizing the possibilities of the moment! He practiced what He had preached all His life! He turned His hell into a heaven. For here was His chance to save the soul of a lost thief who was being crucified beside Him.

This was a spectacular opportunity to dramatically teach all men and women of all ages to come that death can be a grand reunion with God! That scars can become stars!

Today the cross is the positive symbol of the happiest

religion in the whole world. Persecuted? You and I can choose to be happy—anyway! For we believe that Jesus was resurrected on Easter morning! My personal conviction is this: Jesus Christ is alive this very moment!

What does Christ's persecution, crucifixion, and resurrection mean to us? It means that if we allow Christ to live in us, then it will possible for us, also, to:

- Turn our problems into opportunities.
- Tackle our opportunities and succeed!
- Dream great dreams and make them come true!
- Switch from jealousy and self-pity to really caring about others who are much worse off than you are.
- Pick up the broken hopes and start over again!
- See great possibilities in those unattractive people!
- Become a truly beautiful person—like Jesus!

Now that you've studied all eight of the Be-Happy Attitudes, let me ask you a final question: *Are you really happy?*

Happiness—that deep inner strength that is made up of courage, faith, hope, and peace. Mix them together, and you have happiness!

Happiness—the courage to hang on in the face of severe adversity!

Happiness—the faith that God will have the last word, and it will be good!

Happiness—the hope that, even though you can only see the shadow, someday the clouds will clear away and the sun will shine again!

Happiness—the quiet sense of self-esteem that comes when you know you have done your best.

Happiness—the assurance that you have been merciful and kind to enemy and friend alike.

Happiness—the quiet assurance that God will be merciful and kind to you, too.

Happiness—the beautiful belief that this life, no matter how difficult it may be, is not your final destination.

Your life here on earth is only a pilgrimage. Heaven—
life with Jesus forever—is our eternal destiny.

> I'm going to be happy today!
> Though the skies are cloudy and gray.
> No matter what comes my way—
> I'm going to be happy today!*

In Christianity, we talk about "making a commitment"
to Jesus Christ. When we make that commitment, we
raise the sail of faith. We sail and make this voyage in our
little vessel across the turbulent ocean of life. But remember this: No sail has ever moved a ship. *The wind moves
the ship.* The sail only catches the wind.

I'm asking you now to raise the sail of faith, and you
will capture and harness the power of the spirit of God.

Now that you have raised that sail of faith, keep it up
there, even when you're in the spiritual doldrums. In
God's good time the breeze will come. New positive feelings will replace the drab, old, boring, depressing, negative emotions. Fresh enthusiasm for life will come like a
brisk breeze surging through you. You will experience a
rebirth of youthful joy, energy, and excitement.

Here's how to make all this happen; pray this simple
prayer: "Jesus, I need a friend as I journey through life.
Right now I'm asking You to be my best friend and to
keep the Be-Happy Attitudes flowing through my mind.
Amen."

* Ella Wheeler Wilcox

May
our beautiful Lord
give you
an
unexpected surprise
of joy
before
every sunset
of your
life!

To Arvella Schuller,
my first wife and still
my wife today who more
than anyone else I
know lives a life
that reflects the best
that's in this book
and makes it easy
for me to believe
"God is love"

# CONTENTS

# God
# Loves
# You . . .

---

*You shall love the* LORD *your God with all your heart, with all your soul, and with all your mind. . . . You shall love your neighbor as yourself.*

—*Matthew 22:37, 39*

# LIFE:
# A JOURNEY OF
# JOY—
# IT'S POSSIBLE!

*Discover God Loves You . . .*
*And So Do I*

T

he call came late in the evening. John Wayne was facing surgery the next morning. It could be serious. He asked me to come and pray with him. I had met him socially on more than one occasion, but now "the Duke" wanted my prayers as a pastor and friend. He was fighting a recurring battle with cancer.

As I drove alone the next morning through the early darkness, I mentally checked through all the possibilities and prayed, "Dear God, what should I say to him? What can I tell him? Ask him? What prayer shall I pray with him?"

After the twenty-minute drive I arrived at Hoag Hospital in nearby Newport Beach. His room was well guarded. I was told to wait at the door. From inside the voice that all of America loves boomed out, "Let 'im in!"

I walked in and was greeted by his familiar grin. It was strange to see the man who personified the words *tough—true grit—* lying in a hospital bed, so strong and yet so vulnerable.

He lifted a long arm and stretched open his palm to slap and grasp my hand warmly. We talked frankly about his condition. As I began to pray, I watched his face, wanting to see the sight of a soul drawing near to God. His face clearly displayed anxiety; I had seen that creased brow in many tense moments on the movie screen.

"Oh Lord, I believe that John Wayne knows who Jesus is," I prayed. "Deep down in his heart he respects, admires, and loves

Jesus." At that point his face was transformed! The anxiety and tension faded, and his expression became as soft and gentle, tender, kind, and peaceful as the face of a child asleep in his crib! It was the most amazing sight! "And now, Lord," I continued, "Duke is putting his life, his body and soul—his future—into the hands of his friend, Jesus!"

A sweet hint of a smile appeared! When his eyes opened to meet mine, a tear glistened in each. Once more up came that powerful right arm and hand to grasp my hand. Once more the booming voice reverberated through the hospital room, "Thanks, Reverend Bob. I'll be O.K. now!" The smile was wide. The joy—genuine! The happiness—real!

A few days later I received an autographed photo that hangs on my wall to this day. It is Duke Wayne in a cowboy hat. Inscribed are these words: "Keep putting in a good word for me, Bob, I need all the help I can get."

I had no idea how soon I, too, would need all the help I could get.

❦   ❦   ❦   ❦

It was horrible! I was in Korea. My thirteen-year-old daughter Carol was in Iowa. There had been an accident. "We're amputating her leg, Reverend Schuller," the doctor in the emergency room in Sioux City said. My wife, Arvella, and I rushed to Iowa. In a matter of days letters of support and comfort came. Telegrams. Prayers. We all needed them.

Later, Carol was transported by a private hospital jet from Sioux City to Orange, California. It was a painful trip. After we arrived there were more cards, more gifts. And in the pile, amongst letters and photos of celebrities—politicians, professional athletes, entertainers—was an autographed picture of John Wayne. His eyes twinkled under the well-worn cowboy hat and scrawled across the bottom was this simple but profound message: "Dear Carol—Be Happy! You Are Loved!—John Wayne."

I only had to look around that hospital room, overflowing with expressions of love, and then to look at the face of my daughter, who was reveling in all the attention, to see that Duke Wayne was absolutely right. Carol could be happy. She *was* loved! Her face was beaming! Yes, she was wounded! Yes, her stump was in traction! But she was happy in her hurt!

"Was she *really* happy?" you ask. "How can that be?"

Well, she was genuinely happy—according to my definition of happiness:

**Happiness is *not* . . .**

Hollow Hilarity,
Giddy Gaiety,
Loud Laughter,
Flippant Frivolity,
Shallow Smiles,
Frantic Fun,
or
Chemical Cheer!

**But Happiness *is* . . .**

Genuine Joy!
Enjoyable Enthusiasm!
Serene Self-esteem!
Tender Tears!
Lasting Love!
Affectionate Encouragement!
Healthy Hope!

Affirming Faith!
Perceiving Possibilities!


Yes, happiness *is* . . .

Having a hand to hold!
Finding a heart to heal!
Leaning into tomorrow with love!

And, so I can say with total integrity that:
John Wayne was happy, in spite of a terminal disease. Why?
Because he was loved!
Carol Schuller was happy, in spite of losing a limb. Why?
Because she was loved!
And the good news I have for you is—no matter what it is you
are facing, no matter what condition you are in, no matter who
or what you are—you *can* be happy. For you, *too*, are loved!

## Even If You Think You Have LOST EVERYTHING— Someone, Somewhere, Needs Your Love!

The other day I was in my office studying when the
telephone rang. Since it was late and the secretaries had gone
home, the call came straight into my office, which seldom
happens. But if there's one thing I can't ignore, it's a ringing
phone!
I picked up the handset and the operator said, "This is a long
distance, person-to-person call for Robert Schuller."
"Go ahead; I'll take it."
"No," the operator responded, "it's for Robert Schuller. Are
you Robert Schuller?"
"Yes."
The voice at the other end said, "You've got to be kidding!

Everybody said I would never get through to you! It's a miracle! Are you really Robert Schuller?"

"Well," I said, "do you know me?"

"I watch you on television," she reported. "And I've got a terrible problem. I'm about to lose everything that I have."

"Do you have a tumor on the brain?" I asked her.

"No."

"Well, you're not in danger of losing your eyesight, are you?"

"No, not that, but . . ."

"Do you have cancer? Do they have to operate?"

"No."

"Well," I said, "let's see, you've got your eyes, your hearing, your sanity, and you aren't facing a debilitating surgery. Are you able to walk or are you confined to a bed—stiff, rigid, and paralyzed?"

"No, I can walk."

"Well, then," I replied, "you can walk, you can talk, hear, see, and laugh. Why, you've got everything going for you. You've got faith, too. You must believe in God, and you must believe I will respond with love, or you wouldn't even be listening to me! Or at least you wouldn't have called me!"

"Yes," came a feeble reply over the sound of sniffling tears.

"Then you still have what is most important; you have a love connection, right now!" I assured her. "Now affirm out loud: 'I am loved!'" She moaned and mumbled pathetically, but the words did come out!

"Now, can you think of one other person whom you love? A child? A neighbor? A delivery person? A grocer? A relative? An old and lonely person in a rest home? Is there someone you know who is in a hospital? Is there someone you can think of who has had surgery this past month or year? Or lost a husband? A wife? A child? Is there someone who got married recently? Can you think of someone who had a birthday or is going to have a birthday? Take a piece of paper and pencil and make an inventory of 'My Love List.'" She didn't respond. "Please, do it now! I'll wait!"

"O.K.," she said weakly. I heard a piece of paper rustling. Some moments passed.

I had no idea how long I already had talked with that woman! All I knew was that she was in a state of emotional panic, on the edge of desperation! Oh, how I felt for her! What compassion I felt for this woman, who—though she was a stranger—seemed to be one of my dearest friends. Why did I feel so close to her? Why did I care? Where did my authentic compassion come from, for a person whose face I could not see and would probably never see?

"Now read your list to me," I said, finally. She began to read her love list, a litany of love! It was a nice, long list! "So you haven't lost everything—because you still have someone," I assured her. "Your voice sounds stronger now! You do feel better than when we first started talking, don't you?"

"Yes," she answered, "I really do." Her words were stronger.

I was impressed. "Now, will you do something for me?" I asked. She agreed, not knowing what she was being set up for. "I've got a problem," I said.

"You do? Can I help you, Dr. Schuller?"

"So many people need my love," I answered, "and I'm so far from them that I cannot touch them. I get so many letters from unhappy people; they need someone—they need *me*—to call on them, talk with them, hug them, encourage them, kiss them gently on the cheek, but I'm too far away! And there are too many of them!"

"That's really something, Dr. Schuller; you must feel overwhelmed," she said. I sensed the caring—for me—in her voice!

"Will you help me? Please! To pass my love and God's love on to those around you who are unhappy?"

"I'll try," she answered sincerely. "Yes! I really will!" she assured me.

"Thank you," I said. "Now let's pray: Thank you God that *we haven't lost everything, if we still have someone left who needs our love!* Amen."

"Amen," came her voice—strong again.

"You have not lost everything, my friend," I added, "as long as you still have the best job in the world—sharing love. In a world where there is so much hurt and heartache, it doesn't make sense for anybody to say 'nobody needs me.' Someone not far from you needs your tender touch, your simple smile, your holy hug today."

## Even If You Have FAILED IN LOVE—Someone, Somewhere, Can Give You the Courage to Try Again!

Have you suffered the disgrace of a broken relationship? A broken marriage? Are you afraid to try again?

You are not alone! Somewhere, there is someone whose love can overpower your feelings of failure and fear and give you the courage to love again.

I had the joy of marrying the celebrated pianist Roger Williams to his lovely bride, Louise DeCarlo. They stood facing each other, after dating for over *eleven* years. My eyes filled with tears as they said the vows they had written for each other.

*Louise:* My darling, I love you more than life itself. I know how much time you spend on your music, and that's a lot of time spent away from me. But it's that quality time that we spend together that's most important to both of us. I could never think of living my life without you. I shall love you till the day I die. And if God wills, I shall love you even better after death.

*Roger:* My darling, you're my girl. And you'll always be my girl. Because yours is the love that I hoped and prayed for, for all these many years. And yet, when I finally found you I was afraid. I was afraid because my first marriage had failed. I was afraid because, most of all, I hate to fail. Only your love, only your patience, only your understanding helped to turn this loser into a winner again. There's so much to say I can't find the words, except for these—I love you. I love you with all my heart. And darling, I'll be true, so help me God."

Roger added, "I asked my good friend Andrew to sing his composition, 'Winner's Song,' because today, Louise, I've become a winner again!

You're beautiful as a rose can be,
You're living in the love of my heart,
You're family, you belong to me
And nothing's gonna keep us apart,
Oh, nothing's gonna keep us apart.

I don't know a better way for life to go on,
You have made a loser sing a winner's song.
It's the beauty of your love that makes me so strong
With a winner's song!

You knew that I was a helpless child
Who happened to be needing a friend.
But win or lose you were there to prove
Your love would make me win in the end,
Your love would make me win in the end.

I don't know a better way for life to go on,
You have made a loser sing a winner's song.
It's the beauty of your love that makes me so strong
With a winner's song!

—Andrew Culverwell*

## Even If You Have FAILED IN LIFE—Someone, Somewhere, Cares!

Bankrupt? Facing a financial catastrophe? Lost the family farm? Such failure hurts, but the only people who never *trip* are those who never *try*! I have met people who have failed miserably, yet they have recovered a lost happiness!

Could any failure be worse, more shameful, than going to prison?

One day in a bookstore, where I was autographing books, I looked up into the happy face of a man in his forties, I guessed. He looked so excited, so enthusiastic.

"Your book and the television ministry have saved me from total despair," he said. I listened and looked deeply into the warm eyes that were misting. "Dr. Schuller, I was an awful failure. Let me just tell you. I am in jail—today! I've been there a long time. But . . ." he tilted his head, nodding at a tall stranger who stood silently behind him, guarding him . . . , "they let me come out to meet you and thank you! I love myself—anyway! I have found God and have decided to turn my scars into stars! I'm your missionary in prison; I've got lots of tough guys listening to you! They're getting saved too! I have another seven months to go. When I'm out I'm going to try to keep going back to do the missionary work! I'm so happy! Thank you! Got to go! Goodbye!" He waved and was gone.

## Even If You Are RIDICULED AND REJECTED— Someone, Somewhere, Accepts You!

Some years ago I flew to the Orient on a mission for the United States Air Force. As I put my foot down on earth after the last nine-hour leg over the Pacific, the man who stepped forward to shake my hand was a black officer with an eagle on each shoulder. He smiled and said, "Dr. Schuller, I am Bill King."

Colonel King, who became my host in Okinawa, was one of the greatest human beings I had ever met. At the conclusion of those few days, when we were driving to the airport for my trip to Japan, I thanked him for his graciousness, his hospitality, and his kindness. He looked at me and said, "Dr. Schuller, I want you to know that we don't give you good treatment to impress you. We treat you well because you're a human being."

Then he stopped to allow a group of children to cross the street. After they had crossed, he said, "And there is only one way to treat people and that is *first class!*"

Bill King has known racial prejudice in his lifetime. He has been ridiculed and rejected on occasion—simply because of his color. Yet, he has had friends and loved ones who loved him for the beautiful human being he is. As a result he has chosen to treat people everywhere one way—*first class!*


## Even If LIFE HAS BEEN UNFAIR to You—Someone, Somewhere, Needs You the Way You Are!

"I've been handed a bad deck of cards," a man once said to me, disfigured, deformed, and bitter!

"But that's no excuse for choosing to be miserable and un-happy," I chided him. I remembered Mary, whom I'd met not long before in an eastern city. I first had noticed her face. She was a gorgeous girl, with beautiful red hair and dark brown eyes. Her make-up and her hair were like a model's. She could have just stepped from a magazine cover. Then I lowered my eyes from her glamorous face to the wheelchair below. She was tiny, and I couldn't see any shoulders. Propped in the chair was a little body, covered by a small dress. There wasn't anything there to hug.

I knelt by her wheelchair and said, "Mary, you're so pretty," and kissed her on the cheek. "What do you do?"

She said to my astonishment, "Well, I have my master's degree; I have a very successful business. I have joined your Eagle's Club! I've watched you on TV for twelve years. I know all the slogans: *Who can count the apples in one seed? . . . Look at what you have left, never look at what you have lost. . . . There is no gain without pain. . . . It takes guts to leave the ruts!* Dr. Schuller, thank you!"

I was astounded, amazed! This courageous woman reminded me of Max Cleland. Max is a guy who got on the wrong end of a grenade in Vietnam. The explosion blew off an arm and both legs. Now he works from his wheelchair, with one arm. He could so easily have turned his face to the wall and his eyes to the ground and quit, but he didn't. Recently, I asked him, "Max, what are you up to these days?"

"Oh," he said, "I wish you could be in town tomorrow night; I'm having an *Alive party*."

"Alive party! What's that?"

"It's to celebrate my *alive* day. That's the day when I lost my arm and legs."

"You *celebrate* that day? Like a birthday?"

"Oh, yes! That's the day I should have been killed and I wasn't! God kept me alive. So, I celebrate my alive day."

## Even If You Are POOR—Someone, Somewhere, Will Treasure You!

There is poverty in America, and some people are severely underprivileged. Many feel they are trapped, that there is no way out. Do you see yourself in this predicament? You are not alone! Others have been where you are—but they broke free!

Take, for example, Dr. Rodrigue Mortel, an Horatio Alger

Award winner. Dr. Mortel has the distinction today of being the only foreign-trained black medical doctor to head an academic department in one of our 127 American medical schools. He is university professor and chairman of the Department of Obstetrics and Gynecology at the Milton S. Hershey Medical Center in connection with the Pennsylvania State College of Medicine.

Dr. Mortel was born and raised in Saint Marc, a small town located near Port-au-Prince in Haiti. The town had no electricity. His home had no water, no sanitary facilities. His father, who had only a fourth-grade education, was a self-employed tailor earning $30 a year.

Dr. Mortel's mother could not write nor read, but she helped support the entire family with profits made by buying and reselling vegetables in open air markets, using either the train or the family donkey as transportation. Since there was no electricity, Rodrigue had to study by the light of a kerosene lamp.

When Rodrigue went to Port-au-Prince to attend college and medical school, he boarded in a home that had electricity. However, the house was so crowded that Rodrigue had to study under the street lights or in the quiet of the park during his medical school years.

Finally graduating from medical school, Dr. Mortel practiced for two years in rural Haiti and then decided to leave Haiti for postgraduate training in the United States.

After eight years of postgraduate training in America, he became an obstetrician and gynecologist and a specialist in female cancer.

He then entered academic life and devoted his entire professional life to teaching, to cancer research, and to care of women afflicted with this dreadful and deadly disease.

Dr. Mortel attributes his supersuccess today to the faith instilled in him in his early childhood. He always was aware of the persistent presence of God in his life, as well as the powerful impact of prayer.

Today, Dr. Mortel exports to Haiti medicine, hospital beds, x-ray equipment, and whatever else he can obtain in this country that will help his former countrymen.

You, too, can go anywhere from where you are.

## Even If You Are TRAPPED—Someone, Somewhere, Can Liberate You with Love!

As a pastor for thirty-six years I've met and counseled with thousands of persons who felt trapped—in a bad marriage, in an unfulfilling job, in an unpleasant neighborhood, in a hospital bed.

Again and again I have watched their moods change from despair to joy when they allowed their attitudes to change from the negative to the positive!

"I may be a shut-in—but I'm not shut out!" a bedridden young man said to me. "I've got lots of friends." And he gestured to the telephone and to the mailbox outside his window.

Sometimes, when we least expect adverse circumstances, in a flashing instant an unexpected event drastically upsets our cozy routine. We are trapped!

But love can set us free! Captain John Testrake, whose TWA Flight 847 was hijacked out of Athens, found that "love memories" liberated him from fear and depression before he was set free by the hijackers.

You read the headlines! Beginning on June 14, 1985, 145 passengers and a crew of eight were held hostage for seventeen days. Captain John Testrake was the pilot of that flight, and he has been hailed as a hero for his role in that drama. He has said that at the moment the wild-eyed gunmen came bursting into the cabin, amazingly he wasn't afraid.

But when they landed in Beirut for refueling, there were snags in getting the fuel, and the hijackers came close to hysteria. At that moment, with a pistol at his neck and a grenade in his face, Captain Testrake reached out to Jesus Christ, to whom he had given his life many years before. He decided to trust Him completely.

As John Testrake said in *Guideposts* magazine:

There was nothing new about the faith that kept me steady that first day. It was a part of me, just as knowing how to fly a plane was a part of me, but it had grown stronger over the years with each crisis, each sadness. In 1955 my infant son, William, was killed in an auto accident that nearly killed me, too. In 1976 my first wife, Patricia, died of cancer. My faith was there during that long year I was a single father to my four children, Debra, 23, Alan, 19, Diane, 18, and John, 14, all the while flying regularly for TWA and all the while making sure that we stayed close to our church in the little town of Richmond, Missouri. And there in that same church one Sunday, standing among some new members, was Phyllis Hisler. It was as if God touched my shoulder and said, "John, I have brought her here for you."

We married, raising children from both our families. Then, my oldest son, Alan, age 27, died suddenly. Once more I leaned upon the Lord and He was there. Each time I seemed to grow closer to Him. Little wonder that during the hijacking of Flight 847 I knew for certain that God was with me and I with Him. [*]

The flight engineer on Flight 847 was Christian Zimmermann, an ordained Lutheran minister. Both Captain Testrake

[*]Excerpted with permission from *Guideposts* Magazine. Copyright © 1986 by Guideposts Associates, Inc., Carmel, New York 10512.

and Flight Engineer Zimmermann spent their time in captivity reading the Bible and sharing inspiration. And on Sundays these two brave men had worship services for themselves. John led the singing of hymns, and Christian gave sermons that spoke of hope, of joy, of love for God.

What does Captain Testrake remember of those traumatic days? As he said in the *Guideposts* article, "I remember the constant presence of Jesus. He kept me from being afraid. He comforted me. He gave me hope. He gave me freedom, though I was a captive. And He is with me still as I continue to fly for TWA."

## Even If You Are GRIEF-STRICKEN—Someone, Somewhere, Can Fill the Void!

I'll never forget the day I was in the Holy Land with a study group. I called home to see if everything was all right, only to hear that one of the young fathers in our church, Bob Trueblood, had lost his wife and his three children in an automobile accident.

Pam and Bob had married in 1969. They spent fifteen beautiful years together and were blessed with two sons and a daughter. Their home was one of love. On October 22, 1984, Bob took Pam out to dinner to celebrate her thirty-sixth birthday. The next morning he kissed her and the children goodbye as he left for work. That was the last time he saw them.

He arrived home after working late. The phone was ringing. Pam had gone down to pick up the children from their gymnastics class, about a two-mile drive from their house. The person on the phone was the mother of one of the children whom Pam was to have picked up. They should have been home an hour earlier.

Bob got in his car and drove to look for them. He stopped at a police barricade where he learned that a young man, who was

drunk and driving eighty miles an hour, had struck the car
carrying his family. He was told that his wife, his oldest son
Eric, and his daughter Kerry were dead at the scene. His
youngest son Scotty was at a local hospital where they were
trying to save him.

The police raced with Bob to the hospital, but by the time he
got there, Scotty had also died. Bob told me later, "As far as I
was concerned, my life was through. My whole life had been
built around work, my family, and church; all the loves of my
life were no longer here."

It was a difficult night, a difficult week. Bob shed many,
many tears. But at the end of the funeral, he said,

I began to realize something. I had lost my entire family,
but two thousand years ago my Heavenly Father had sent
His entire family, in the form of Jesus Christ, down here to
die on a cross and that was done on purpose. Now, Pam's
death and the deaths of my children were certainly not on
purpose, but God loved you and me enough so that two
thousand years later, I could go to a funeral and realize that
while I was there with the bodies of my family, they were in
heaven with Jesus and they were fine. I don't know how I'd
have made it through the week without that realization. I
looked to God and I had a choice to make. I could either
blame God for what happened, and shake my fist at Him.
Or, I could fall into His open arms and allow Him to love
me through it. And that's what I chose to do.

Pam and Bob had been members of a Sunday school class at
the Crystal Cathedral, the Becomers, and there were many
events going on at that time because of the approaching holiday
season. Attending those activities helped Bob a lot. At one of

the events Bob began to talk with a young woman named Diane Moyer, who had been recently widowed and had just moved from Ohio. She understood Bob's pain because a year before she had watched her husband die of cancer. Six months after Pam's accident, Diane and Bob were married. With her came her daughter, who had the same birthday as Bob's! And then, on May 1, 1986, a son, Robert Henry, was born.

Bob said, "The good Lord gave me a number of things to help me through the biggest hole I've ever been in in my life—certainly one I never hope to see again. He gave me the support of this church, the support of a Sunday school class, the support of cards and letters, but more than anything else, it was the internal security of knowing Jesus Christ."

## Even If You Are DYING—Someone, Somewhere, Loves You Forever!

Steve Miller is a handsome, young, articulate member of the Crystal Cathedral. He also is winning over muscular dystrophy.

When he was in his mid-teens, an energetic and athletic young man, all of a sudden Steve started getting tired. Some of his coaches thought he was just lazy. But when they took him to a doctor, a battery of tests showed that he had myasthenia gravis.

Steve was told that he could not be as active as he used to be, that his life would change drastically. He was put on medication and told that he would at best regain just 70 percent of his strength, stamina, and endurance.

Steve followed the instructions, but then one day an idea popped into his head. "What would happen if I developed myself to the point where my 70 percent was equal to a normal person's 100 percent?"

So with his doctor's approval, Steve started to build himself back up physically, mentally, and spiritually. Then Steve encountered two young people with muscular dystrophy who affected him deeply.

He met the first one in a hospital in Arizona. He went to visit a friend one day and in the next bed was a girl lying flat on her back and hardly able to move. Not wanting to be unfriendly, Steve went over to say hello to her. On the nightstand next to her he noticed a prescription for the same medication that he was taking. Steve was curious about why she was lying there flat on her back. When he asked her, she replied, "Because I have myasthenia gravis and the doctors told me that this is where I need to be." She told him that she was taking twelve pills a day, which seemed like a lot except that Steve was taking thirty-six and he was up and around, still active.

The second of Steve's profound experiences came when he was a volunteer staff member at one of the summer muscular dystrophy camps. Steve told me later,

At those camps, the staff has to bed check the kids every night. Some of the more severe forms of the disease, such as Duchenne dystrophy, cause muscles to atrophy and turn to fat. People with this form cannot move, even in their sleep. Just as we are, they can be uncomfortable at night. We just roll over, but they can't. The camp staff tried to help these patients stay comfortable.

So, we would bed check the kids every hour. One morning at about four I went in to check on a young girl. She was obviously in trouble, laboring to breathe. You see people don't die of muscular dystrophy; they die of suffocation. She was really having problems, so I called for help. I set her up to get the weight off her chest. The whole time that I was holding her there, she kept apologizing for keeping me up so late.

Tough times never
last . . .
Tough people do!
****

Just remember—
God loves you . . .
And I do, too!

Then she said, "I know I'm gonna die. But that's O.K. I'm happy. I've had a great time."

You know, Dr. Schuller, she *was* happy! She just kept on saying, "I'm not afraid, I'm happy." And then she died while I was holding her.

That was tough on Steve. But he said,

I didn't know it at the time, but later on I realized what a valuable learning experience that was. On one hand I had met one girl in a hospital with my disease and she had given up on life. But the other girl with the same terrible disease kept on being happy until the very end. They both had a *choice* as to how they would react to their situation.

You see, Dr. Schuller, I believe we are responsible for our actions, but we're also responsible for our *attitudes*. Good things happen to us and bad things happen to us and we can choose how we want to react.

I asked him, "Steve, you have a tremendous outlook. How did you develop such a healthy attitude?"

"Well, I believe that in our lives we are all given glimpses of greatness, glimpses of the ability to really step beyond, to go one step outside our comfort zone. It is not only important to do it for ourselves, but it's important for us to do that for other people too. We need to be an inspiration for each other."

Steve is thirty-four years old. He has lived triumphantly with his disease for twenty years. He believes that God has healed him!

Oh God!
When I lost my love—
What a hole was left!
And the hole is so deep,
so empty, so dark, so black.


But the sun is going to rise again!
Until, at high noon it shall fill the
dark, empty hole with light,
warmth—love!


I'm waiting for the sunrise.
It's coming.
Nothing can stop it!

Hallelujah!
Amen.

Many of the people I've just told you about, who have
learned to find love and happiness in spite of enormous
obstacles, appear to be extraordinary. But in reality they are just
like you and me. They are people who have had pain and who
have hurt but have learned to rise above them.

How did they do it? Well, if you knew them as I know them,
you would see that they all have three things in common: 1) a
healthy love for themselves, 2) a harmonious love for God, and
3) a wholesome love for others.

As Jesus once said, "Love the LORD your God with all your
heart, with all your soul, and with all your mind . . . . [and]
your *neighbor as yourself*" (Matt. 22:37, 39, emphasis added).

Sound simple? It is. No matter what your situation, no
matter what your position, you can learn to love and be *loved*
that way. You can be loved! You can be happy—anyway!

# JUNCTION ONE:
# LOVE YOURSELF—
# AND BE HAPPY!

"The happiest place on earth," they call it—Disneyland, California. I arrived in California in 1955, shortly before this joyous place opened only a mile and a half down the road from where later we built the Crystal Cathedral. The first thing Walt Disney built was the great communications loop, a railroad that encircled the park. Disneyland is many "lands"—Fantasyland, Frontierland, Adventureland, Tomorrowland—all tied together by the railroad. There are only a few stations. You can get on the train at any stop, but you will not experience fully the happiness of Disneyland if you get off the train at the first station you come to. It is very easy to be distracted by the alluring and enticing attractions and to disembark. You may revel in the fun at one station and forget that the clock is ticking. But later you will find out that your time has run out and you must leave the happy place and cannot finish the entire circle. Back at home you'd probably report, "*Yes,* I had great fun, but *no,* I didn't get a chance to have the full experience."

In much the same way, a life of happiness is found on the train called "love." There are three junctions. You can conceivably enter and exit at any of these three stations. One junction is called "Love Yourself and Be Happy!" Another is named "Love Your Neighbor and Be Happy!" A third carries the banner "Love God and Be Happy!"

In all cases love requires both giving and accepting: Love

flows when you *give* love to yourself, your neighbor, and your God and *accept* love from yourself, your neighbor, and your God.

You can enter the love train at any junction. But if you get sidetracked by the attractions and satisfactions and feel happy at any one stop and miss taking the whole trip, I must caution, even warn, you that the joy will only last if you make the entire loop.

But where does one really get on? Is it best to board at "Love God and Be Happy"? Perhaps. I know persons who have had amazing religious conversions. Before they learned to accept and love themselves or their neighbors, they were transformed by the love of God! This was their first experience with a nonjudgmental, nonmanipulative, honest, caring LOVE! For them this was the entry point to the happy life.

I know others who entered from the platform at "Love Your Neighbor and Be Happy!" They were confirmed agnostics or atheists, incapable of religious beliefs or feelings until they encountered authentic, unconditional love from another person. Malcom Muggeridge, the famed British author and television personality, comes to mind. While sipping tea in his cottage in Sussex, England, he once recounted to me how he was swept away by the love he saw in the life of Mother Teresa, a woman who personifies sacrificial love. Her love annihilated his cynicism, intellectual skepticism, and arrogant elitism and led him ultimately to a childlike faith in God.

"Love Yourself and Be Happy!" is the station where others step on the train. The primary hangup that kept these passengers from believing in love was their own lack of self-esteem or self-love. They were incapable of approaching God or others until they felt they had some value. So deep and entrenched was their lack of trust in their own potential value that they subconsciously turned off all loving signals sent their way. The first step these people needed to take, before they could have a happy experience in love, was to learn to love themselves.

## WHERE SHOULD I GET ON?

There is a main entrance to the Disneyland railroad; it is at the front of the park, and if you had your choice of junctions, this would undoubtedly be the best place to get on the train. When it comes to the train of love, however, one can speculate, argue, study, which station on the love railroad, if any, is the central depot!

My specialty for thirty years has been a ministry passionately appealing to negative-thinking, impossibility thinkers who suffer from low self-esteem, lack of trust, and a profound lack of faith in themselves, in others, in God!

For that reason—call it strategy if you will—let's enter the "happy railroad that makes the love loop" at the station called "Love Yourself and Be Happy."

## LOVE YOURSELF AND BE HAPPY

This station may not be the main entrance or the central depot or the most popular junction, but for many of us it is the place to begin. Until we can love ourselves, we'll never be able to love God or those around us.

*The Person Who Does Not Love Himself Is Too Empty Of Love To Give It Away . . . And Feels Too Unworthy To Accept It From God Or From Others.*

So I ask you now: "Do you love yourself?"

If your answer is a doubtful "yes" or a definite "no," then how can you expect others to love you? And if you don't believe others will love you, won't you miss the first sensitive signals of affection when they are sent your way? Won't you inadvertently nip love in the bud, in the first, fragile, tender stage?

Self-esteem is foundational. Therefore an inferiority complex is the first problem that has to be corrected! Before you can love or be loved—before you can ever hope to be happy—you need to achieve deep inner security. *You* have to discover your real intrinsic worth as a human being.

Self-love is an essential requirement for healthy living. It is a vital ingredient to long-lasting relationships. It is the key that can unlock the door to a life of genuine joy. Self-esteem is the deepest desire of our hearts.

Are you leery of this station because you wonder: *Will self-love lead to narcissism?* Narcissus, as you may know, was the Greek mythological character who tried to meet his need for self-esteem and self-love by *focusing on the material image of the self,* that is, the body. The material image of a person is what Swiss psychiatrist Paul Tournier calls the "personage." Narcissism focuses on the material solution to what is essentially a *spiritual* problem!

A great deal of "self-esteem" literature today misses the point right here! If loving yourself means admiring your body, your shape, your style of hair, your jewelry, clothing, or accessories, then indeed we are, like Narcissus, getting on the wrong track. Futility and frustration and eventual failure are the dismal, disillusioning, and despairing end to the counterfeit self-esteem offered by narcissism. At best it is cosmetic psychology, and what is needed is not a cosmetic treatment, but conversion: The heart of a human must be changed!

I must believe that I have value as a person! No matter who I am, I can be an encourager! I can be a spreader of hope! I can be a spirit-lifter to disheartened people! I can be a conduit, a channel for God's love, joy, and peace to flow to other human beings! I can love others and myself with God's love! I *can* do it, if I'll be a *conduit!*

The truth is that any person who has achieved self-love based on sacrificial love for others has acquired the best preventive treatment against narcissism.

A favorite picture of mine in my study is a picture of only the folded hands of Mother Teresa. I love it. The fingernails are all broken! Unfiled! Here then is a portrait of spiritual, healthy, self-love. Can you see any narcissism in it?

You may be cautious at the "Love Yourself—and Be Happy" station because *you were taught that self-love will lead to pride.* Wait a minute! If that thought holds you back from loving yourself, you are a victim of the frailties of language.

What we need to realize is that *pride* is a word in the English language that is both positive and negative. Therefore, it is confusing and dangerous. Destructive, *negative* pride is the very opposite of self-love. It is arrogance! It is egotism—the very opposite of self-esteem.

But *positive* pride generates tremendous generosity! A strong self-respect motivates a person to unselfish liberality! Only persons with an abundance of inner spiritual resources dare to give themselves away, investing their love and caring in a variety of human lives. Only these persons can afford to lose!

Perhaps, you are afraid of this station because *you have been mistreated, maligned, rejected, and hurt by people you loved.* A young woman named Mary I once knew would understand how you feel. A bride-to-be, Mary had mailed the invitations to her wedding weeks earlier. Her dress and the gowns of her four attendants were already purchased. The wedding cake, baked and frosted, was waiting to be cut the following day. She was wrapping her gift for the groom when the telephone rang. It was he! "Mary." The voice was strained.

"Hi, John. Aren't you excited?" she asked.

"Mary," he continued painfully, "I can't go through with it. I mean it's all off. There isn't going to be a wedding tomorrow. Don't ask questions. I'm sorry. Goodbye."

The stunned young woman went to her pastor's office.

"What is wrong with me? I know there must be something terribly wrong," she said. Her slender shoulders trembled as her head dropped. "I'm so embarrassed. I can't face anyone anymore. Somewhere, I failed terribly."

I have heard virtually the same words from a man who had just come through a divorce; from the mother of three children whose husband had quietly deserted her; from a millionaire who had suffered financial reverses and subsequent bankruptcy; from an executive who was mysteriously "let go" from a firm he had served faithfully for years; and from more alcoholics than I can remember.

When these kinds of life situations hit and you feel inept and unsure of yourself, you can recapture lost confidence. A way out and up is always possible.

Go for it! Get on the train. Head for the junction, "Love Yourself and Be Happy." Discover in the process the rebirth of your self-worth.

## A REBIRTH OF SELF-WORTH

No matter what has happened in your life you are *not* a "complete failure," a "hopeless sinner," a "total washout." After twenty years in the field of people-counseling I have heard that exaggerated, distorted, destructive lie repeated many hundreds of times, and a lie quickly becomes a truth if you believe it. In almost every instance I was able to see and point out worthwhile qualities in the person who was unfairly, unreasonably, and unlovingly self-condemning.

*There are vast undamaged areas in every human life.* You will discover them in this station if you will board the train one step at a time.

*Your freedom to
choose
a positive attitude
is the
one treasure
God will let no one
take
from you!*

## Step I. Stop Putting Yourself Down!

It is important to realize that although you may not be able to change what has happened, you *can* control how you *react* to what has happened. Remember that you will never again be the person you were before you experienced any trauma. You have two options. You can decide that you have nothing left to live for. Or you can say, "I may have failed, but I am still a person of worth."

Self-debasing thoughts will come naturally to your mind. Restrain them. Whatever you do, do not believe them. They are extreme, emotional exaggerations. By all means, resist the destructive inclination to welcome, nurse, feed, and strengthen these self-destroying feelings. The depressed person tends to strengthen self-debasing thinking by deliberately choosing to believe the worst about himself. The emotionally "down" individual deliberately goes on a self-degrading mental rampage—listing all the failures ever encountered; pointing up all the weaknesses; recalling from the long-forgotten past any and every blunder ever made.

In this crazy, self-destroying mental activity, the depressed man or woman—

- Exaggerates the significance and the reality of these real or fancied shortcomings.
- Accepts personal blame almost entirely and mercilessly for all these failures, stubbornly refusing to believe or remember how other persons contributed to the mistakes.
- Makes certain worthy virtues and accomplishments are forgotten or discredited and belittles, berates, and betrays noble character qualities. The value or the reality of all the positive qualities in this person's life is angrily scorned when some friend calls attention to them.

Why do we tend to despair and further degrade ourselves with self-destructive thinking? Are we seeking sympathy to nurse our wounded pride? Do we hate ourselves so much that we want to mentally liquidate, eliminate, and eradicate that which we hate? Does an irrational subconscious suppose that it will love itself if it mentally destroys the self it hates? Or are we trying to atone for the guilt of failure? Do we deliberately inflict this mental punishment upon ourselves, hoping finally to awaken a feeling that we are redeemed through the crucifixion of self-condemnation? Whatever the reason, it is important to understand that we cannot rebuild self-love by destroying the undamaged areas of self-worth that still remain.

### Step II. Select Self-respect, Not Self-pity!

You certainly do not rebuild self-love by indulging in self-pity. Self-pity focuses on the unhappy past, keeping alive the very experiences which must be forgotten and left behind. Self-pity focuses on what has happened. While you are concentrating on the unfortunate past, you are in that moment enslaved, controlled, and dominated by the self-demoralizing past. Something regrettable may have happened, but don't allow yourself to *remain* trapped in that experience by self-pity.

If unpleasant things come to pass, by all means let them pass! Quit holding on.

Why are we so inclined to self-pity? Are we trying to tenderly nurse a wounded ego? If so, we must see that self-pity only keeps the wounded pride raw and open. In our own self-pity we hope to gain the pity of others, mistaking sympathy for respect. We crave to reassure the faltering self that it is worthy after all.

Or do we indulge in self-pity—trapping ourselves in the past—for fear of moving ahead into the future where we might suffer additional assaults? Is self-pity a deceptive defense mechanism willfully experienced to protect us from new risks we may encounter if we start to think of beginning again?

You will never rebuild self-love until you *liberate yourself from self-pity and the tyranny of unpleasant memories.* You must stop thinking and talking about them. *Do not allow them to control you.* Banish such thoughts as "I'm finished . . . I'm a failure . . . I'll never do anything worthwhile . . . I bungled every chance I had . . . I hate myself . . . I'll never amount to anything."

When such thoughts occur, REMEMBER:

### Failure Is No Disgrace

It takes courage to try. It is more honorable to try something worthwhile and fail than never to attempt any worthy venture. Play-it-safe people seldom win the applause and the respect of others; they never do anything to merit congratulations!

I have a motto that applies to this:

### It's Better To Do Something Imperfectly Than To Do Nothing Perfectly!

Another of my slogans may also be helpful:

### I'd Rather Attempt Something Great . . . And Fail, Than Attempt Nothing . . . And Succeed!

If you have tried but don't feel you have succeeded, you should feel proud of yourself! You are great! You had the courage to dream! You had the guts to try! You have succeeded in dreaming!

### Failure Is Proof That I'm a Human Being

Tell yourself—"If I have suffered failure, I am in good company. I can be sure that I am a member of the human race!"

Every person has failed somewhere, even if it was the failure to see and seize a great opportunity. That often is the most costly, although unrevealed, failure.

Nobody's perfect. Yet everybody seems to have an inclination to be perfect. They wish they were perfect or they would like to give people the impression that they're perfect.

The truth is: *Everybody's imperfect*, but most people don't want to admit it. And average human beings go through a lot of mental and social games, wearing masks, trying to give people the impression that they are almost faultless. The tragedy is that such persons never become authentic. The most beautiful thing to me about the gospel is that it shows how we can be accepted by God even though we are imperfect and sinful.

One of the exciting things about the Bible is that it makes perfectly clear that the great people whom God used were far from perfect. For instance, Noah was a drunkard. Moses committed murder. Joseph was arrogant. David, who was called a "man after God's own heart," was guilty of adultery.

Now, if these great men of God conspicuously, glaringly, and publicly had their sins and imperfections, yet God was able to redeem, change, and use them, I suggest this ought to be a source of great encouragement to you and me! We can be reassured that *nobody is perfect*. Everybody sins, even the nicest people.

# In love's service— only broken hearts qualify . . .

P.S. Have you earned your credentials?

### Failure Can Be Fruitful

If my failures teach me something, they will have positive value. I can learn from my weaknesses. I can learn something about other people or, if nothing more, I can learn patience, compassion, and humility. A failure may turn out to be the greatest thing that ever happened to me.

Have you had a failure? Has your company gone under? Has your marriage fallen apart? Have you been stood up at the altar? Have you lost a loved one through death? Is your heart breaking?

Is there someone who needs you, who could benefit from what you learned through your pain? Your loss? Your failure?

"Turn Your Scars into Stars," by turning your hurts into halos, by using your pain to help ease somebody else's.

When my daughter Sheila was in her freshman year at Hope College in Holland, Michigan, three thousand miles away from home, she went through a devastating experience.

Because of an overflow attendance at the college that year, nine freshmen, along with a dorm resident advisor, were housed in a cottage (an old home adjacent to the campus). These nine freshmen didn't know a soul when they stepped on that campus. And thrown together as they were, they formed a tightly knit group.

Their personalities were as different as night from day, and their interests and values were also frequently dissimilar, but since they lived separately from the other students the friendships grew.

One of the girls, Linda, was not the easiest person to get along with. She was outspoken and sometimes surly. She seemed to be groping for identity and affection and always had a tough shell around her, though there were times when she seemed to be daring someone to crack it. One night she approached my daughter and said, "Sheila, do you really believe in God? I mean, you're always reading your Bible and stuff, and I know your father's a minister, but do you *really* believe in God? Do you feel Him deep down inside?"

Sheila looked at Linda with surprise. Linda had made no pretenses about where she stood on such matters as religion, dating, and drugs.

"Yes, Linda," Sheila answered, "I do believe in God. And I do feel Him deep down inside. I know He loves me as much as I love Him. Do you believe in God, Linda?"

Linda burst out, "I wish I could! I really wish I could!" And off she ran to her room. Although Sheila tried to talk to her further, Linda made it clear that the discussion was over.

One afternoon when Sheila arrived home from studying she was greeted by one of the other girls who said, "Oh, Sheila! It's terrible! It's so terrible!"

"What is it? What's happened?" Sheila asked.

"It's Linda! We don't know if she's going to make it or not!"

"What do you mean?"

"She took a whole lot of pills. She's in the hospital. She's in a coma."

Sheila was stunned. She prayed, "Oh Linda! You've got to make it! There's still so much I have to tell you about Jesus and His love for you!"

Providentially, I was at the college at that time for a board meeting. Sheila ran along the icy sidewalks across the campus to the hall where the board was meeting. Sheila stood outside the room and prayed frantically for the meeting to end. Finally, when a student aide brought me a message that Sheila wanted to see me, I hurried out of the meeting to find my daughter looking visibly shaken. She buried herself in my arms and poured out the whole tragic story.

I took her by the arm and led her out to a lone sidewalk where we could walk off the grief and talk without interruption.

Finally, I said, "Sheila, trouble never leaves you where it finds you. It will either leave you a bitter person or a better person. Do you remember the phrase I taught you, 'In love's service, only broken hearts will do'?"

"Yes."

"Well, you are experiencing today the real hurt and agony that comes with a broken heart. Only people who have experienced what you are feeling now can be compassionate enough to help others. Let God take your hurt and use it to make you a better person, a special person—one who's fit for love's service."

As Sheila told me later, "I resolved then and there not to let Linda's life go to waste. No matter what the outcome, whether she lived or died, I would let God use the hurt."

Linda's life hung in the balance for three days. One night, the chaplain came over and met with the girls in the living room of their cottage. "She's gone," he said.

Linda's life was short, but it had a tremendous impact on Sheila's. In fact for seven years after she graduated from college Sheila worked as a counselor to troubled young girls in our church. She spent her summers working with girls at campgrounds and took numerous young girls under her wing, becoming a big sister to many.

Sheila told me, "In my life I have seen many 'Lindas.' Most of them have not physically taken their lives, but many of them are dying inside. Whenever I see a girl who is hurting, confused, or lost, I remember Linda; and I remember your words, Dad: 'In love's service, only broken hearts will do.' And then I know what to do. I can sign up for love's service, for I know how fatal a broken heart can be."

Just because it looks as if you have failed, it doesn't necessarily mean that you still won't succeed. So don't give up! Don't make an irreversible negative decision that you may later regret.

## Success Is Never Certain
## And
## Failure Is Never Final!

Remember those words. Burn them into your subconscious. A time will come when you will need them.

Several years ago, when the "Hour of Power" first went on television, we gave away a most challenging gift. Knowing that the olive trees in California were originally from the Holy Land, we knew a tiny olive tree would be special and precious to our viewers. The gift was attractive, helpful, and within our budget, but it was next to impossible to package and mail!

After making the offer we were overwhelmed with tens of thousands of requests for the tiny olive trees. The trees were sent. Two weeks later we were deluged with tons of negative mail. To our dismay most of the trees had arrived dead or dried out. But one letter impressed me:

My Dear Friend,

I have received the olive tree and wish to thank you. Permit me to take a moment of your precious time to tell you about my experience. What a thrill I had when the postman delivered the little box. I was so excited and happy. I gently opened the carton and to my surprise found a plastic bag with a tiny plastic box and a dried-out twig! What a letdown! I could have cried. I felt as though this little innocent olive tree had smothered and withered inside this plastic bag on the long trip from California to New York.

Well, I read the instructions carefully and for some reason I didn't throw it away. I transplanted that olive twig. While doing this I felt so sorry for it because it had dried out and withered and the leaves were folded down. Most had fallen off. I soaked the poor twig thoroughly and placed it on a table facing the east sun. I felt foolish keeping this twig and giving it so much attention. But after several days, a surprise! The leaves had lifted and a tiny branch had turned itself to the sun.

I am so delighted now, words can't express my gratitude to you. I just love it.

I wonder how many olive trees were thrown away as dead twigs because people didn't have the faith to believe there was still life in those withered roots?

Is your life bare? Has a dream died? Has your self-esteem been shattered? Don't throw it all away! Don't give up yet! There's still life in the roots. Tap into them. Drench them with faith in yourself and in God.

## Failure Is Never Total

"I'm a *complete* failure," the self-degrading person wrongly claims. But *no* person is ever a *total* failure!

Any person who claims complete worthlessness is absolutely wrong. The late Dr. Smiley Blanton, an eminent psychiatrist, once said to his colleague Norman Vincent Peale, "There are vast undamaged areas in every human life. These undamaged areas must be discovered, then used as the base for a new beginning."

Psychiatrists have long noted that mental illness never seems to be total. Freud wrote that even patients with severe hallucinations later reported that "in some corner of their minds," as they expressed it, "there was a normal person hidden, who watched the progress of the illness go past like a detached spectator."

In World War II an asylum in France that housed 158 persons considered hopelessly and incurably insane was liberated by advancing armies. All the inmates escaped. Years later it was discovered that fifty-three were living normal lives, apparently recovered.

*No matter what your condition*—you *can* rebuild a meaningful future! You *can* reconstruct a self-love-generating life.


## Step III. Start Believing in Yourself!

You only have one more step to climb before your self worth will be reborn! It is time to act! You must believe in *you*!

You are filled with many wonderful possibilities. Look for them! You will be amazed at what you will discover.


### *Discover Your True Identity*

Look at the history of the great families: the Medicis of Italy, the Hapsburgs of Germany, and the Stuarts of England. You may say, "If I carried one of those family names and had that identification and those connections, I'd really be somebody. I know I would have self-esteem."

Well, I have good news for you. You can be identified with the family of God. God can be your father! If God's your father, and you're His child, you must be somebody terrific! You carry His honorable name!

During the French Revolution on separate occasions King Louis XVI and Queen Marie Antoinette were escorted to the guillotine in a square in Paris and beheaded. A tale is told that at one of the executions the crowd watching went crazy, screaming joyously! "Bring out the prince!" they bellowed. "He's next!" The young boy was terrified! He was only eight years old, but he was to be the next king and so the mob thought he had to be eliminated, too. He stood on the platform trembling in his black velvet coat and patent leather shoes. His golden curls, which fell over his shoulders, were damp from his tears. "Down with him! Kill all kings!" screamed the furious horde.

But then out of the crowd came a vicious voice. "Don't kill him! You'll only send his soul to heaven. That's too good for royalty. I say, turn him over to Meg, the old witch! She'll teach him filthy words. She'll teach him to be a sinner. And then, when he dies his soul will go to hell! That's what royalty deserves!"

So, according to legend, that's exactly what happened. The officials turned the young prince over to Meg, the witch. But every time she tried to teach him vulgarities, the prince stubbornly stamped his little feet until his curls shook, and with clenched fists he said, "I will not say it! I will not say those dirty words! I was born to be a King, and I won't talk that way!"

The problem with many people today is that they don't realize who they are. If you are a child of God, *He's your father!* Do you feel close enough to God to call Him your father? Do you feel close enough to go to Him at any time for any reason? I have five children by birth. They can come to me anytime. They have inside connections. They have my most private, unlisted telephone number. I am their father! They are my children. *You* can have that kind of relationship with God!

### Discover Your Innate Dignity

When you know who you are, you will live an ennobled life! When you have a tremendous sense of self-respect, you won't stoop to crime; you won't use profane language; you won't abuse the people around you. It will be beneath your dignity. There are some things that the Schuller family doesn't do. It's the same way with God's family. When you consciously know that you belong to the family of God, you develop the most healing, helpful, and divine sense of righteous pride. It will not be a sinful pride; it will be a redemptive pride.

Let me illustrate this with a story I read in high school years ago. A farmer's young son had been outside playing one day and came home with a large, odd-looking egg. The boy proudly showed it to his father and asked if he could keep it. The farmer didn't know exactly what to do with it, so he went to the barn and carefully placed it under a mother goose that was nesting. A few days later the father and son were leaving the house when they saw the mother goose parading across the barnyard followed by six beautiful baby geese. It was a comical sight, because the tiny newborn creatures were trying frantically to keep up with their mother.

The boy and his father smiled and started to turn around . . . but then something caught their eyes. One little goose was trailing behind the rest. His beak was not flat, it was pointed and twisted. He could hardly walk, because he had claws instead of delicate webbed feet. Instead of having lovely white plumes, he was an ugly brown color. And to top it off, he made a terrible squawking sound. He was a freaky bird, ugly and disfigured!

Then one day, above the barnyard flew a giant eagle. He swept lower and lower until the strange, awkward little bird on the ground lifted his head and pointed his crooked beak into the sky to see what it was. The misfit creature then stretched his wings and began to hobble across the yard. He flapped his wings harder and harder until the wind picked him up and carried him higher and higher. He began to soar through the clouds! He discovered what he was! He had been born to be an eagle, but he was trying to live like a goose!

You were born to soar! You were created in God's image! The tragedy is that too many human beings have never discovered their divine heritage so they live like animals. God loves you— He created you—you are His child. Do you know it? Have you claimed your divine heritage?

### Discover Your Latent Possibilities

Every situation contains within it the seed of a possibility. If you were born in poverty, if you are part of a minority, if you apparently lack resources—don't give up on yourself. You have possibilities within and around you. Look for them. Discover them. It may be to show compassion; it may be to help somebody who is hurting. In the process you will be blessed because problems combined with possibility thinking can propel you to do great things. And when you have overcome obstacles and turned problems into opportunities, you will be amazed at how good you will begin to feel about yourself.

### Discover Your Unique Ability

Everybody has been created with a special gift, a very personal, unique ability to do something great for God. And until you discover exactly what it is that makes you special, you will feel inadequate, insecure, even inferior. It's up to you to discover what it is that makes you the wonderful person you are. It's up to you to take inventory of your talents, gifts, and unique abilities.

One word of caution. Many people get hung up on the word *talent*—they think it's something you are born with. I contend that frequently talent is something you acquire, like experience or wisdom. It can be developed through hard work, like studying. Frequently, talent is spelled W-O-R-K.

Sherrill Milnes is the leading baritone of the Metropolitan Opera, as well as of the other leading opera houses of the world, and a good friend who has sung magnificently for us in the Crystal Cathedral. This famous singer was the son of a preacher, born and reared, like me, on a farm in the Midwest.

Anybody who has been reared on a farm knows all about the work ethic. It is drilled into a child from early in life as the entire family works together from sunup to sundown, milking the cows, feeding the various animals, gathering eggs, pitching hay, working the fields. I asked Sherrill once when we were together, "Do you think your boyhood farm experience affected you any way in your successful career?"

Sherrill smiled and said in his deep baritone voice, "I think it did very definitely. Life on a small family farm teaches you the value of hard work, and personally I think that the only way that one can fulfill his talent and his ambitions is to work at it."

"But, Sherrill," I said, "I think most people look at you and say, 'Well, you've got the talent. You just open your mouth and sing.'"

"Oh, that's just not true!" he replied. "It takes a lot of work and a great deal of discipline to be a leading singer with the Metropolitan Opera Company. I vocalize *daily*. I also have to take good care of my instrument, my voice, which is with me wherever I go, of course. That means I have to make sure that I get plenty of rest. If performances are scheduled too close together, I have to be careful that I budget enough time for that rest and for rehearsals. *Talent,* you see, is *hard work, discipline, common sense,* and *keeping yourself in good physical and mental shape."*

Recently I had dinner with famed lawyer Louis Nizer. He said to me, "I have often lectured at the greatest law schools in America. At those lectures I enjoy telling the students—'I want to introduce you to a mystic word. It will perform miracles for you. It will open portals for you. This marvelous, mystic word will turn the *stupid* student into a *bright* student, the *bright* student into a *brilliant* student, the *brilliant* student into a *steadfast* student! This word will guarantee great success for anyone. The mystic word is W-O-R-K!'"

Talent? *Everybody* has it! Hard work? *Anybody* can apply themselves diligently if they decide they really want to. Discipline? It's just a choice between doing what will make you feel better about yourself or doing what will make you angry with yourself.

You can be somebody special! In fact, you *are* somebody special! It's up to you to find out what it is you're especially good at, and then do it the very best you can. It may be to sing like Sherrill Milnes. It may be to listen. After all, what good is a singer without an audience?

Your talent is not more nor less important than the talent of someone else. God made you—YOU—for a special reason. Ask Him to show you what that is.

## Discover Your Divine Destiny

"For I know the plans I have for you, says the Lord. They are plans for good and not for evil, to give you a future and a hope."

(Jer. 29:11 TLB)

This Bible verse says plainly that God has a plan and a dream and it includes you. You were born for a purpose. You are here for a reason. When you discover God's dream for your life, then you will be well on your way to discovering your worth as a fellow human being, sharing this planet called earth.

Donna Stone Pesche discovered her destiny, and millions of children will now live without fear and pain because of her efforts. You may have heard of Donna. Her father, W. Clement Stone, is renowned for his many contributions to worthy projects, as well as his P.M.A. (Positive Mental Attitude) seminars and books.

Donna died from cancer in 1985, but not before she was able

to set in motion the National Committee for Prevention of Child Abuse. Donna was always interested in child welfare and children with unmet needs, but her greatest motivation came from the fact that her mother, Jesse, had been an abused child. Jesse's last remembrance of her father was the police taking him away after he had chased her mother with a butcher knife. When Donna heard that story, it made such an impression on her that she decided to do whatever she could to prevent all kinds of abuse, but especially child abuse.

As Donna said to me in 1981, "Reverend Schuller, child abuse is a tremendous problem. We believe that child abuse affects over a million children every year in the United States. And we estimate that it kills at least five thousand to seven thousand children a year. It's a tremendous problem. Next to sudden infant death and accidents, abuse is the number one killer of children in America."

"What kinds of people would beat a child?" I asked Donna.

"These parents are not monsters. They are people who have their own unmet needs. I like to think of them as people who have only half a cup. If you have almost nothing emotionally, it's so hard to give to other people. They are usually people who are immature, who have a very low sense of self-esteem. They have no pride in themselves. Usually, they have been abused as children themselves. They are people who have unrealistic expectations of their own children. And they are people who are suffering, in crisis, and need help."

"What can be done to help prevent child abuse?" I asked.

"Well," Donna said, "as more people become aware of the problem, we hope and pray that the problem will gradually diminish. Certainly, it must get better, for we have found that 90 percent of the people incarcerated in the prison system have been victims of abuse or gross neglect. So we have to work with children. Another way we're trying to help is by starting self-help groups, like Parents Anonymous. Your help-line, 'NEW HOPE,' [at the Crystal Cathedral] is an excellent prevention."

*Perfect love
perceives
people—
not as problems!
But—
as possibilities!*

Only a few years after this conversation took place, Donna discovered she had breast cancer—shortly after my wife, Arvella, lost a breast to cancer. I remember Arvella's calling Donna and praying with her, supporting her in the tough struggle against this horrible disease.

Then I remember my last meeting with Donna. I was told she could meet me at the Admiral's Club of American Airlines at O'Hare Airport. By now she was battling the cancer furiously, and because the treatments had caused a hair loss, she wore a turban over her head. She was as vivacious as ever! We went to her home. She told me the cancer had entered her brain. I looked at her and said, "Oh, Donna, you can still see."

"Yes!"

"You can still hear."

"Yes!"

"You can still talk."

"Yes!"

"You can still feel." She had her hands on mine and I had mine on hers.

"Yes!"

She interrupted me and said, "But, Dr. Schuller, best of all, I can still *give!*"

This was the secret to Donna's sense of self-worth. She had discovered her destiny. She had discovered what she was meant to give to the world. And she derived a tremendous amount of joy and self-esteem from giving of herself to others until the very end of her life.

## NOW—BELIEVE IN YOURSELF AND BE HAPPY

- YOU have your own *identity*; none of us is exactly alike.
- YOU have your own unique fingerprints; YOU can make your own unique impression on the world!

- YOU have an innate sense of *dignity*. Do not suppress it. Cultivate it! Hold your head up high.
- YOU have latent *possibilities*. Find a need and fill it. With all the hurt in the world today, there is no excuse for feeling useless.
- YOU have unique *ability*. YOU can find it if YOU will look in the right places.
- YOU have a divine *destiny*. YOU were created with a specific purpose in mind. God chose someone special—YOU! He believes in someone special—YOU!

God believes in YOU. YOU can, too.

So take the first step: Head for the love train. Enter at the station "Love Yourself and Be Happy!"

# JUNCTION TWO:
# LOVE GOD—
# AND BE HAPPY!

**"I** would love to believe in God, if I knew it was the truth," an intelligent young Japanese said to me as I finished a lecture in Tokyo. He continued, *"Prove* God to me. That's what the unbelieving world is waiting for. We're scientific. We want *proof* before we believe."

"But that's a contradiction," I answered. "If there is proof, there is no longer room for belief. For faith believes in that which cannot be proven." I looked into this bright young man's shining black eyes and said, "Let me put it this way:

WHEN PROOF IS POSSIBLE, FAITH
BECOMES IMPOSSIBLE!
AND WHEN PROOF IS IMPOSSIBLE, FAITH
BECOMES POSSIBLE!"

At this second junction of the Happy Railroad we will see that loving God is a two-fold process. We need to *believe* in God and we need to *love* Him. We need to deal with our *beliefs* as well as our *feelings* about our Creator. We do that when we make a commitment of our whole being—mind, will, and emotions to God. And so we will obtain our ticket at this station when we choose to believe, and we will board the train when we begin to love our Creator.

## PICK UP YOUR TICKET—CHOOSE
## TO BELIEVE!

Now let me say this—*if you are looking for proof about God*—
you will not be able to board the Love Train at this station—and
if you boarded the railroad at some other stop, your journey on
this loop of love will be stopped by derailment at this point. You
need to choose to believe if you want to explore and discover
true love and genuine joy. You do have three options open to
you, you know:
1.  There is *a* God. This is theism.
2.  There is *no* God. This is atheism.
3.  "I don't know; therefore I'm not going to commit either
way." This is agnosticism.
    It's important to be honest when discussing the existence of
God, for there is no firm, final proof for any position. Both
theist and atheist have made commitments to a belief system
without conclusive proof.
    The atheists and the theists both are believers and have faith.
The difference is: Atheists are negative in their faith; theists are
positive in their faith. The atheist says "No." The theist says
"Yes." The atheist says "There is nothing." The theist says
"There is something."
    The atheist says "All believers in God, without a single
exception, in all of human history have been mistaken. I am
wiser than they. I say they were wrong, I am right!"
    The theist says "All believers in God, in all of human history,
cannot *all* without a single exception have been wrong! What if
they are right? I could make a tragic error if I arrogantly reject
their collective testimony! Jesus Christ believed in God! I
suspect He knew something we don't! I'll trust Jesus in humble
faith before I'll trust the atheist."
    The honest fact is either there is a God or there is not a God.

Either the theist or the atheist is right. Both at least have the courage to take a stand. This is more than can be said for the agnostic. He runs with the hares and dashes with the hounds. He vacillates and remains indecisive. Proudly he applauds himself for "rising above the battle." In fact he cowardly avoids an issue that will not go away. *No* decision is certainly not the *right* decision. The evasive position of the agnostic is surely not an answer. And does any bright, sensitive person want to go through an entire lifetime avoiding or evading life's ultimate question for fear of making the wrong decision?

This choice to believe will require honesty and courage. To be honest is to admit that there are no final proofs. To be courageous is to choose to believe—anyway!

For those of you who are afraid of appearing ignorant if you believe in God, let me remind you that many of the world's greatest scientists are believers in God. Take Dr. Michael DeBakey, for example, who is one of the world's leading heart surgeons. His accomplishments in the last forty-nine years have led to revolutionary advances in treatment for cardiovascular diseases. Dr. DeBakey created the pump that makes open-heart surgery possible and has developed more than fifty different surgical instruments. You can't go into a surgical room anywhere in the world without picking up an instrument that bears the name "DeBakey."

What drives this man? What motivates him? If you ask him, he'll tell you it's his faith in God and his faith in humanity. I recently had the privilege of meeting this great man. I took hold of his hands and asked him, "Dr. DeBakey, how many human hearts have these hands held?"

He said, "Oh, over fifty thousand."

I thought, *fifty thousand? That can't be! He'd have to perform over eleven hundred surgeries a year. That's got to be impossible!*

Just then he said, "Dr. Schuller, I have a surgery going on right now. I think you'd like to see it. It's in Dome 4."

I followed him through a door that opened onto a balcony. I looked down through a glass ceiling into an operating room. Suddenly I understood how he had done it! Surgeries were going on in Domes 1, 2, 3, and 4. He moved from one team of surgeons in one room, to the next, to the next, and to the next. Fifty thousand hearts was probably an understatement!

For the first time, from my perch on the balcony, I looked down at a man who was having open-heart surgery. All I could see was a table, surrounded by nine doctors and three nurses, all wearing green masks. The table was covered with green cloth. There in the middle of all this green was something that resembled a bowl. In that bowl was a huge red chunk of something that was moving. I said, "Dr. DeBakey, could that be a living human heart?"

"Yes!"

"His *living* heart?"

"I hope so," he said with a chuckle. Then Dr. DeBakey looked at me, put his arm around me, and said with a moist eye, "Bob, look at that! Isn't it beautiful? What a temple! I have done this for forty-nine years, and not once have I failed to feel the presence of God when I have seen the heart.

Faith in God! Some of the most intelligent men and women in the world have decided that the smartest choice to make is to believe in a God—of *love*—no less!

## "I WANT TO BELIEVE—BUT I HAVE QUESTIONS!"

Our faith—although it is a leap over the chasms where proofs elude us—is not *blind*. It is based on solid evidence and premises. As a pastor I am aware of the three major questions that many people struggle with.

## Question #1: If There Is a God—Why Did He Put Everything on a Faith-only Basis?

The answer to this question is simply that God wanted to allow us to be possibility thinkers, persons, believers—not puppets nor computers. The Bible says that the human being was designed to be a decision-making creature. That's the meaning of Adam and Eve. God deliberately gives us the choice to obey or disobey, because if there is no choice, there is no development of character. Unless there is more than one possibility offered, we will never learn to live by faith. Faith is choosing a possibility before we can be sure that it's the right one.

Living life on the faith-only basis is what makes life worth living. It gives life its meaning.

Faith is often called a "leap." How appropriate! How else could you possibly move from one point to another when there is no direct link? How else do you cross over a crevice when there is no bridge?

Faith is leaping across gaps that exist between:

- the known and the unknown;
- the proven and the unproven;
- the actual and the possible;
- the grasp and the reach;
- the "I've got it" and the "I want it";
- the knowledge and the mystery;
- sin and forgiveness;
- life and death;
- time and eternity.

Faith is making decisions before you've solved all of the problems.

Faith is making commitments before you can be assured everything will work out right.

Faith is moving ahead before you have answers to all the questions.

Faith is taking a risk without being fully insured.

Faith is choosing to believe before there is total proof.

## You Will <u>Never</u> Have <u>All</u> the Answers!

If we are open-mindedly seeking the truth about life and God, we must leave room for mysteries and unanswered questions. Life and religion is a compilation of facts and mysteries. Even science has to leave room for mystery.

And thank God for mystery! If we knew *all* the answers, if we knew the way everything worked, how boring, how cold, how calculating life would be. Perhaps you've heard the little ditty that shows this so succinctly:

> Twinkle, twinkle little star,
> I know exactly what you are:
> An incandescent ball of gas,
> Condensing to a solid mass!

## The Negative Answers You Have May Be Wrong!

Louis Kahn, the great architect, once said, "If when I am ready to begin a new project, if I then have all the answers, some of my answers are wrong."

Check the neat little negative answers you have lived with so long. What if those answers are wrong and others' answers are right? Do you want to go to your grave having lived your entire life by the wrong answers? "O.K.," you say, "but how do I know if my answers are right or wrong?"

Well, if an answer is right, it will check out. If your bank book is accurate it will balance. If a scientific deduction is correct, it will fit the test results. If you doubt that God's love exists I challenge you to consider some evidence I have gathered.

In my work I have blessed thousands upon thousands of human beings with a look, a word, and a touch. Some have been in wheelchairs, some with crutches, some with limbs missing. Some speak with difficulty because of brain damage incurred in accidents. And yet, in spite of the pain, in spite of the difficulties, in spite of the battles with cancer and other physical infirmities, these people—who have every reason to be bitter, depressed, and angry at the world and at God—are *genuinely happy.* How do you explain that?

Sure, they still hurt. Yes, there is still pain. But beyond that there is HAPPINESS! Why? Because they all believe that they are truly loved. They believe that God loves them. And that authentic, real love gives them the reason for their joy. They have chosen to believe in this positive answer to the awesome, often troubling questions we all have about life.

If you cannot believe in a God of love, perhaps you are living with the wrong answers. There are people who do believe in happiness, in goodness, in *love!* What if these people are right? What if you are wrong?

## Question #2: How Can I Believe in a God of Love in an Evil World?

That's the wrong question! The right question is, *"How can I doubt God in a world that is this good?"*

Now! I ask you, which question is the more constructive? Creative? Redemptive?

If we're going to find faith we need to get an accurate, positive perception of reality. It is true that:

- The world is filled with suffering!
- We are surrounded by selfish people!
- The world is under the threat of missiles, terrorism, and thermonuclear destruction.

However, it is *also* true that there is a lot of good in the world! There is suffering. There is selfishness. But there is also an immense capacity for love within the human family.

Ken Kragen is wonderful evidence of this. Ken was the driving force behind "We Are the World" and "USA for Africa." Ken, who is the manager for such star performers as Kenny Rogers and Lionel Richie, gathered together his clients and many other entertainers to record a song that raised nearly $50 million for the starving people in Africa.

As Ken shared with me the excitement of this incredible feat he said, "I went to Africa with the first shipment of food and supplies, and when I came back, everywhere I went in this great country people said to me, 'That's wonderful what we're doing for Africa. It's necessary—it is important—but we have things here at home that need to be done. When are we going to do something for America?' Then I knew we had to do something even bigger for our own country."

Ken did that with "Hands Across America." On May 25, 1986, millions of Americans stood hand to hand in a glorious link-up from the Pacific Ocean to the Atlantic Ocean. The chain wound its way through the Crystal Cathedral during our Sunday service. We joined hands in this incredible outpouring of love to make a difference in this country. All of the money raised was given to the homeless and hungry right here in America.

"What I have seen, Dr. Schuller, through all of this," Ken said, "is that *people want to give*. People do care enough to do something for those less fortunate."

I applaud Ken Kragen. "Hands Across America" represents

the best of American tradition, where we care about our neighbor—we help, we build a house, we rebuild the barn that burned down. During my childhood my family lost everything in a tornado; I remember what it was like when people brought us blankets, clothes, and food.

People like Ken Kragen are proof of the fact that "God loves you and so do I!" Look around you. Anytime you show me a horrific tragedy, I will show you an example of tremendous compassion. Always remember *to check the love that is in the human race*—love that is unquenchable! Indestructible!

There is a wonderful Bible verse (Song of Sol. 8:7) that I learned as a boy:

> Many waters cannot quench love
> Nor can the floods drown it.

"Waters" such as hurt, deceit, anger, and bitterness exist—they threaten to destroy love. But time and again, history has proven that love is the stronger force. Love always wins out in the end.

There is a love loose in this world that no amount of evil can ever imprison. And so long as there is love, I must believe in a God who will never let love die.

## Question #3: How Can I Believe in a God of Love When Personal Tragedy Overwhelms Me, When "All Hell Breaks Loose"?

Again, I must ask: What's your perception of reality? There are positive and negative perceptions of every reality. The negative perception sees only the human tragedy. The positive sees the impulsive, instinctive, intuitive eruption of a caring and sharing spirit that occurs because of the tragedy. This explains why, in the darkest hour, this scenario unfolds time after time:

Catastrophe strikes!
The news is confirmed and reported.
Compassionate friends appear from everywhere and seemingly nowhere.
They huddle with the hurting heart and cry together.
They take time to pray together, eat together, and—almost always—laugh together!

Yes! Laughter in the trenches! Laughter in the emergency room! Laughter in the living room, where family and friends have gathered for a wake. I have heard laughter at the reception of almost every funeral I have ever attended or presided over.

This laughter—is it irreverence? No! It is a natural expression of joy breaking forth after the dark gloom of tragedy has lifted. As the Bible says,

> Weeping may endure for a night,
> But joy comes in the morning (Ps. 30:5).

Recently on a TV talk show, the host asked me, "Are you always happy, Dr. Schuller? And how can you be happy when things are so bad?"

His question triggered a thought, an explanation that had never occurred to me before. It amazed me, for in it I saw a basis for understanding the psychological and spiritual reactions we have to our world around us. This was the answer I gave my host: "I can be happy because *it's not the reality that is important— it's my perception of the reality that really matters. I can be happy no matter what happens to me, if I can maintain a positive perception of that reality.*"

Many of you women who have been hit with the reality of

breast cancer know what I'm talking about. My wife Arvella knows, too, because she has not been spared from this disease. When she was diagnosed as having a malignancy of the breast with surgery required, she had to decide how she would perceive this reality.

One of her perceptions of her very real breast cancer could have been, "Oh, this is going to devastate me. I will no longer be attractive to my husband. I'll probably get cancer in some other part of my body in a few years and die." If Arvella had adopted that reaction, she would have lost hope, and even if she lives a long life, it would be a life filled with fear and pain. This would be a negative perception of a reality.

Mercifully, this was *not* the reaction Arvella chose. She chose to believe she could conquer cancer. She chose to believe she could be whole and well again despite her mastectomy. And she is alive and happy and very, very busy in the ministry of the "Hour of Power."

When your perception of reality is positive, you can be happy, no matter what happens. If today you have no money, if you're poverty-stricken or on the verge of bankruptcy, you need to examine your perception of this condition. On the one hand, you can decide this is a total tragedy—you're wiped out, you're finished. On the other hand, you can look upon this as an opportunity to make some much-needed changes.

When you change your thinking, when you develop a positive perception, an amazing thing happens. Suddenly the reality is no longer as disastrous. After all it's not a disaster unless you *think* it's disastrous.

If you will perceive your problem as a possibility in disguise, then a stumbling block can become a steppingstone. The obstacle will now be an opportunity. The problem is a challenge, and fatigue is replaced by a new rush of energy.

You can apply this principle to physical and economic conditions. It even works with personal relationships. Perhaps you have to work with or live with someone whom you can't handle. This person grates on your nerves.

I won't argue the point. But I will challenge your perception of what that reality means.

Negative perceptions block, obstruct your imagination from the positive possibilities. All you can see is the problem. You are blinded to the solutions, the possibilities for something even better. All you see is the hurt and the anger. You can't see the love and the joy that is hidden—waiting to be released.

On the other hand, a positive perception can unlock, reveal, release hidden possibilities. Suddenly you can see that life isn't so bad after all. Maybe things will work out. Maybe this is just God's way of guiding you. The positive perception looks for LOVE!

Where does this love come from? It comes from God Himself. Consequently, the deduction is clear: *If there's a lot of love in the world, there must be a lot of God in the world!*

So when I am asked, "How can you believe in God when all hell breaks loose?" I answer that question this way: "How dare I *not* believe in God when all hell breaks loose? I have enough problems without adding dangerous blinding doubt!"

*Remember: God will allow nothing—and no one—to rob you of your option to react positively!*

Faith then is the intelligent choice! Faith is the courageous choice! Jump onto the train. Choose to believe—in God—in a God of love!

## BOARD THE TRAIN—CHOOSE TO LOVE GOD!

Several influences and misconceptions hold people back from loving God. As a pastor I have heard and seen these time and again, and I must say that most of the hindrances were

## Crystal Cathedral Prayer

Lord,
Make my life
A window
For Your light
To shine through

And a mirror
To reflect Your love
To every person I meet.

subliminal. The people were unaware of what was keeping them from a loving relationship with God.

More often than not, people are unable to love God because they suffer from negative perceptions of God. Are you having trouble loving God? If your perception of your Creator is negative, then you must ask yourself some crucial questions.

## To What Extent Is My Negative Perception of God a Result of My Negative Perception of Myself?

Emotional pollutants can distort our perceptions of God. These pollutants are guilt and shame and lack of self-esteem.

Remember: *Perception is a mirror.* Perhaps you have not visited Junction One—"Love Yourself and Be Happy!" You are not adequately loving yourself and are therefore crippling your ability to appreciate and love God.

When people say to me, "Oh, Dr. Schuller, you're such a beautiful person," I chuckle and answer them this way: "Wait a minute. That is only your perception of me. Perception is not a window; perception is a mirror. If you see beauty in me, you are seeing your own beauty in me. It takes one to know one!"

"Beautiful" people are quick to spot "beautiful" traits in somebody else. The opposite is true as well. When you see something unattractive in somebody's life, perhaps it bothers you so much because that same quality exists within you. *Perception is a mirror.*

How you see God will depend a great deal on how you perceive yourself. Angry people either don't believe in God or believe in an angry God. On the other hand, loving people believe in God and believe in a loving God.

## To What Extent Is My Negative Perception of God a Result of My Ancestry?

Was your negative perception of God born in your family? Did your parents have (1) no faith at all or (2) a very negative and destructive faith? You probably need to know that embracing a faith that appears to violate your inheritance of knowledge and understanding will not be easy.

Most of us live with the tension of the pull of tomorrow and the tug of yesterday. To what extent are we responsible to carry on the lives of our ancestors? To pursue their projects? To fight their wars? To nurture their life's work? To propagate their doubts, their unbeliefs, their negative perceptions of God?

Tradition and perpetuity have validity only if they protect and advance truth. You may say, "I don't think I could become a believer or a Christian because my parents were not. And I wouldn't want to offend them or embarrass them, even if they are dead!"

Then I must ask you this question: "Do you not honor your parents if you improve on their beliefs? If you left a flawed inheritance to your children, would you not feel honored to see them lovingly correct your imperfect work?"

Dare we modify our parental heritage? Many of us don't, but if we improve our parents' perceptions, prejudices, ignorances, or inaccuracies, do we not improve our ongoing family history?

We have to understand this because it helps us understand some of the reasons why the wars keep going on in Northern Ireland and in the Middle East. It may be what keeps us from loving God, too.

Positivize your perceptions of God. Don't miss out on faith just to be faithful to family history and traditions!

## To What Extent Is My Negative Perception of God a Result of My Spiritual Habitat?

If we have negative perceptions of God, it could be because we human beings are out of our natural habitat.

Mountains are hidden by the fog. But that doesn't mean that the peaks are not there. The sun is often shadowed by the clouds, but that doesn't mean it isn't shining. Likewise, our perceptions of God may be tainted by emotional pollutants in our spiritual environment; but that doesn't mean God does not exist or that He doesn't care.

Do you realize how much your spiritual environment is affected by your physical surroundings? Have you stopped to think why it's often more difficult to find God in crowded cities than in the peaceful countryside?

I first learned of the great impact our physical surroundings have on our spiritual environment when I was introduced to Neutra's theory of bio-realism. Richard Neutra was, of course, a great architect who designed buildings in coordination with the landscape in order to create environments that were conducive to positive emotions. Neutra taught that when you take human beings out of their natural habitat, surround them daily with concrete and steel, and bombard them with the noise of traffic, the silver voice of God is drowned out.

Neutra's theory is substantiated when I meet people who say, "Reverend, I must tell you honestly—frequently, I feel closer to God on the golf course than I do in church."

There is some truth to that statement. That's why I contracted Neutra to design our walk-in, drive-in church where the sounds and sights of moving traffic are eliminated from the senses and replaced by views of tranquil garden settings. In effect, through architecture, human beings in such a building are brought back to the environment for which they were created. It is an environment that lifts the fog and allows the spirit within man to feel and to hear God clearly, free from the environmental pollutants.

These are some of the causes of negative perceptions of God. If you suffer from any of them, it's important to understand that they are *miss*-conceptions: If you allow them to affect your relationship with God, you'll *miss* love! You'll *miss* life! You'll *miss* laughter! You'll *miss* joy!

On the other hand, the positive conceptions of God are the *true*-conceptions. The truth is that: God *is* Love! God's love *is* unconditional! God's love *is* non-judgmental!

Are you still skeptical? Let's spend just a little more time at Junction Two!

## GOD DOES NOT SAY, "I'LL LOVE YOU *IF* . . ."

On Sundays in the Crystal Cathedral we stop during the service and ask those present to say to at least one other person, "God loves you and so do I!" We don't say, "God will love you *if* you are good and worthy of His love." We don't say, "God will love you *if* you can perfectly follow the Ten Commandments." We don't say, "God will love you *if* you will come to church every Sunday."

No! We don't have to prove ourselves to win the love and approval of God the Heavenly Father. His love and grace and eternal life are not prizes that we need to qualify for or promotions that need to be earned.

We have all heard the story of Pinocchio. Geppetto, the kind wood carver, longed for a son of his own. One day he "wished upon a star" and asked that the puppet he had made, Pinocchio, be turned into a real boy.

That night, as Geppetto slept, a fairy came and brought

Pinocchio partially to life. He was able to walk and talk without any strings. But he was still made of wood. She promised him that if he could prove that he was a good boy, she would return and make him into a *real* boy.

That's not how it is with God. We don't have to earn our love from Him. We don't have to prove ourselves to Him. He does not say, "I'll love you *if* you'll live an exemplary life." He loves us exactly as we are—right now!

One of the most well-known Bible verses is John 3:16: "For God so loved the world that He gave His only begotten Son, that whoever believes in Him should not perish but have everlasting life."

Notice that this verse does not say, "God so loved nice, good, perfect, holy people."

No! It says, "God so loved the *world*!" That means that He came, He lived, He loved—for *all*! J. Wallace Hamilton once said, "Jesus Christ is walking the highways of life looking for the riffraff, looking for the sinners like you and me—hounding us until He catches us, not to point an accusing finger, but to remind us who we are—children of God, for whom He died, whom God wants to use as His princes and princesses in His kingdom."

## GOD DOES NOT SAY, "I'LL LOVE YOU *WHEN* . . ."

God doesn't wait for you to love Him. He loves you now! He doesn't say, "I'll love you *when* you love me!" No—aware that you may flee from His love—He still makes the plunge; He makes the commitment; He makes the decision to love you.

Thank heaven that God decided to become involved with you and with me anyway! The act of sending Jesus to earth, the Incarnation, was only one of the decisions God made. Before that God decided to create human beings—people with the freedom to choose or not to choose, to reject or to accept, to run to love or to retreat from love. God made the human being a most unique creature.

Then, when we messed up the creation and allowed sin and negative forces to enter in, God made the decision to correct the situation by sending His Son to teach us the truth about living. This son, Jesus, not only told us the truth, He lived the truth. He was as He said, "the way, the truth, and the life."

God made the decision to send Christ to this world to save us knowing that it would cost Him the life of His one and only Son. He made the decision knowing that many would turn their backs on the love and the life He was offering them. But He didn't wait for us to ask Him to do it. Knowing full well that many would never accept it, He decided to give His Son's life *before* we knew we needed it.

## GOD DOES NOT SAY, "I'LL LOVE YOU *BUT* . . ."

God doesn't say, "I'll love you, *but* you must earn it."

This is an extremely difficult concept for most of us to accept. After all, as children we were taught to obey the rules. Our parents, whether they meant to or not, frequently conveyed the idea that their love had to be earned. When we were bad, their love was withheld. Even the best of parents are guilty of this tactic at one time or another, for certainly who among us can mask our disappointments and frustrations when our children fail to live up to our expectations for them? That doesn't mean we love them less; however, that is the message that children frequently receive.

There is a beautiful word in the Bible: *Grace*.

"What does that word really mean?" I asked my seminary

professor, Dr. Simon Blocker. I'll never forget his answer. It was so sound, psychologically and religiously!

"Grace," he answered, "is God's love in action for those who don't deserve it."

Grace is a gift. It can't be bought. It can't be earned. It is freely given. But a gift isn't really a gift until it is accepted! God offers to *all* the gift of grace. He offers the gift of love, the gift of a new you. Can you think of a better gift?

God's beautifully wrapped gift of grace came just in time for a woman I know named Sherrie. During the turbulent sixties she was a college student at Berkeley where she had begun using LSD. When her parents asked her to come home for a visit, Sherrie agreed, with one provision—that she would be able to return to Berkeley and never come home again. I received a telephone call from her parents urging me to talk with her while she was home.

The entire family came to my office together—father, mother, and daughter. Sherrie looked terrible. Her beautiful young face was distorted. Inner tensions, guilt, and her hardened attitude had altered her appearance. With sincerity she declared to me, "I have found God in LSD. Every Friday night we have our services. It's beautiful. You don't know what God is like until you've found God in LSD."

"I believe I have found God in Jesus Christ," I replied. "You claim," I continued, "that you have found God in LSD. Who's right? You or me? Let's put God to the test."

She nodded her head approvingly.

"God is love—do you agree?"

She said she did.

"Love is helping people," I added. "Do you agree?"

She nodded her head again.

"How much money have you collected in your LSD services to feed the hungry, to help the crippled, to find a cure for cancer?" I asked.

She was silent.

"I must tell you, Sherrie," I went on, "because of the Spirit of Jesus Christ that lives in the people in this church, we have been able to convert thousands of dollars over the past twelve months into help for human beings with problems. The Christian church has built hospitals and institutions to treat the blind, the sick, and the lame and has provided care for millions of unhappy people."

A sad look of disillusionment began to appear on Sherrie's face.

"Let's all stand, hold hands, and pray," I suggested. Father, mother, daughter, and I joined hands in a circle. I offered this simple prayer. "Jesus Christ, Your Spirit of Love lives within my heart. I pray that You will come into the life and heart of this beautiful young woman."

As I finished, I saw a tear slide from her eye. I reached over with my finger and picked up the wet drop of warm emotion from her soft cheek. Holding it before her, I exclaimed, "Sherrie! Look what fell out of your eye! Didn't you feel beautiful inside when this tear was forming and falling? This is the deepest and most joyous experience a human being can know. It is religious emotion. It is the movement of the divine Spirit within you. Christ is coming into your life, Sherrie. Let Him come in. Don't be afraid of Him. Nothing good ever dies inside when Christ comes in.

"Look at the sky—it is blue. Look at the grass—it is really green. Look at the flowers—they are really red. While you had this high trip, which put this beautiful tear in your eye, you were not in complete control of yourself. This is reality. It is not artificially induced. It is authentic. The world around you is not distorted or hidden in a psychedelic fog. You can trust this Christ." At that point tears were flowing freely from Sherrie's eyes. She felt the love of God for her.

Almost immediately her facial expression changed. The

narrowing eyes of suspicion and rebellion changed into the round, open, beautiful eyes of wonderment. The face, which had been tight, tense, and older than her years, relaxed. Once more the cheeks had the full blossom and the warm, rounded shape of a pretty young maiden.

As I write this, Sherrie is now a beautiful young wife and mother. She has devoted much of her life to helping others discover the supreme joy of knowing Jesus Christ.

The Love of God—it is there, a priceless gift, for you and for me. He doesn't say, "You can be saved, but you'll have to earn it." He doesn't say, "You can have my love, but you'll have to pay me for it." No! He only says, "You are loved! My love is a gift! Pure and simple; free and clear; no down payment necessary!"

John Newton said it years ago. Singers still sing the timeless words today:

> Amazing grace, how sweet the sound
> That saved a wretch like me!
> I once was lost, but now am found,
> Was blind, but now I see.

## GOD DOESN'T SAY, "I'LL LOVE YOU *AFTER . . .*"

God doesn't say, "I'll love you *after* you see the error of your ways, *after* you come back to me on your hands and knees." No! He goes out looking for you. You are His creation. He made you. He loves you. He wants to welcome you as His child into His arms.

You may remember the traditional story of Helen of Troy. There is an alternative legend in which this beautiful queen was captured and carried away and became a victim of amnesia. She became a prostitute in the streets. She didn't know her name or the fact that she came from royal blood. But, back in her homeland, friends didn't give up. One Greek man believed she was alive and went to look for her. He never lost faith.

One day while wandering through the streets, he came to a waterfront and saw a wretched woman in tattered clothes with deep lines across her face. There was something about her that seemed familiar so he walked up to her and asked, "What is your name?" She gave a name that was meaningless to him. "May I see your hands?" he pursued because he knew the lines in Helen's hands. She held her hands out in front of her, and the young man gasped, "You are Helen! You are Helen of Troy! Don't you remember?"

She looked up at him in astonishment.

"Helen of Troy!" he repeated. The fog began to clear. There was recognition in her face. The light came on! She discovered her lost self! She put her arms around her old friend and wept. She discarded the tattered clothes and once more became the queen she was born to be!

God searches for you in the same way. He uses every method possible to look for you and try to convince you of your worth to Him.

## GOD DOES NOT SAY, "I'LL LOVE YOU *THEREFORE* . . ."

God doesn't say, "I love you . . . *therefore* you are favored in my sight and will never suffer; never hurt; never experience pain, rejection, setbacks, or grief!"

Unreasonable, confused expectations, more than anything else, can rupture relationships. If you expect that because God loves you, *therefore* you should never experience heartbreak, your expectation is unrealistic and your relationship with God will turn sour. The truth is—God will give you grace to become a more beautiful and loving human being if you keep trusting Him through tragedy.

"You always seem so happy," I said to my dear friend, Art Linkletter. "I remember when your daughter, Diane, committed suicide at the age of seventeen. Then, I remember not too many years ago when your thirty-one-year-old son was instantly killed in an auto accident. I don't know how often you and I have been together since those two tragedies, but I always experience powerful vibrations of joy in your presence. Explain it to me. How can I interpret this to my readers? I'm totally convinced you're not a phony. I know you are a sincerely happy man."

"Oh yes, Bob," Art replied with that great, happy grin of his. "I've never been happier anytime in my life than I am today. I can't go anywhere without somebody approaching me and telling me of their pain. And I find my joy in comforting them. There's no doubt about it; I am a more compassionate human being. The loss of my children makes me want to love everybody, and that's what makes me happy!"

## GOD DOES SAY, *"I LOVE YOU"*—PERIOD!— EXCLAMATION POINT!

Love? It's there! It's unconditional! It's free, no strings attached! But you'll never be able to know it or see it or feel it until you come to terms with your Creator. He created love. He is the Source of love. And you will not be able to grow in your love for yourself or for others until you reach out and accept His love, until you can say "God loves me! This I know!"

If you have trouble believing that you are loved by God, if it is hard for you to see how much you mean to Him, then maybe this story will help.

Once there was a little boy who made a sailboat. He carefully carved the hull from wood, then lovingly sanded it smooth and delicately brushed on the paint. Next he cut the sail from the whitest cloth. When he finished it he couldn't wait to see if his boat was "seaworthy," so he took it to the lake. He found a grassy spot by the edge of the water, knelt down, and gently set the boat on the water. Then he blew a little puff of air and waited.

The boat didn't move, so he blew a little harder until a breeze filled the tiny sail and the boat pulled away from the shore. "It sails! It sails!" he cried out, clapping his hands and dancing along the side of the lake. But then he stopped. He realized he had not tied a string to the boat. He watched as his creation moved farther and farther away until it was out of his reach.

The little boy was both happy and sad—thrilled that his boat had sailed, but saddened because it was now out of his reach. He ran home crying.

Sometime later the boy was wandering through town when he passed a toy shop that sold both new and old toys. There in the window was his boat! He was ecstatic. He ran in and said happily to the shopkeeper, "That's my boat! That's my boat!"

The man looked down at the little boy and said, "I'm sorry. I bought the boat. It is for sale, though."

"But it's my boat," the boy cried out. "I made it! I sailed it! I lost it! It's mine!"

"I'm sorry," the shopkeeper said again. "If you want it you will have to pay for it."

"How much is it?" the lad asked. When he found out the price he was shattered. He had only a few coins in his bank at home. His head drooping, he left the store.

But this little boy was very determined. When he got home he went to his room and counted his pennies, nickels, dimes, and quarters to find out how much more money he would need before he could buy back his precious boat. So he worked and

**Grace**
**is**
**God's love**
**in action**
**for**
**those**
**who don't**
**deserve it!**

saved until finally he had just the right amount. He ran back to the store, hoping the boat would still be there. He laughed with joy; there it was sitting in the window just as before.

He ran into the shop, dug into his pockets, and placed all of his money on the counter. "I want to buy my boat!" he exclaimed.

The shopkeeper lifted the little sailboat out of the window and placed it in the excited boy's hands. The boy grasped the boat tightly to his chest and ran home proudly, saying, "You *are* my boat. You *are* my boat! You're *twice* my boat! First, you're my boat because I made you, and second, you're my boat because I bought you!"

If you were that boat you would know that you were loved. The news I have for you, my friend, is this: You are that sailboat! Jesus Christ is the little boy. And the cross is the price! You are God's child twice over. First, you were God's child because He made you. Second, you are God's child because He bought you on the cross of Calvary, and He will go to all lengths to get you back!

One of my favorite illustrations of this unconditional redemptive love of God is the musical drama *The Man of La Mancha.* In the musical, Don Quixote meets a woman of the streets, a wild, wanton wench named Aldonza. The man of La Mancha stops short, looks at her intently, and announces that she is his lady. He will call her "Dulcinea." She responds, with mocking laughter, that she is hardly a lady.

Still Don Quixote sees the seed of potential greatness and tries desperately to give her a new self-image of the person she really is—if she can believe it. He *insists* that she is his lady.

Angered and hurt, with wild hair flying over nearly naked breasts, she screams that she is only a kitchen maid! She is *Aldonza,* not Dulcinea!

She runs from the stage as the man of La Mancha whispers again and again that she is his lady. At the close of the play Don

Quixote is dying. He feels he has failed. The good he has tried to give has been rejected. The love he has offered has been shunned. But, then to his side comes a "born-again" Aldonza. She is now lovely with a new gentleness. Confused, he does not recognize this lovely stranger until in a warm voice she tells him that she is his Dulcinea. She has been saved from self-hate and has been taught self-love.

God's love is like the man of La Mancha's! He sees you *not* as you are, but as you can *become*! He sees the lady in *every* woman! The gentleman in *every* male! He sees you as the gentle, caring person who is loved and who can love in return! He sees the beauty in you—and will help you become the person He wants you to be.

Now then, it is possible to believe in a God of love! And when you see all that He has done, don't you think He deserves to be loved by you?

Don't pass by this all-important junction on this journey of love! Choose to believe in God! Choose to love God—and *be happy*!

# JUNCTION THREE:
# LOVE OTHERS— AND BE HAPPY!

A conductor of the train at Disneyland has made the loop hundreds, perhaps thousands, of times. He has watched the people wait eagerly for the approaching train. He has seen them surge happily through the gates in response to the call, "All Aboard!"

In contrast, when we are invited to take the trip on the Happy Railroad's train of love, most of us hold back. We may approach the junctions hesitantly, suspiciously. Some of us turn and run away.

Why is that? If love is so beautiful, so profoundly satisfying, so happiness-producing, why doesn't every normal human being instinctively, intuitively, irresistibly race to embrace fellow humans with a holy hug? Why don't we rush headlong into happy relationships? Could it be that we're afraid to get on board at "Love Your Neighbor and Be Happy!"—afraid of rejection? Of failure? Of involvement? Of oppression?

And what is fear? It is simply a lack of faith.

## DON'T HOLD BACK! ONLY BELIEVERS CAN BE LOVERS!

Possibility thinkers are people of faith who dare to believe that anything is possible. They dare to run risks! They have the

329

faith to love, and that's important because *only believers can be lovers.*

Another question comes to mind. If lack of love is fear, and if the presence of fear is lack of faith, then why do we lack the faith to plunge into a life controlled by love?

One of the reasons—shockingly—is that some people have *never* experienced healthy, honest love! It's painful to face up to—but it does happen. There are people who have gone through an entire life and have *never* known love. Perhaps their birth was the result of a night of passion between a man and a woman. So they never were truly welcomed and loved in birth or childhood or in their teen-age or young adult years.

Widespread child abuse is the most tragic reason why some are afraid of love. Social institutions, meanwhile, have often failed as well. Educational, political, even religious institutions have established priorities and prejudices that leave little or no time for ebullient, effervescent expressions of affection. So some people lack the faith to love because the concept is totally foreign to their perception of reality!

No wonder many, if not most, living human beings cry out, "Yes, Dr. Schuller, love may make you happy, and that's why I'm unhappy—*nobody* loves me!"

I dare you to have the faith to believe that there are in this world people who are trying to reach you, to love you. They honestly and deeply care about you more than you could ever know. There are fellowship groups, intimate colonies of caring Christians, scattered around this world.

You tried and were hurt? Disillusioned? Try again! And the fact that you have never experienced love doesn't mean you can discount its reality.

Remember this: Never judge reality by your *limited* experience. I have never been to Mt. Everest, yet I believe it is there! I trust the verified reports of those who have climbed its icy, rocky face. As you believe in the seas even if you have not sailed them, so you can believe in love, even if you have never experienced it.

In other cases faith in love has been shattered by crude encounters with counterfeit love. Tragic stories can be told of the innocent lover who has been exploited, manipulated, used, ripped off, and left lonely, bleeding, shocked, bitter! More often than not, this person was a victim of a love that was a selfish "I need you" or "I want you" display of passion.

If the only encounter a person has with love is a "commercial," interpersonal relationship, where love is only given to get something in return, then of course it would be difficult to acquire the faith to love.

Or if "getting love" or "being loved" always has a "price tag," this is judgmental "love."

- The teacher "loves" me when I do a good job!
- My parents "love" me when I obey.
- My religious authorities and God (as I interpret Him) "love" me when I live by the rules.

Love, at this point, has become a reward to be handed out! And withholding of love becomes a silent and cruel form of punishment! No wonder many persons yield to a natural inclination to shyness. A fear of intimacy takes over. People take the attitude that sex may be O.K. but intimacy is out! So they choose to "make love" without revealing their names.

Such an attempt to protect ourselves is terribly dangerous. A cold, hard shell will inadvertently be built around the heart and soul. The result: A deep-seated fear of loving. Love and happiness are lost.

If we are asked, *"What, then, is real love?"* we could offer one of these three answers:

### 1. *"I love you because I need you."*

Love relationships do fill mutual needs—and that's O.K! But if love rises no higher than this "I need you" level, it is, indeed, basically selfish. The dangers of selfish love are obvious: This path leads to jealousy and extreme possessiveness. Fear is the end result—the fear of losing a prized possession!

### 2. *"I love you because I want you."*

Passion does have a proper place in all healthy love relationships. But passion alone can be sheer lust. This path too will generate enormous negative tension. Passion does not deserve all the credit that it has been given by romance novelists and soap operas. Passion is *not* proof of love, anymore than lack of passion is absence of love. So let us not be deceived. Let us see real love as it is. As the poet William Blake wrote:

> This life's dim windows of the soul
> Distorts the heavens from pole to pole
> And leads us to believe a lie
> When you see with, not through, the eye.

I am reminded of a man who is unmarried. He is in his fifties, and he was despairing to me recently because his life is lonely; he has never had a family. "The trouble is," he said, "I once knew a young girl, but there wasn't the passion for her that I thought should have been there. So I foolishly thought I didn't love her. However, I deeply respected and trusted her! Now, in retrospect, I see that this was love, but I didn't know it. So I let love pass me by."

How often have we passed love by because we have not recognized it for what it is?

### 3. *"I love you because you need me."*

This is REAL love! This is the love that releases the hidden possibilities. This love wipes out fear—FOREVER!

Why does real love cast out fear? For one simple reason: Real love is a self-*less* love. Self-*ish* love always produces fear. If I love you only because *I need you,* or if I love you only because *I want you,* I'm going to be afraid that I might not win you or hold you. So I'll live in the fearful anxiety of losing you.

But! If I love because I want to give something to you, I'll never be fearful or worried or tense, *for a giving love can never lose!*

Give love, and if it's accepted, you have succeeded! If love is rejected, you still have your love to give to someone else who is waiting to accept and appreciate it!

## WHY SHOULD I RUSH TO BOARD THE LOVE TRAIN?

There are two very good reasons to rush to love. The first is that *real love releases my hidden possibilities!*

Although love can hurt, although love can bring disappointment, pain, and rejection—*real* love also brings with it *possibilities!* As Amanda McBroom says so beautifully in her song, "The Rose":

Some say love, it is a river that drowns the tender reed.
Some say love, it is a razor that leaves your heart to bleed.
Some say love, it is a hunger, an endless, aching need;
I say love it is a flower, and you its only seed.

It's the heart afraid of breaking, that never learns to dance.
It's the dream afraid of waking, that never takes the chance.
It's the one who won't be taken, who cannot seem to give;
And the soul afraid of dying, that never learns to live.

When the night has been too lonely,
And the road has been too long,
And you think that love is only for the lucky and the strong,
Just remember, in the winter, far beneath the bitter snows,
Lies the seed that with the sun's love,
In the spring, becomes the rose. *

We should rush to get on the Love Train because we all long to bloom like the rose. We must be willing to take the chance that, in spite of the challenges and risks, we will discover the real love that can melt the snows and wake the slumbering possibilities swelling within us.

With the warmth of real love, confidence is born within me. I feel loved, and I project that love to others. In the process this love becomes a magnet. It attracts happy and creative people who bring with them inspiring ideas, and in their presence we find inspiration, enlightenment, insight! We are left with an expanded imagination! Latent possibilities emerge in our thinking!

We rush to love because it draws us to new people who stimulate our settled minds with new ideas. Suddenly our minds are opened to fresh possibilities. We discover new doors opening to new relationships! Eye-opening insights! Even faith in God! In ourselves! And in others! So, in the presence of love, the creative process proceeds. "Impossible" situations become challenges that beckon as great possibilities!

The second reason we rush to get on the love train is that *real love releases and encourages the greatness that we all have within.*

---

We all want to be great at something! Whether it be a great husband, wife, parent, employee, or employer, none of us *really* wants to be mediocre. And nothing releases greatness within people more than love.

You may remember seeing Ed Burke carry the American flag and lead America's Olympians into the Los Angeles Coliseum for the 1984 Olympiad. Ed Burke is a great hammer thrower, a great husband, and a great father. What you may not know is that Ed's greatness, as well as the fact that he was in the coliseum that day carrying the flag, is a result of the loving support of his wife, Shirley.

Ed told me after the Olympics, "Dr. Schuller, Shirley and I carried that flag in *together,* and I believe the fact that I was chosen to carry the flag validated what we have done together, which is a lot of very hard work, inspiration on her part, help in coaching, and a marriage commitment for over twenty-five years. I think the Olympic Committee wanted to tell America that it's possible! 'This couple did it.' That's why I say that she was with me every step of the way."

Shirley's support of her husband has been extraordinary, to say the least. In 1961, Ed and his bride were students at San Jose State where Ed was a young hammer thrower, the best collegiate thrower in the country. One day he asked Shirley to come watch him throw for the newspapers and be interviewed. A newspaper photographer wanted one more picture. Ed threw the hammer. It was a very good throw. Ed was performing better than ever before.

The photographer left. Since it was cold, Shirley walked to the car. Ed wanted to make one more throw, but this one went completely out of control. The hammer ripped from his grasp and careened one hundred feet into the automobile where Shirley was sitting. The hammer struck her in the head with full force.

Ed thought he had killed her. It was the most tragic moment in his life. He drove his unconscious wife to the hospital.

Although Shirley regained consciousness and suffered no long-term side effects from the injury, Ed was devastated. He felt he could never throw the hammer again.

But, Shirley believed in him! She loved him! She saw the possibilities in him. She knew that he had promise. He was going to be a good hammer thrower. In order to get him back on the field, she coached and worked with him herself. The two of them worked together so successfully that Ed was actually able to enter the 1964 Olympic games. Shirley then coached Ed through the American record and the longest throw in the world in 1967.

The Burkes continued to work together until the 1968 Olympics in Mexico City. At that event, however, Ed became disenchanted with the program because of the political upheaval among the athletes. So he quit. Ed became a good businessman, a good teacher, a wonderful father, but that was not enough for Ed. Eleven years later, as Ed was turning 40, Shirley could see that he was becoming more and more restless.

One day, while watching the world games on television, Shirley saw some Russian hammer throwers. Shirley noticed that they weren't very big men. This was intriguing because experts believed that an athlete would have to be bigger and bigger to be able to throw farther and farther. But the Russians had found a new way of throwing that was more fitted to a smaller man.

Shirley called Ed to the television. Their daughters watched as well. They had never seen their father throw the hammer, and they begged him to throw the hammer for them. Ed said, "No!" But the girls found an old rusty hammer in the garage, took sandpaper and SOS pads and cleaned it up, and again begged their dad to show them.

This time Ed could not refuse. He took his family in a truck to a large field at San Jose State. He threw once, twice, and again. The neuromuscular patterns were still there. Ed threw ten times before he was ready to go home. A vision of himself walking into the Los Angeles Coliseum for the next Olympics came clearly to him. He had marched twice before in the middle of the Olympic parade and remembered how wonderful it was to represent his nation. He turned and looked at Shirley. As if she read his mind, she said with a smile, *I know!*

Once again Ed and Shirley Burke embarked on a training schedule. Here was a man in his forties challenging young men half his age. But once he made his intentions known, many other men his age and older throughout the world contacted him. He became their champion.

Of course he made the team and was selected by the American team's twenty-two captains to carry the American flag in the opening ceremony. Shirley and Ed talked about how he should hold the flag—high! For two reasons: First, because he wanted to present his country's flag as high as he could; and secondly, because he wanted to hold it up high to the heavens, thanking God and praising God every step of the way.

The great day came, and when Ed entered the Coliseum he was floating. The music and the roar of the crowd held him up. Shirley, who was watching from the sixth row, slipped out of her seat and maneuvered her way to the side of the track. As Ed came by, with all the love and pride she could muster, she shouted, "Hold it higher!"

Ed admits that his wife's love brought him out of self-imposed, fear-induced, guilt-inspired retirement to take the path that led to his glorious moment!

## HERE'S A TRIP THAT WILL TRANSFORM YOUR LIFE!

The junction, "Love Your Neighbor and Be Happy!" attracts a variety of passengers.

People who choose to love people really change! No wonder they discover real happiness! Some who board at this stop are "I-I" people. Others are "I-It" people. What a happy change awaits both of them!

## "I-I" People

The "I-I" person tries to find emotional fulfillment in feeding an insecure ego, satisfying selfish pleasures, and making sure he gets his own way. When faced with decisions, this kind of person asks questions like:

- "What's in it for me?"
- "What will I get out of it?"
- "Does it fit in with my plans?"

It does not matter if others like it; it does not matter that others could be helped; it does not matter that others are hurting.

This is the nonsharing, noncaring, no-burden-bearing person. Someone is crying? Someone is dying? Tough! Rough! "I've enough problems of my own" is the answer this person gives. Instead of, "Oh! Let me help you!"

There is a great deal of evidence to indicate that by nature most people tend to be "I-I" persons.

A person's entire character is affected by the "I-I" attitude.

*The "I-I" attitude affects the value system.* "I want what I want when I want it the way I want it" sums up the value system in one selfish sentence. "Do your own thing, I'll do mine" is another expression.

*The "I-I" attitude molds the emotional life.* Such self-centered people soon discover that very few people sincerely care for them. Hence, they become insecure, defensive, oppressive, suspicious, and cynical. They yield to a frenetic pleasure drive

If you are not for
yourself—
who will be?
But, if you are for
yourself alone—
what are you?
—Rabbi Hillel

in a neurotic effort to escape from facing a self they are not proud of. Or they drive themselves toward more power, foolishly believing that power and position will make people look up to them. They mistakenly think that they will then truly respect themselves as well. Too late, sometimes never, these people learn that the "I-I" route never builds self-respect.

The "I-I" person cannot give—so he cannot accept. For accepting always requires giving. You have to give your honest, humble attention to accept advice, criticism, and suggestions. You have to give a heartfelt concern before you can accept the burdens of others and be able to say, "I care about you." You have to give your freedom before you can accept involvement in worthy causes. You have to give your time, talent, and treasure before you can really accept responsibility.

One of the greatest lessons we must learn today is that humanity is an organismic unity. We are all in the same boat on planet Earth. What hurts others will ultimately hurt us. All people are closely linked on the spacecraft on which we live. An explosion occurs and you hear the bad news and see it on TV. It will distress, anger, worry, or frighten you. It is affecting you! You may eat and be merry, but you'll hear people who will talk about the terrible things that are happening.

Mass communication has helped make humankind realize that the world is also an emotionally organismic unity, like it or not! NO MAN IS AN ISLAND! We all have to live together. And really, it's for our own good that we do. Consider if we could be true, pure isolationists; if we never needed to interact with our neighbors, would we then be happy? No! For then we would be "I-I" people and "I-I" people can never be happy! Why? Because they miss out on real love!

## "I-It" People

"I-It" persons relate primarily to things. They try to find emotional fulfillment in material acquisitions.

- Want joy? Get something new.
- Bored? Go shopping.
- Guilty? Buy a gift.
- Fearful? Buy a gun.
- Insecure? Build a bigger savings account.
- Need to impress people? Cars. Clubs. Cocktails will do it.
- Lonely? Go to a movie, a bar, or a motel.

To such individuals, even people become things, not persons with hopes, feelings, or dreams. People are toys to be played with, tools to use, trinkets for amusement, treasures to buy, or trash to be thrown away. Here's what happens to the person with an "I-It" outlook:

*The "I-It" person is never emotionally satisfied or fulfilled.* When things rust out, wear out, wrinkle, grow old, or go out of style, this individual never discovers that things do not feed self-respect or self-esteem on any lasting basis.

*The "I-It" attitude also determines the value system.* What's the salary? What are the fringe benefits? How much will it cost? These are *the* important questions.

*The "I-It" person is never truly free,* but is forever trapped by the tyranny of things. "Paint me. Paper me. Patch me. Repair me. Replace me," these things shout!

*The "I-It" person never really loves.* "I love you because I *want* you" or "I love you because I *need* you" is the limited depth of the love relationship of the "I-It" person. Other people are not known on a deep level; life is shallow, ultimately meaningless.

If "I-I" people and "I-It" people want to find love and to be happy, they'll have to become "I-You" people.

## "I-You" People

"I-You" people have chosen to love their neighbors. They see people as persons who have dreams, desires, hurts, and needs. When an "I-I" person or an "I-It" person becomes an "I-You" person, what a change takes place:

The housewife becomes a homemaker!
The sire becomes a father!
The lover becomes a husband!
The lawyer becomes a counselor!
The teacher becomes a person builder!
The doctor becomes a healer!
The truck driver becomes a transporter of vital material!
The salesman becomes a supplier of human need!
The businessman becomes a job-opportunity creator!

One of the happiest and most well-loved men I have known was Theo Weaver. He was a friend for over thirty-five years, and the best neighbor anybody could ask for.

In 1955 when I came to California with my wife and $500 to start a church, Theo was the first man I met. At that time the church was only a dream. I met Theo at a restaurant. I told him who I was and why I had come to town. He agreed to help me. Sure enough, on that first Sunday, March 27, 1955, there he was handing out the printed programs and taking up the offering. He was our first usher. He went on to become a faithful member of the church board and stood by me, even when he didn't agree with me, through all the tough growing times in the church.

He was an "I-You" person, always willing to serve and put

others above himself. As I came to know Theo better, I learned how he gave of himself.

In addition to being a steadfast husband and father, he never missed a day and he was only *late* for work twice in the thirty years he worked for the Bell Telephone Company. When he died suddenly from a heart attack at the age of sixty, the Crystal Cathedral was filled with men who openly wept at the loss of this loving coworker. Widows whom he had helped by mowing their lawns grieved at the loss of their beloved neighbor. Opal, Sharla, and Glenn said goodbye reluctantly to their adored husband and father. I have officiated at thousands of funerals and memorial services in my life. Many of them have been for great statesmen, some have been for celebrities. None of these people was more *loved* than Theo.

His friend, Vernon Riphagen, wrote a poem when he heard of Theo's death. The family asked me to read it at his service. It summarizes the loving, happy life of a good friend and neighbor.

Our Father in Heaven we thank thee today
For having Theo Weaver pass by this way.
He would give of himself, he would give us his trust,
He'd go extra miles as all angels must.

A family man, husband, grandpa, and father,
His family was all, the worries didn't bother.
His friendship was deep, he was sincere
With all who knew him and held him so dear.

Loyal and faithful, employed by Bell
On Tuesday his heart wasn't working too well.
Then Wednesday his local life line was shattered.
He was plugged in to Heaven, and that's all that mattered.

We thank thee, Dear Lord, for caring for me
By sending such people as an example for me.

May we be as faithful, may we be true
When we make the long journey over to You. *

Theo was an "I-You" person, a loved person, a happy man. How do you become an "I-You" person? You become an "I-You" person by becoming an "I-*Him*" person.

What do I mean by "I-*Him*"? I believe Jesus Christ lived to show us true love! I believe He died to demonstrate true forgiving love. I believe He lives today, and I can pray to Him. He hears me! He cares about me. He loves me! I have a one-to-one relationship with Him. Now I have the courage to love others too!

In 1959 when we purchased the property on which the Crystal Cathedral stands today, I went to the post office and tried to get an address people could easily remember. "You'll need five numbers, Reverend Schuller," I was told.

"O.K., I'll take 1-1-1-1-1," I said.

"Sorry, the second number must be 2," the official declared.

"O.K., I'll take 1-2-3-4-5."

The man just laughed and shook his head, rejecting the idea outright.

"Well, then," I tried again, "1-2-2-2-2!"

Disgusted, he shot back at me—"No way! Now here is your address—take it or leave it—1-2-1-4-1!"

I left. Twenty years later I discovered the hidden, divine blessing. Why, the numbers said it all—what our joyous faith is all about: "one-to-One-for-one!" I relate to Jesus, so now I can relate to you! Of course! That translates "God loves you . . . and so do I!"

The invitation to be happy and loved was offered to everyone—everywhere—by Jesus Christ when he said, "You

---

*Used by permission.

shall love the LORD *Your* God . . . [and] *your neighbor as yourself*" (Mark 12:30–31). That invitation still stands today.

In this Bible verse, you have it: Three love opportunities open to you and every person! Three glorious possibilities to enter into a trusting and mutually affirming relationship: With yourself! With other human beings! With God!

Now, isn't that a trip that gets you excited and enthused? Then let's prepare for life's greatest journey by learning what "love" and "being loved" are all about.

Before you take your first trip to a strange place or a foreign country, you probably do what I do—get a guidebook and read up on the customs and culture. On the subject of love, the single most inspiring and illuminating guidebook ever written in any language is a chapter in the Holy Bible, 1 Corinthians 13. Let's look at it together: We'll learn lessons on love that will make our one trip on planet Earth a truly loving and happy venture!

# . . . And
# So
# Do
# I!

**IF I SPEAK** in the tongues of men and of angels, but have not love, I am a noisy gong or a clanging cymbal.

And if I have prophetic powers, and understand all mysteries and all knowledge, and if I have all faith, so as to remove mountains, but have not love, I am nothing.

If I give away all I have, and if I deliver my body to be burned, but have not love, I gain nothing.

Love is patient and kind; love is not jealous or boastful; it is not arrogant or rude. Love does not insist on its own way; it is not irritable or resentful; it does not rejoice at wrong, but rejoices in the right.

Love bears all things, believes all things, hopes all things, endures all things.

Love never ends; as for prophecies, they will pass away; as for tongues, they will cease; as for knowledge, it will pass away.

For our knowledge is imperfect and our prophecy is imperfect; but when the perfect comes, the imperfect will pass away.

When I was a child, I spoke like a child, I thought like a child, I reasoned like a child; when I became a man, I gave up childish ways.

For now we see in a mirror dimly, but then face to face. Now I know in part; then I shall understand fully, even as I have been fully understood.

So faith, hope, love abide, these three; but the greatest of these is love.

I Corinthians, Chapter 13

# THE ROAD OF LOVE:
## TAKE IT!
## IT'S
## THE *RIGHT*-WAY!

*Love Is the Greatest*

*"The greatest of these is love."*
  *1 Corinthians 13:13*

"**G**od loves you . . . and so do I!" Two simple phrases. Alone each one is great—but together they combine to make a *life-transforming* prescription for joy!

In Part I, "God Loves You," you boarded the train, made the full loop, and saw how you can be happy and loved. Now get ready for the *real* journey! You can't stay in Disneyland forever! You need to get onto the road of life.

Now, the rugged, raw, real road of life is a far cry from Fantasyland. There are mountains that need to be climbed, rivers that must be crossed, bridges that will have to be built, walls that must be scaled.

The journey of life can be rough and it's easy to get lost, discouraged, and worn out. Personally, if I'm going to a great deal of effort to get somewhere, I like to check my location periodically and ask myself if I'm going the *right*-way. It doesn't do any good to keep going if you're on the *wrong* road or if you're going in the *wrong* direction on the *right* road.

So, on this journey of life, I ask myself two questions:

1. Am I on the right road?
2. Am I going in the right direction?

To help us navigate this challenging trip called life, God gave to us, through St. Paul, a road map. It's found in 1 Corinthians 13. This classic passage of Scripture clearly outlines for us how to find the right road and which direction to take.

351

# AM I ON THE RIGHT ROAD?

You are on the right road—if you are on the road of love. Paul wrote ". . . *the greatest of these is love.*"

It sounds too simple, and it is so easy to get distracted and to think of the road to success, the road to faith, the road to riches as more important than plain old love.

A housewife and young mother named Ann woke up one day terribly depressed. She felt overwhelmed—by her children and by the schedules and demands that life heaped on her. It seemed that all she did was nag at her children. She barked at them and scolded them incessantly. When she stopped and looked at the mother she was portraying, she was a shrew. In the midst of her tears, she cried out to the Lord. Her answer came through the Bible: "If I speak in the tongues of men and of angels, but have not love, I am a noisy gong or a clanging cymbal. And if I have prophetic powers, and understand all mysteries and all knowledge . . . but have not love, I am nothing. If I give away all I have, and if I deliver my body to be burned, but have not love, I gain nothing" (1 Cor. 13:1–3).

Five words leaped out at this young mother, challenging her. She wrote them on her calendar. She posted them on her refrigerator. She taped them on the dashboard of her station wagon. They said, "WITHOUT LOVE I AM NOTHING!"

It meant nothing that supper was served on time, or that the laundry was all done, folded and put away, if her work was done with an attitude of drudgery. It meant nothing that she was able to juggle the schedules of her husband and children, as well as her own part-time job and hobbies, if she had no time left for a kind word, a loving touch, or even just a smile.

She realized that the single most important thing that she could ever do was to love her family. This was what the Lord wanted her to do. Those five words were so simple, yet so life-transforming. One day she told me, "Dr. Schuller, I began to live my life by love. I began to run my home on love power. It was as transforming as when I accepted Christ into my life. It brought happiness back into my life and into my home."

Without love, you are nothing. Whether you are a young mother, a doctor, a teacher, a psychologist, a businessman, a service man, a truck driver—whatever it is you do, whoever it is that you are—discover the simple truth that my friend, the young mother, discovered: *Without love I am nothing!*

Is love the right road? Is it really the greatest? Consider the answers to these questions:

**Q:** *What is society without love?*
**A:** *Society without love is a conglomerate of people who work, live, shop together—but never become a caring community.*

I remember a recent trip to Russia. While I was there, I could see how the Communist Party had tried to educate persons into being cold, calculating, intellectualized, rationalized creatures. It is like creating a person who basically becomes a computer responding to someone who pushes the button. Such a philosophy doesn't give humans enough credit. The Communist doctrines say that the human being, the emotional creature, is weak. It is at this point that Communism and Christianity are totally irreconcilable.

I subscribe to a couple of wire services and several years ago this story came over the wire service: "A religious fever is spreading across the Communist Soviet Union. In what is called 'an upsurge in religious practice in the Soviet Union,' tens of thousands of religious believers swarmed into the churches this past Easter. There they ate wafers, made crosses, and sang hymns to celebrate the resurrection of Jesus. Moscow's fifty-four churches, guarded by police and militant groups, were packed."

Why has such a phenomenon of social retrogression appeared in a so-called developed socialist country, in the land of the great Lenin? We know the answer: The normal, natural, healthy, whole human being is a creature whose emotional life has been allowed to blossom! Positive emotion is a mark of emotional health! By contrast, persons whose open, effervescent, ebullient, emotional instincts have been educated out of them or frozen out of them by society—such persons are not complete, healthy humans!

And what of the Nobel Prize-winning author Aleksandr Solzhenitsyn? Think of it—he was a product of Russia's educational systems, its indoctrination, its dialectical materialism. He had been protected from Western influences. Yet he has made this statement: "I myself see Christianity as the only living spiritual force capable of healing my land."

Incredible! Even after more than half a century, a totally repressive society based on total mind control has not been able to change the human being's deep heart hunger for love.

**Q:**  *What is success without love?*
**A:**  *Success without love is empty.*

Mary Nemec Doremus grew up in Palm Beach, Florida, where her family lived between the Kennedys and the Guccis, right on the ocean. She lived a privileged life, and by the time she was twenty had her own television show and was interviewing the "best" and most prominent Americans.

Then her father suggested that they go to Czechoslovakia to visit the land of their family's heritage. Her father's ancestors had been the gamekeepers and courtiers to the king there.

Shortly after they arrived in Czechoslovakia, however, the Russians invaded. Mary and her family heard shots being fired all night and day and witnessed children being blown apart.

One young boy they saw was proudly holding the Czech flag when he was shot. As the flag fell, another young boy picked it up.

Mary and the others were fortunate to get out of Czechoslovakia, and as they came across the border, after spending time lying on the floor with mattresses over their heads and tracer bullets ricocheting off the walls, these words came to Mary:

"Let the words of my mouth and the meditation of my heart be acceptable in Your sight, O LORD, my strength and my redeemer" (Ps. 19:14).

Mary Nemec's life was changed! Suddenly it didn't seem very important to see her name in lights. Suddenly it was very important to her to live! No longer was she interested in a movie career. She wanted to make her life count. She wanted to do something for her country and her God.

As soon as Mary stepped into the free world she was interviewed on the Huntley and Brinkley TV news program. Later, she gave over three hundred speeches around the United States. She encouraged young people to begin thinking about their country.

Ten years passed, during which time she met a young man named Ted Doremus, fell in love, and got married. She gave birth to two sons. Then Mary's parents urged her to join them on another trip. "Mary, China is just beginning to open up," they said. "We'd like to take you and the family to China to compensate for the traumatic visit to Czechoslovakia."

In China, Mary became ill with a virus. After she suffered from irritability, a low-grade fever, extreme weight loss, and intense pain all over her body for a year, doctors found a mysterious virus in her brain, her blood, her skin, and her cerebral spinal fluid. The result? Today, Mary relies heavily on the use of a wheelchair to conserve her energies and must take medication every twenty to thirty minutes during the day and several times at night for stabilization of her condition. Without it she becomes "limp," paralyzed and totally dysfunctional.

Her reaction? "Rather than groveling in my navel and demanding to know 'Why' from God, I've always tried to say, *'What do you want from me? Where am I supposed to be going?'* I knew there was a purpose that would be revealed to me at the right time. When I gave up the need to know, that was the healthiest thing that ever happened to me."

When I visited with Mary, I was so impressed with her beauty! She radiates genuine joy! She also told me, "I found that, from my bended knees in prayer comes the greatest standing I've ever done. I found that to be able to say that Jesus is my Lord and Savior is a very, very important thing for me to be able to say. This has been the basis for everything that I've done in life, including the National Challenge Committee on Disability. Through this organization, we're changing the way that America perceives individuals with disabilities. We're not childlike and dependent, but we're strong. And what we look or sound like has nothing to do with what we are able to do.

"When I sit here, the last thing I want you to notice about me is my disability. The first thing I want you to notice about me is my abilities. And I like to say that there's life *after* disability!"

Mary Doremus—what a wonderful example of someone who has discovered the beauty of living and living a life with love at the core. She has known what it is to be celebrated in society. She has known what it is to be a successful television personality. She has known what it is like to be superwealthy. And yet, as she discovered in Czechoslovakia, all of this is nothing without love. Even health was not as important as being able to give of herself to her country and to other disabled persons.

**Q:** *What is eloquence without love?*
**A:** *Eloquence without love is mere patter.*

In my chosen career as a minister, the ability to communicate ranks high among the gifts I sincerely desire. God only knows how often, how fervently, how passionately I have prayed, "Give me the gift of eloquence, Lord."

And God only knows how often He has answered that prayer. But I know this—He has answered it more often than I have deserved! And when I've experienced this exciting answer to prayer, it has been a "spiritual high!"

Why was the experience so fulfilling?

The answer I have found is that a beautiful feeling comes when a healing and comforting love is allowed to flow unobstructed through a human life.

I experience this same joyous emotion even more intensely and sincerely when I am alone as a pastor praying with a solitary soul in a private place.

What do these two different experiences have in common?

In both instances, whether the audience has been large—hundreds, thousands, even millions at a time—or whether it has been an audience of one, my happiness came from sharing a comforting, healing *love* with someone else!

Consequently, I am convinced that the happiness I am feeling at those times when the Lord grants me the gift of eloquence comes from the *love* I am feeling, not the oratorical experience. For the words, however colorful, however powerful, are nothing if they are not words that encourage, uplift, heal, and restore.

**Q:** *What is faith without love?*
**A:** *The most dangerous thing in the world!*

What is possibility thinking without love? If I have faith so that I can move mountains but do not have love, then you'd better watch out. Faith without love can be the most dangerous thing in the world! But faith, together with love, is a powerful, life-changing combination. The two go hand in hand. Faith and love are twins.

For years I believe I misunderstood a portion of 1 Corinthians 13. When I used to read the verse—"And now abide faith, hope, love, these three; but the greatest of these is love"—I thought Paul was in essence presenting three lovelies in a beauty contest. One was Faith, one was Hope, and one was Love. And when the judging was complete, Love won the crown, Hope was the first runner-up, Faith came in second. In other words, I had the mistaken impression that Faith, Hope, and Love were in competition with each other. That's not true; the three are a Holy Trinity, and love is what wraps them all together.

In a previous book, *The Be Happy Attitudes,* I put it this way:

> In the presence of Hope—
>     faith is born.
> In the presence of Faith—
>     love becomes a possibility!
> In the presence of Love—
>     miracles happen!

### Love: The Power Behind Faith!

Love is the power center behind a mountain-moving faith. When love is at the core of your faith, it puts five miracle-working powers into your belief.

### 1. Love Puts Renewing Power in Faith

When love is so strong it won't allow you to doubt for long, then it puts power at the center of your faith. Some people ask me, "Where do you get your faith?" My answer is simple: "I love Christ too much ever to doubt God!"

If love is at the core of your faith—for your work, for your project, for your dream, for your cause, for your husband, for your wife, for your children, for your friends—that faith will never quit. Where there is a passionate love, faith always comes back and renews the dream, tries again. Driven by authentic love, you will settle for nothing less than success. You will reorganize; reschedule; revise; reexamine; rededicate. But you will not *resign*! The kind of faith that never quits, the kind of faith that is constantly renewed, is faith that has love at the center.

### 2. Love Puts Realigning Power in Faith

When love is at the core of your faith, you constantly realign your faith to make sure that you are focusing on others, not *yourself*. And that's crucial.

I recently had to have my tires realigned. These were still new tires—only four months old and without many miles—but I could hardly drive down the freeway without the car almost jiggling apart. After my front wheels were realigned, though, the car no longer shook and was easy to control.

You and I must do this constantly with our faith. Realign your faith to make sure it's focused on service and not on self. Love at the power center will keep you smoothly on track.

### 3. Love Puts Restraining Power on Faith

Love keeps your faith from running over people just to get what you want. Remember, love without faith is impossible; and faith without love is unacceptable.

Once after I had finished one of my lectures at a sales conference, a businessman said to me, "I've got a problem. You know, I really believe I could expand my business to cover the whole country! But if I did it I would put a lot of little guys out of business. As a Christian I don't think I should do that, do you?"

"I don't think so either," I answered.

### 4. Love Puts Redeeming Power in Faith

When love is at the center of your faith, then your faith becomes a redeeming power. Instead of hurting people, you help people! Instead of being a destroyer, you become a builder! Instead of just being a teacher, for example, trying to draw your maximum salary and maximum benefits, you're primarily concerned about how you can mold and build complete persons out of those kids. And as a doctor you're not primarily concerned about how many fees you can attract, but how you can heal the whole person. And as a businessman you're not primarily concerned with profit margins, but how to serve people and their needs by delivering quality goods and services. And if you're a lawyer, you look upon yourself as a counselor helping people with distressing problems. And if you're a laborer or service technician, you really want to help people by doing great work honestly and at a fair price.

Faith is continuously *renewed*—when love is at the core.
Faith is continuously *realigned*—when love is at the core.

Faith is continuously *restrained*—when love is at the core.
Faith is continuously *redeemed*—when love is at the core.
Faith is continuously *rejoicing*—when love is at the core.

## 5. Love Puts Rejoicing Power in Faith

What good is faith if it leads to despair? With love—faith rejoices!

All of us have known of people who were positive and were terrific possibility thinkers. They made their goals, they achieved success, they were wealthy, they had power. And then, tragically, they ended up dead from an overdose. All the possibility thinking in the world is dangerous unless at the core there is love. It is love that gives the rejoicing power which keeps you energetic and joyful in your success! For after all, what is ultimate success but letting God's love and power flow through you! To summarize:

Faith *Stimulates Success!*
    I think I can!
    I think I'll try!
    I'm going to go for it!
Hope *Sustains Success!*
    I'm not going to give up!
    I'm going to be an H.I.T.—
    Hang-In-There person!
    Things will turn around!
Love *Sanctifies Success!*
    I'm going to share my success!
    I'm now able to help others!
    Now—I have something to give!

## AM I GOING IN THE RIGHT DIRECTION?

Well, if you're going in circles, NO! You are not going in the right direction. Likewise, if you are standing still, the answer is NO!

If you insist on staying where you are, you'll waste the precious gift of love God has given you.

Oscar Hammerstein wrote in *The Sound of Music:*

> A bell is no bell til you ring it.
> A song is no song til you sing it,
> And love in your heart
> Wasn't put there to stay—
> Love isn't love
> Til you give it away."

Pass love on to someone who needs it. If we choose to be a reservoir of God's love, without allowing ourselves to be a channel of His love, we will soon see that love fails to generate joy power.

I recall standing at the bottom of Hoover Dam outside Las Vegas, Nevada. The guide was explaining the enormous turbines. "How much energy is being generated right now?" I asked. "Oh, nothing now," he answered. "The gates are closed; only when we allow the water to pour out of the reservoir through these turbines is energy generated!" Love's power comes as we allow love to pass through our lives to others.

Likewise, on my first trip to the Holy Land, the guide asked the question, "Do you know why the Sea of Galilee is alive with fish while the Dead Sea to the south of the Sea of Galilee is dead—salty, incapable of supporting any life? Remember, both

lakes are filled with the very same water from the Jordan River."
When no one offered an answer, he explained, "The Sea of
Galilee gives all its water back! It takes the Jordan in from the
north and gives it out as an extended Jordan River to the south.
The Dead Sea takes in the water of the Jordan and holds onto
all of it. It gives nothing back!"

---

## *Love Generates More Love! Love Generates Happiness!*

---

Frank Laubach, a "world-class" missionary to the hungry, the
illiterate, and the unlovely, once likened the human being to a
common lawn sprinkler head. "It's worth about eighty cents,"
he said, "but attach the sprinkler head to a hose, let the water
flow through, and it makes flowers grow. It makes the grass
green. Suddenly you have parks, beauty, and food! Who can
calculate the worth of that?"

Laubach continued, "God's plan for your life is to be a
sprinkler head for Jesus Christ, letting His love flow through
you, filling your world with happy love! Then every life
becomes invaluable! The possibilities are endless! Then you
can begin each day with a prayer I often pray: "Lord, show me
the person you want to touch through my life today. Amen."

## HERE, THEN, IS THE RIGHT WAY TO GO!

This is God's purpose for you, whoever you are, wherever you
are. You can be a person through whom our Lord spreads His
love and joy. Nothing else can compare with this satisfaction.

There are few people who have impressed me as much as my
dear friends, Ole and Pat Nordberg. In fact, their story brings
tears to my eyes every time I relate it. Their story summarizes

the essence of this book, *Be Happy—You Are Loved!* It tells the *reality* of love, the *power* of love, and the *responsibility* to share love with others.

Pat was only thirty-two years old when the doctor faced her grimly in his office. Her husband Ole gripped her hand. The doctor looked at this bright young couple, the parents of a five-year-old boy. "Mrs. Nordberg," he said, "you have an aneurysm in the most inaccessible part of your brain. Your condition will get no better. You could die anytime. You might be lucky and live if nothing is done."

He paused and looked at their faces, which were numb with shock. Anticipating the inevitable question, he said, "Surgery? I'd say there's a ten percent survival possibility—that's all. I shall have to move the brain aside with my hands. If my finger slips or I don't handle it correctly, you could be paralyzed, blind, or a mental vegetable—if you live."

Pat and Ole could not speak. They were dazed as they somehow managed to walk out of the doctor's office. The drive home was silent, as speechless love flowed from heart to heart.

"Mommy, Mommy," their son cried as he ran into the waiting embrace of his beautiful mother. It was her son and husband that made the decision so difficult for Pat. Should she choose surgery with only a one in ten survival possibility? Should she let things go? Hope and pray that the next headache would never come? She remembered the first one some months before. She had felt the blood vessel break. She had felt the warm liquid flow around her brain under her skull before she lost consciousness.

New x-rays were taken. The diagnosis was the same as before. The aneurysm was still there.

"Why me? What have I done? I've been a good person." Self-pity mixed with anger as Pat wept alone in her bedroom.

"God is our refuge and strength, a very present help in trouble. Therefore, we will not fear, though the earth be removed, and though the mountains be carried into the midst of the sea; . . . God shall help her, . . . Be still, and know that I am God." These words came like sweet music into her mind. The verses from Psalm 46 brought with them a divine peace to the woman faced with a decision that no person should have to make. Now, with the power and strength of these words, she had her answer.

Pat called Ole. "Honey," she said, "I am no longer afraid. I know that if I die, God will provide someone better than I to love my son and my husband." She paused and with utter calmness said, "Ole, I am going to call the doctor and give him my decision—to operate."

Ole knew Pat's decision was the right one. Terribly concerned about the gravity of Pat's surgery, Ole immediately asked everyone he knew to pray for her. The neighbors joined in a circle of love. They spread the word of Pat's surgery from house to house on their street. "Ole is driving her to the hospital tomorrow. They don't give her much chance of ever coming back alive or with a normal mind, but she says this is the decision God led her to make."

The next morning a pall settled over the houses on the street. Children left for school, husbands went to work, but the women at home watched their clocks carefully. A neighbor called the other neighbors and said, "Let's all step out on our front steps and wave to Pat as she leaves and throw a prayer to her with a smile and kiss."

Quietly, coolly, and calmly, Pat entered the car as Ole carried her small overnight suitcase. He opened the garage door and backed out into the street. Pat saw them then, her neighbors all up and down the block, on both sides, waving and throwing her prayers with a smile and a kiss.

From house after house on both sides of the street, as Pat and Ole drove slowly away, neighbors waved goodbye, for the odds were that they would never see her again. Pat smiled. *She was loved.* It gave her strength and the peace to go through with an incredibly difficult, terribly dangerous, probably fatal surgery.

The surgeons cut Pat's skull open. Reaching into the cranial cavity, the doctor took the young mother's brain in his hands and ever so delicately removed the weak section of the major blood vessel that was threatening to blow. Delicately, gently, tenderly he returned the brain to its proper place, putting a protective plate over the hole in the skull. The entire skin of the scalp, peeled away for the surgery, was rolled back into place and stitched. Her hair would grow back in time—if she lived!

The surgeon, his task done to the best of his ability, went to face Ole. "Mr. Nordberg? It's all over for now. All we can do now is wait and pray. It may be days before we will know if Pat will live and what her condition will be."

Ole sat by Pat's bed. Her shaved head, wrapped in white bandages, still and unmoving in the center of the pillow, gave her a deathly appearance. Round the clock, hour after hour, day after day, nurses on duty waited, hoping for a sign of consciousness. Would her eyes open? Would her lips move? Would she be able to speak?

On the morning of the fourth day after surgery, the nurse on duty had turned her back for a moment when she heard a low but clear voice behind her. "Could you bring me some lipstick please, nurse?" Whirling, she looked at Pat, whose eyes were open and alert and, the nurse thought, who was mentally healthy enough to want to look pretty.

If only the sentences had kept coming so clearly. Over the next few weeks, Pat's wounded brain was unable to sustain normal speech. Words got mixed up and out of proper sequence. To compound the problem, her body was poorly coordinated. Would she ever be able to live a normal life?

Months passed. She was able to ride with her family to church again. "Pat," a church member stopped and asked her, "could you help out as a volunteer in the church school for our

*Love without faith—*
*is impossible!*
*And*
*faith without love—*
*is unacceptable!*

handicapped children's class? We need one adult for each child. Would you try, please?"

Pat didn't need to be asked twice! Here was a chance to prove that although her speech and body movements were unreliable, she could still be helpful. The events that occurred in that classroom changed her life. Soon after Pat volunteered she noticed an eight-year-old girl who was receiving little, if any, attention. When Pat asked about the girl, she was told, "Mary is only a vegetable. She has no potential for ever developing." Pat was deeply troubled. It was difficult for her to think that there were people who had no potential whatsoever.

One day, feeling empathy for Mary, Pat sat beside her on the floor, watching as Mary tore up pieces of paper and fluttered her mumbling lips with a finger. Then, when Mary looked at Pat, Pat smiled. Mary stared at Pat's smiling face, and then a miracle happened! The little girl crawled over and buried her head in Pat's lap and sobbed and sobbed.

Pat lovingly stroked Mary's head and back; she thought, *Dear Lord, if love alone will do this to a child, what would love plus an education do?*

She decided then and there to become a child psychologist. A long and impossible road lay ahead for Pat. Her first hurdle was to learn to drive a car so she could get to class. In order to develop the physical coordination to drive a car, Pat took Hawaiian dancing lessons. She passed her driver's test and enrolled in California State College in Fullerton.

Classes posed a new obstacle for Pat and her wounded mind. Remembering was a real problem for her. But she would not quit. She worked and worked and worked until she accumulated enough units to get her degrees. It took six long, tedious years, but she did it! Drawing from her aphasic experience, she wrote her master's thesis under the title, "Counseling Parents of Aphasic Children."

And along the way she learned tricks to help her with her

speech problem, until today her speech is perfect. People who meet Pat now are unaware of her past condition and have no idea what tremendous physical difficulties she has overcome.

Today, Pat, with her well-earned master of science degree, works with exceptional children in the public schools as a practicing school psychologist. She faced enormous challenges, yet she was happy. Why? Because she was loved! She was loved! Oh, was she loved! But she didn't just rest on that love. She gave it away as soon as she could, thereby multiplying her love as she shared it with children who were hurting.

"Be Happy—You Are Loved!" Does this statement describe you? Are you loved? Then give it away! When you do, you will find your life transformed from self-centeredness to other-centeredness. Attitudes will change from a greedy, "grab-all-I-can" attitude to a "What-do-you-need, How-can-I-help?" attitude.

In the assessment of any person—success or failure, saint or sinner, winner or loser, achiever or underachiever—the final judgment is not based on academic degrees nor honors nor medals nor talent nor training. No! The final exam is: Can you give and receive real love?

How do you become a "1-2-1-4-1" person? A "one-to-One-for-someone" person? A "God loves you . . . and so do I" person? For neither recognition nor fame nor wealth nor power can compensate for the lack of love coming into and flowing out of your life. No wonder St. Paul wrote, *"The greatest . . . is love."*

You are on the right road! Now get ready to turn onto the *free*-way!

# THE ROAD OF LOVE:

# BE BRAVE! TRAVEL THE *FREE*-WAY!

*Real Love Liberates*

*"Love is patient."*
     *1 Corinthians 13:4*

There is a strange paradox in love; a mysterious contradiction; a mystic ambiguity! To make love work we must release what we want to possess!

Some of my most delightful memories as a small child are the springtime days when baby chicks were delivered to our Iowa farm. I used to take the soft, fuzzy, newly-hatched little birds and rub what felt like silky fur against my cheek. Sometimes I would squeeze too tightly because I loved them so much and didn't want them to get away. "Don't hold so tight," my father warned.

"But I love the chick so," I protested.

"If you love it so much, you have to let it go," he said.

If you really love your wife, don't be so possessive; if you love your husband, don't be so jealous. Real love is not possessive. It does not manipulate or intimidate. *Real love liberates!* For it wants the object of its healthy love to blossom to its full potential!

It takes courage to love enough to let something or someone go. That's why this chapter title says, "Dare to take the *freeway.*"

Where I live in Southern California, freeways are an essential mode of transportation. This interconnecting web of lanes ties Southern California together from San Diego to San Francisco. These freeways, which are "free" of stop signs and traffic signals, allow motorists to whizz by on overpasses—and sail through cities.

373

The *free*-way road of love is a risky one. And its dangers and casualties frighten many from ever attempting it. Instead, they cautiously cling to the side roads, where their "love" is held in check by slower speed limits and *stop* signs!

I once sat in a class taught by the late psychotherapist, Erich Fromm. He pointed out that not all that passes for love is authentic or healthy! Some love is so possessive that it is the neurotic expression of an insecure person. Take the "possessive mother" or the "clinging vine" for instance! This possessive "love" arises from deep inner insecurities, low self-esteem, and fear.

Conversely, authentic and healthy love dares to take the *free*-way! A liberating love is reluctant to inhibit, prohibit, or solicit. Rather, it attempts to give the "green light" whenever possible. It encourages and patiently supports the person receiving the love.

I think that's what Paul meant when he said, "Love is patient." A patient love respects a person's need to take time and understands a person's need to grow. A patient love accepts the other person as he or she is, today! A patient love liberates in that it has faith that a person can change and can make it; it hopes that the one loved will someday respond to love; and, finally, it will work to help the one who is loved become what the person longs to be.

## A LOVE THAT LIBERATES—IS A LOVE THAT *RESPECTS!*

Love respects—it respects the other person's need to take time to learn, time to grow, time to develop, time to improve.

Have you ever watched a young mother walk across a busy intersection, holding the hand of her little child, who hesitantly takes one wobbly step after another? You can sense the impatience in the drivers of the cars who are waiting to turn right. Patience is a virtue that many persons lose as soon as they get behind that mask of the windshield and are shielded from confronting people who will never be known or seen again.

On the other hand, with great patience, the mother appreciates her toddler's need to learn to walk, the child's need to grow gradually into an independent individual.

## A LOVE THAT LIBERATES—IS A LOVE THAT *UNDERSTANDS!*

When you understand persons, you must respect their need to be themselves. It is encouraging that society has grown to the point where men and husbands are beginning to understand a woman's need to express herself through a career. I personally think it is a great thing to see women doing and accomplishing all that they can.

People are sometimes amazed when they look into the workings of the "Hour of Power," our television ministry. Several women hold prominent positions in our organization. And Arvella Schuller has been a partner with me in my ministry since we were married.

I met Arvella, who was the organist at the little Iowa church where I was a guest minister, when we needed to discuss the hymns and the music for the first service I would be conducting. Today, Arvella and I are still meeting to discuss each week's service. Arvella is program director for the "Hour of Power." She oversees a creative team of directors, musicians, and technicians who put together a worship service seen by over three million people every Sunday.

I understand and applaud Arvella's need for a career. Mixing a schedule as busy and complicated as ours requires a lot of give and take for both of us, but the rewards of such a partnership have been immeasurable—a thriving mutual love, admiration, and respect.

A liberating love understands, and when it understands, it is that much more prone to accept those who are loved and let them be who they are.

## A LOVE THAT LIBERATES—IS A LOVE THAT ACCEPTS!

There are some things you cannot, will not *ever* change about your loved one, be he or she a child, a friend, a coworker, or a spouse. Can you accept that person as is—today? Even if the person stays that way for life?

A dear friend and employee of the "Hour of Power" is Shannon Wilkerson. Today, Shannon is vibrant and confident, which is a miracle considering that Shannon's early life was marred by physical and emotional abuse, mostly as a result of her mother's alcoholism.

In grade school, when most children went home to a smiling mom offering milk and cookies, Shannon went home to a mother who frequently was drunk and lying on the floor, unconscious. The few PTA meetings her mother attended were disrupted by her obnoxious behavior. Soon, parents of Shannon's schoolmates told their children not to play with the daughter of the drunken woman.

Believing that she was a freak, Shannon withdrew from friends and life in general. Her best friend became the television set in her bedroom, where she locked herself in at night to avoid her mother's verbal abuse.

Shannon's father was also a thorn in her life. Whenever he was home, Shannon avoided him because of his anger. Many times the young girl hid under the dresser in her bedroom to escape her fighting parents. At an early age Shannon learned that she couldn't trust anyone.

Then in junior high, and later in high school, Shannon started experimenting with drugs and alcohol. Shannon recalls, "I wanted so badly to be accepted by the other kids in my school. And smoking and taking speed helped me forget about the pain in my family."

Still addicted to TV, Shannon turned the set on one Sunday morning. "I awoke to a beautiful choir singing and a minister saying, 'Don't turn that channel. God loves you and so do I!' That caught my attention. I watched the 'Hour of Power' for the first time. I heard that Jesus loved me in spite of any wrong things I had done—even though I lived in a home full of turmoil."

Shannon's concept of God was transformed. No longer was God someone who punished people when they were bad and rewarded them with gifts when they were good. Instead, Jesus became real and personal—helping Shannon learn to accept herself. "Suddenly I knew," she says, "that I did not have to be a product of my parents and my home. I could be somebody special with God's help!"

With a new faith, Shannon withdrew from drugs and alcohol. She began to absorb herself in wholesome activities— the school band, Future Farmers of America, and gymkhana (barrel racing with her horse). Soon her efforts paid off. She earned the position of first-chair clarinet in the band, and working with animals helped her handle her resentments and fears.

"I knew I could be what God wanted me to be," Shannon says. "As I built up my self-esteem, I was able to prove to myself that I could make it. Every little success reassured me that I was right, made it easier to give up the drugs and my old negative patterns."

As she progressed through high school, Shannon continued to develop her young Christian faith. "The Lord showed me that I could trust Him," she recalls, "so I decided to ask Him for the biggest miracle in my life. I wanted my mother to be sober. I prayed and called New Hope, the telephone counseling ministry of the 'Hour of Power.' I wrote the ministry and they sent me literature on alcoholism, explaining that it was a disease, one for which I was not responsible. I read the literature in earnest and attended meetings for teen-agers of alcoholic parents. What I learned was that I was a co-alcoholic. A co-alcoholic is not someone who drinks, but someone who, by reactions, feeds the disease in the lives of the alcoholic in the family.

"As a child you want your parents to be there for you. But mine never were. I remember once when I was riding my horse and my dog ran out into the street and was hit by a car. I was so upset that I rode my horse to the front of our home. I wanted to cry in my mother's arms, but she had passed out on the floor.

"I learned to swallow my emotions. I grew up quickly. The bills were not always paid, so my brother and I had to take over that responsibility. The day the dealer came to repossess our cars, the two of us just sat on the fireplace and cried."

Convinced that she could get her mother to stop drinking, Shannon would search the house for empty bottles and wave them in front of her mother's face. Half-empty bottles of booze were dumped out and refilled with lemon juice, rubbing alcohol, or vinegar. But what Shannon thought would help her mother face her problem only aggravated her.

The problem came to a climax one rainy evening when Shannon took her mother's last bottle and dumped it down the drain. As Shannon talked on the phone to her best friend, her mother awoke from her drunkenness.

"She came up behind me and said in an angry voice, 'Shannon, I hate you and I'm going to kill you!' I turned and saw the knife in her hand. She was serious. I ran to my bedroom. Mother stumbled and fell as she chased me down the hall. Safely in my room, I stood in shock. Through the door I could hear her repeating how much she hated me. And then it happened—the knife came plunging through the door.

"I fell in a clump on the floor and cried. I was angry at God! I had read the literature. I had prayed. I had watched Dr. Schuller. I had done all I could do. What was wrong?"

Shannon's despair was suddenly interrupted by a quiet inner voice urging her to get up. She knew God was telling her to love the woman who had just tried to kill her! Pulling herself to her feet, Shannon opened the door to a very sick, very ugly woman, once more unconscious in the hallway. Shannon's emotions were in turmoil, her love struggling against her hate. "I am sorry it is like this," she found herself saying. "I love you very much and I am sorry."

At that moment a great burden lifted from her shoulders, and a sense of peace surrounded her. She knew her mother's disease would no longer control her life.

"Suddenly, I knew that everything was in God's hands. It was really 'letting go and letting God.' I had spent all my energies and time trying to fix her problem. Now, I began to invest my energies in myself. Instead of worrying about our arguments or trying to figure out how to make her sober, I decided to live my own life to the fullest. I refused to surrender to my mother's disease."

A year later Shannon's mom finally hit bottom—something that every alcoholic has to do before realizing he or she needs help. One morning this poor, sick mother decided she no longer wanted to wake up being sick! She called Alcoholics Anonymous, and together mother and daughter attended meetings to find physical and emotional healing. Shannon's initial doubts concerning her mother's sincerity were soon replaced with hope, and sixty days later Shannon's mother received special recognition for her sobriety. One year later a birthday cake celebrated the first anniversary of her freedom from the oppression of alcohol.

Eleven years have passed since Shannon's mother took her last drink. Three years ago, mother and daughter were baptized together in the Crystal Cathedral. Today, Shannon still finds the miracle hard to believe. "I never would have dreamed that such a total healing could take place," she says. "I always had faith that someday God would heal her, but the real miracle is the *forgiveness* that has taken place."

Shannon's mother is now remarried to another recovered alcoholic, and the two of them travel the country sharing their stories with hundreds of others still struggling to deal with their disease. "It is still difficult for me to listen to my mom speak," Shannon confesses, "because she always tells me how much she hated me—how I represented to her what she wanted to be. But then she always reaffirms her love for me."

## A LOVE THAT LIBERATES—IS A LOVE THAT *BELIEVES!*

I first heard of W. Robert Gehring, M.D., through the letter he sent me in 1982. Now, he has published his story under the title, *RX for Addiction*.

He is a medical doctor. Surprisingly, his life was messed up, shot full of drug and alcohol addiction and demeaning sexual exploits. Then he tried to kill himself. He scrubbed up, pretending to be preparing for surgery, but instead he injected a drug in his veins, planning to end his misery for good.

However, he regained consciousness. Standing at his side was one of the hospital's prominent staff physicians. Dr. Gehring had no doubt that he would be evicted from his position at the hospital.

Imagine his shock when the doctor said to him, "Bob, I have no intention of having you dismissed from the hospital. I've come to try to save you. All I want is for you to come to church with me."

Robert Gehring had tried everything else. He decided to try church as well. To his amazement he found what he had been looking for. He encountered Jesus Christ and was saved—all because a fellow doctor, a Christian man who believed in God and believed in Dr. Gehring, gave him the gift of love and helped him receive the gift of faith.

Have faith in others. They may still be just seeds waiting to sprout. But the potential is there, just under the surface. If a relationship is nurtured with the warmth of love, if it is watered with positive thoughts and affirmations, if the negatives can be tenderly weeded out or choked out by the new positive feelings of self-esteem that will appear as a result of your love, you will be amazed at what will bloom in the most unlikely spot!

If this seems impossible to do, then let me share a prayer that might help:

*FAITH*

Lord, I believe
In the sun, even when
  it is behind the clouds;
In the seed, even when
  it lies unsprouted under the ground;
In faith, even when I have been betrayed;
In love, even when I have been rejected;
In hope, even when I have been hurt;
In God, even when
  You do not answer my prayers.
Amen.

# A LOVE THAT LIBERATES—IS A LOVE THAT *HOPES!*

You can be patient with others if you have *hope* that eventually they will respond to your love. If someone you love is reticent to accept your love, then ask yourself, "Could they be holding back from love because they are hurt, crushed, broken?"

In my office I have a beautiful photograph of Freedom on my wall. Freedom is the famous American bald eagle.

On December 30, 1980, an Iowa farmer walking through his field saw a large wounded bird flapping his wings awkwardly in the snow. The bird tried desperately but couldn't fly. The farmer approached the bird and was shocked to see that it was a bald eagle with a wing badly shattered by some hunter's poorly aimed buckshot. The proud bird, a national treasure that is protected by law, had been left floundering. The bird was four to five years of age and stood two feet high. His wings, even though one was broken, measured six feet from point to point.

The Iowa farmer had heard about the Raptor Rehabilitation Center for birds of prey, connected with the University of Minnesota. So on December 31, 1980, the bird was brought to Raptor. The wounded wing gradually healed, and Dr. Reptick, the founder of the Raptor Center, said that he thought the bird might fly again.

On February 8, 1981, three months later, the bird was sent by airplane to Washington, D.C., where he appeared at Constitution Hall as part of the welcome home to the hostages held in Iran. And later in a special program, a tribute to the men missing in action in Vietnam, he became a famous eagle. He was brought back from Washington to Preston, Wisconsin, where four hundred people looked on as the director of the Raptor Clinic said, "I think we can trust him to live in the wilds again."

The leather thongs were snipped at each foot, and the bird stretched his wings slowly, cumbersomely. He flapped them, flying very low to the ground, and then began to soar over the river and the hills. A photographer snapped the picture, and a famous painter painted the scene and sent me a print. It's entitled simply *Freedom*.

Once this proud bird was healed of his hurts and his wounds, he was able to fly again. Perhaps there is someone you know and love who is hurting and carries deep scars, wounds that keep him from responding. Be patient. There is hope. Believe that healing will come with time and unceasing love!

## A LOVE THAT LIBERATES—IS A LOVE THAT WORKS!

It's not enough just to respect, to accept, to understand, to believe in, and to hope for those you love. You also need to *work* at loving them.

We have a specialized outreach at the Crystal Cathedral to prisoners. Many of our people work year round conveying love to the men and women inmates of Chino. The parishioners' love is patient and kind. They go to the prison every week. They write to the inmates and send them literature. But most of all they bake cookies!

Every Christmas, the Crystal Cathedral congregation gets together to bake fourteen thousand dozen cookies. That's a lot of cookies! They are all handmade—chocolate chip, oatmeal-raisin, peanut butter, sugar, you name it—and they are baked in the kitchens of our people's homes.

Then they are lovingly wrapped and boxed in care packages that include one of the gifts that we give out on Sundays to our television congregation. Some boxes have rainbow suncatchers in them that say, "When it rains, look for the rainbow." Others have crosses. Each Christmas gift box also includes literature, along with stationery with stamped envelopes! Each box is carefully wrapped and individually handed to an inmate by one of our volunteers who shakes hands, looks the person in the eye, and says, "Merry Christmas! God loves you and so do I!"

I have long believed in the beauty and the power of this

simple sentence, but recently I was absolutely shocked to face in an unlikely spot the results of this statement of love and of the prison ministry.

My son, Bob, and I were on our way to lunch when I noticed that my gas tank was nearly empty. Bob said, "Do you have money?"

"No, but I have some credit cards," I answered. With that assurance we pulled into a Texaco station, the first station we came to.

"Fill it up," my son said to the young man who came to serve us. He filled it up. I gave him the credit card.

He looked at it and said, "Sir, this card's no good. It expired three months ago. Do you have any cash?"

I was in a predicament. Bob didn't have enough cash either. I said, "I don't have any cash on me. But look, don't you recognize me?"

"I never saw you before in my life," he said.

"I'll give you a clue. My name is Schuller."

"Never heard of it."

I was at a loss. I finally said, "I don't have anything else to give you. You may keep the credit card. I'm sure Texaco will honor it. My credit is impeccable. And if they won't accept this credit card, you can check me out in the telephone book . . . . You can call me . . . . I'll pay you cash! Plus interest for the trouble!"

He agreed.

Later, while Bob and I were having lunch, I happened to find my *new* Texaco card! I said to my son, "It's a long way back to that gas station, but I think we ought to go."

When we pulled into the station the attendant came running. "Oh, I'm glad to see you!" he said. "I told my boss about it and, boy, did I get it! He told me, 'Everything is on computer today. As soon as that outdated credit card hits the computer, it's going to come back here and you are going to have to pay that bill out of your own salary.'"

The choice
to believe
and love
is a God-given
option
that's always
open
to every person!

P.S. Now then—isn't God
good?!

The agitated young man continued, "You know, I haven't had this job too long. I really want to do good at it. So I really am glad to see you! When my boss looked at the card, he recognized your name. He helped me realize that you are Dr. Robert Schuller. I didn't put it together at first! I just got out of jail. It was while I was in prison that I read the books that were written by a Dr. Robert Schuller. I've got to tell you, you changed my life!"

"Jail?" I said. "Was it Chino?"

"Yes."

"Did you get a box of cookies and gifts?"

"You bet. And, Dr. Schuller, last year in the gift box there was a little wooden cross. That was the only gift I had to send to my little son. I read the three books, and I came to realize that I was in jail because I had a bad attitude."

After I handed him my new credit card I reached in my briefcase, got out a copy of *The Be Happy Attitudes*, autographed it, and gave it to him.

A life liberated! A man saved—because these were "God loves you . . . and so do I" people, "one-to-One-for-one" persons, who loved enough to work at putting someone on the *free*-way to happiness.

# THE ROAD OF LOVE:
## CATCH IT! THE
## *EXPRESS*-WAY!

*Real Love Communicates*

*"Love . . . is kind; love is not jealous or boastful."*
1 Corinthians 13:4


If you ever have found the road of loving relationships to be rutted, narrow, and littered with rocks, you probably need to change roads—to find the *express*-way. You may need to learn how to express love more effectively. I have seen, after years of marital and other counseling, that rocky relationships frequently are a result of misunderstandings bred by inadequate communication.

I heard the other day of a young woman who went to see her lawyer about getting a divorce from her husband. At the first meeting the lawyer said, "Well do you have any grounds for this divorce?"

"Yes, an acre-and-a-half," she answered.

"No," he said, "what I mean is, do you have a grudge?"

"We don't have a garage, but we have a carport."

The lawyer was getting very frustrated with this first meeting. Taking a wild stab he said, "Well, does he beat you up?"

"Oh no! I get up before he does every morning!"

At this point the lawyer threw up his hands and said, "Well, then what's the problem?"

"I don't know," she said, thoughtfully. "We just can't seem to communicate."

Communication is the key to making your relationships with others work. Without it, the doors will remain locked. Feelings will be suppressed. Misunderstandings will abound. Expressing love is an art that I'd like to help you master, but it will take some effort—and some time.

## FIND TIME TO EXPRESS LOVE

Make time to find the *express*-way. Take the time to express love. Schedule "express times" into your calendar.

My wife, Arvella, and I have a date night every week. Mondays are our date nights, and *nobody* interferes. My secretary has orders that absolutely *nothing* can be scheduled on Monday night. My children know it is futile to try to reach my wife or me on Monday night.

This date night is our express-love night. It is the time of the week when we go someplace alone and get to know each other again. In just one week's time, so much can happen, so many misunderstandings can occur that it's vital for us to sit down and lovingly discuss what we've been feeling the last week and what we are expecting in the upcoming week.

In my opinion, this weekly date night has been one of the secrets of my successful marriage of over thirty-five years to my first and only wife!

This is not easy—our schedules are FULL. We are both extremely busy. We are constantly pulled on by our children, associates, friends, social and business obligations, and opportunities in ministry. A marriage can only take pulling for six days. On the seventh, we need a respite—a chance to be together as husband and wife, friend and companion, free from the tensions and distractions of everyday life.

Interestingly, Dr. Joyce Brothers once suggested a similar technique in parent-child relationships. When asked how parents could ease sibling rivalry, Dr. Brothers answered, "Give each child a special night of the week when they get to stay up one-half hour later than their brothers or sisters. Use that time to talk and listen to and love that child. You'll be amazed at how much that weekly time will do for you and your children."

Communicating love takes time, and expressing love requires a certain amount of know-how. In my many years as a pastor, television preacher, author, and lecturer, I have learned something about communication, and when it comes to relationships, there are three sides to expressing love: See It, Say It, and Show It.

## SEE IT!

"All I want is a look!"

We all cry out at one time or another for wordless, matchless communication. We all long to feel the love that can be expressed tenderly and sincerely with a look of love.

This simple, but heart-enriching form of communication is one of the first to be neglected. We find ourselves buried in a television show, needlework, dishes, weeds to pull, bank sheets to balance. We fail to take the moment, the few *seconds* to look up from our work or activities and look into the hearts of those we love.

It is essential that we learn to recapture this art of speaking with the eyes, for love can look deep into the hearts and read the unspoken distress signals. Frequently, the words that reveal the deepest reaches of our soul are too painful to say out loud. But the eyes will tell the truth. When the lips deny, the eyes can frequently see what's really going on within.

The eyes can see the truth, and they also can see if the message is getting across. They let us know if the listener is really listening and comprehending.

When we communicate within our family we make it a point to look each other in the eye. We do not throw out information in passing when the other person is working, reading, or watching TV. We make sure others take a break and stop and listen with their eyes.

Arvella and I were especially concerned with this when our children were small and we were disciplining them. When I used to reprimand one of the kids or was talking to them of love, I often said, "Look at me!" Direct eye contact established the fact that I meant what I said. It insured that my child really was listening and that I had been heard.

So! Let us not fail to understand the ability of the eyes to speak of love—whether it be a loving look of discipline and correction, or a look of loving approval.

I shall long remember my father's amazing ability to speak with his eyes. He was a reserved person, and although he usually sat quietly in any large room filled with his married sons and daughter and grandchildren of all ages, without his saying a word, we all knew how very much he loved us. He was truly a man of few words, but his eyes and face assured us of his love.

A quotation from a woman who had fifty happy years of marriage says it perfectly: "Early in our marriage, we learned to see through each other . . . and still enjoy the view!" (*Reader's Digest*, 1977).

## SAY IT!

Words are the obvious building materials of communication. Once we have *seen* it, it's important to *say* it, for verbalizing our feelings does two things: First, it confirms to the other person that what they believe they are feeling is indeed true. Secondly, just saying "I love you" to someone does require a certain amount of basic commitment from you.

*Saying* that we care, whether it be words of praise or words of correction, is one of the more difficult and challenging parts of communication. Since verbal communication is such an essential stone in the foundation of a loving relationship, volumes have been written on this subject by psychologists and psychiatrists. However, nothing I have read on the fine art of communication has been as practical and as helpful as what I learned from the late Dr. Henry Poppen.

Dr. Poppen was a wonderful friend and served as the first minister to the Keenagers (senior citizens group) in our church. He had been a missionary to China and was imprisoned when the Communists took over the Chinese government. Earlier Dr. Poppen had used his communication gifts to skillfully negotiate with the Japanese captors, persuading them to feed hundreds of thousands of starving Chinese villagers.

One day I asked Henry, "What is the secret to your success in communicating with others?"

His answer was power-packed. "Four words," he answered. "Be *friendly*. Be *fair*. Be *frank*. Be *firm*."

I have followed his advice as a husband, a father, and a pastor, and I have to tell you—it works!

## 1. Be friendly. "Love . . . is kind."

The power of words! They can hurt; they can maim; they can destroy a relationship. On the other side of the coin, words can enrich, save, and heal.

I once knew a girl who had unsuccessfully tried various methods of suicide. Her life was salvaged by three small words. A man whose friendship was very important to her said to her therapist, "I will do anything I can to help her. *She's worth it!*"

Those three words, "She's worth it!" totally transformed this girl's life. She began to see her worth for the first time. She no longer wanted to die. She was valued. She had something to offer to others—herself! She wanted to live.

If only we could all be so thoughtful and generous with our words, and restrained from making negative comments, even in jest. I am amazed at the number of people who callously throw out negative comments about others under the guise of humor. In our family I have long had the rule that we are not to partake in negative humor. We do not call each other names, such as "fatso," or "turkey," or "jolly green giant." For even though everybody may laugh at the time, the other person most assuredly ends up later in the privacy of his room, wondering if there isn't some truth in the jest. After all, if there wasn't some truth in it, then why would everybody laugh!

Be friendly when you communicate. Be kind. Choose your words carefully. If you are dissatisfied with your relationships, I suggest that you take an inventory of your conversations. Are they positive? Are they kind? Do they build others up?

It's interesting in studying 1 Corinthians 13 to note that Paul says "Love . . . is kind," and then almost in the same breath, "Love is not jealous or boastful." Ogden Nash once wrote:

> To keep your marriage brimming,
> With love in the loving cup,
> Whenever you're wrong, admit it!
> Whenever you're right, shut up!*

In other words, "Don't boast!"

I think it's important to mention at this point that at times silence, refraining from speaking, can be the most friendly form of communication.

It's easy to boast and overlook the fact that good news for you may be bad news for someone else. And it takes a great deal of sensitive respect for another's feelings to decipher which is which. Think of it:

- Your promotion, when your friend and colleague has been passed up, may well be good news for you but may be bad news for your friend who is still waiting.

---

*I Wouldn't Have Missed It (Boston: Little Brown, 1962). Used by permission.

- The news of your marriage engagement is good news for you, but it may be bad news for your single friend. Your diamond ring may only remind her of her lack.
- Your pregnancy is good news for you. But it may feel like bad news for your friend who has been trying to have a baby and has been unable to conceive.

It is a rare friend who is able to handle a friend's good news when he is not as fortunate. So before you are quick to share your "good" news, stop and think, "Will this hurt this person or help them? Will it inspire and encourage, or will it discourage and depress?"

If you're not sure what the answer would be—then I would suggest that you keep your good news to yourself!

### 2. Be fair. Love doesn't make unreasonable demands.

Love does not insist on its own way. That is being fair! How do you know what's fair and what's not? My advice (it has worked for me) is be honest and ask, "Do you think I'm being fair? What do *you think* I should do to help you?" Then remember the old American Indian proverb, "Never ask one to walk with you till you have walked one day in his moccasins."

### 3. Be frank.

"How can I be frank and friendly at the same time?" you ask. "There are times when I need to tell those I love that they are having problems. After all, you don't let your wife go out of the house with a tear in the back of her dress, do you? And I can't let my loved ones say things or do things that will ultimately hurt them."

An age-old conflict! A timeless question! Is it possible simultaneously to maintain a sense of loyalty to another's feelings and loyalty to one's own integrity?

If we read further in 1 Corinthians 13, we find a clue. St. Paul writes, "If you love someone, you will be loyal to him [or her] no matter what the cost" (TLB).

*Loyalty* is the key word. Loyalty, by its nature, implies honesty. If you look at any large corporation, you'll see what I mean. A chief executive may have many people working for him. Of these some are true-blue, loyal employees. They are the ones who love the company and the president enough to be honest with him. But there are also the "yes-men" and "yes-women" who care only about their own careers, and consequently, they tell the president only those things that will further their own advancement in the company.

Loyalty and honesty are essential to any love relationship. *Constructive* honesty, rooted in love, can often open the lines of communication in *any* relationship.

I have emphasized the word *constructive* and thereby have chosen to qualify the term *honesty*. I believe that various degrees of honesty do exist, ranging from the constructive to the destructive. We may "speak the truth" and hurt people in the process. Not all honesty is valuable, and not all words of truth are rooted in love.

Constructive honesty builds up, but destructive honesty tears down. Constructive honesty looks for solutions, while destructive honesty points out the weak spots. Destructive honesty hurts. Constructive honesty heals.

Consider the wise words of my daughter-in-law, Donna, who has the challenging task of being a pastor's wife. That kind of position requires the very special gift of being constructively honest. It is a gift I see in my wife, Arvella, and recently I saw Donna exhibit the same ability.

We were all gathered at the family home after a Sunday of morning worship services. Our son Bob had delivered the message for the "Hour of Power," which he does from time to time. We were all relaxing over a delicious dinner that Arvella had made. In the midst of the laughter, Bob turned to Donna and said, "Well, how did I do this morning?"

"Very well! I was really proud of you, Bob!" Donna said.

"Yeah? How did you like the story about . . . ?" He mentioned one of his illustrations.

Donna paused. The story had not gone over that well. Should she be honest and tell Bob that he shouldn't repeat the story—maybe ruining the family gathering, not to mention Bob's day? Or should she lie and tell him how wonderful it was only to hear him repeat it in the future?

I shall never forget her wise answer, "Bob. The story was O.K. But, you know, you have others that I like a lot more!"

Bob's deep baritone voice rolled with laughter. "Don't I have a wonderful wife? Did you notice how beautifully she put that?"

He put his arm around Donna and said, "O.K., honey, I get the picture. Thanks."

Honesty and integrity are rooted in loyalty. The truly honest person remains loyal to the other person's feelings and is aware that it is possible to be honest, frank, and positive at the same time. Recognize this: You don't have to reflect things the way they are *now* to be totally honest. You can reflect things as they have been—reminding a person of when he was exceptional, as Donna did. Or you can project the possibilities and the opportunities of what someone can do and become without losing integrity. We can reflect in love what the person *can be*.

Consider these examples:

- "You can be a really great student!"
  —A father to his child who is struggling in school.
- "You would be a knockout if you lost a few pounds."
  —A mother to an overweight child.

*Real love sees people not as they are, not as they were, but as they can become*. This is love at its best. This is the love Jesus has for us. He sees us not as we are, but as we can become. This love is healing and constructive.

If you love someone, you will be loyal no matter what the cost. Jesus paid the cost of His loyalty to us: death on the cross. He only asks in return that we love others as best as we can and that we reflect Christ's love as clearly and beautifully as possible.

## 4. Be firm.

We have all heard the term *tough love.* Parents, chief executive officers, persons in the final seat of authority know that to vacillate is to send signals of weakness into negotiations, and love is a process of negotiation! "Love . . . is kind; love is not jealous or boastful; it is not arrogant or rude" but love does not mean that we let people run over us and give them exactly what they want. It does not mean that we tell people what they want to hear, even though the truth may upset them.

Indeed, there are principles which you must never compromise. There are moral values that must never be sacrificed. Do you remember Tevye, the father in *Fiddler on the Roof*? He is a tremendous example of compromise. When each of his daughters asks for his permission or blessing to marry the man of her choice, he discusses the difficult matter with himself. He argues both sides of the issue. "On the one hand. . . ," he says, and then he adds, "But on the other hand. . . ."

Often his decision involves compromising his ideas of proper *social* structure. But with his last daughter he reaches the point when he says, "There is no other hand!" When it calls for him to compromise in his *religious* beliefs, he cannot do it. This is a line that he cannot cross.

There is always a point beyond which you *cannot* compromise!

## EXPRESS LOVE: SEE IT! SAY IT! *NOW* SHOW IT!

The gift of touch is a wonderful and unique way to communicate love. It has been shown that children need touch so much that in extreme cases a child may die without it! They need to be cuddled, even as newborns. Perhaps that's why some of the prominent hospitals in Southern California now have baby cuddlers on their neonatal staff. These men and women go to the hospitals and do one thing—they cuddle the newborn babies. While mothers are resting and recuperating and while the nurses are busy tending to the babies' medical needs, the baby cuddlers hold the babies, they stroke them, they talk to them, and they love them.

One baby cuddler was featured recently on television news. She was shown holding a little premature baby, with his stocking cap on his head to keep in his body warmth. His wrinkled little face was cradled in the cuddler's arms. The lovely, white-haired grandmother rocked this baby and talked to him. Suddenly the infant gave a funny, crooked little smile.

"See?" the baby cuddler exclaimed. "He's smiling. He's happy. That's because he's loved!"

Not only the babies benefit from this program; the baby cuddlers say that they do it as much for themselves as for the infants. There are many such programs across this great country. With all the hurting people in the world, there is no excuse for anybody not to take an opportunity to show love to others.

We all need to look creatively for ways to say "I love you" through the things we do. Actions *do* speak loudly.

Dr. Howard House and his brother Dr. William House are the founders and directors of the House Ear Institute, a leading institution for research to help the hearing-impaired. The

House brothers developed the cochlear ear implant, which has enabled children with supposed permanent hearing loss to hear sounds—many for the first time in their lives. Recently at a wedding reception, Howard presented one of his favorite poems, a stanza by Odell McConnell:

> Love is a verb as well as a noun;
> Love means a smile and never a frown.
> To love is to do and not just to feel,
> For unless you express it, love isn't real.

Love in action. That is a love that really communicates. Let me suggest a definition of love in action:

---

### *Love Is My Deciding To Make Your Problem My Problem!*

---

With this definition of love, you don't have to be a minister, a counselor, a psychiatrist, or a doctor to know what I'm talking about. Whatever your profession or career, you can express love for others in whatever you do.

Take Kenneth Hahn, for example. Kenny, who is the supervisor of Los Angeles County, has used his position in politics to live love and express love by creating programs that help people with their problems. You may not realize it, but as a result of his decision to make others' problems his problem, Kenny has saved countless lives—perhaps even yours! No matter what city, what county, what state you live in, if you have been helped by the paramedics of your community, you can thank Kenny Hahn.

The paramedic program in America started in Los Angeles in 1970, because when one man, a wonderful Christian, heard about the problem, he wouldn't let anything stop his solving it.

Dr. Walter Graf, who was Chief of Cardiology at Daniel Freeman Memorial Hospital in Los Angeles, once said to Kenny, "You are good at solving problems. How would you like to endorse a plan where you can save a life a day?"

Kenny responded, "Me? How can a politician save a life a day?"

"I think the county firemen can be trained to render emergency aid, the same as is given by a doctor or a nurse, for the first hour in the field," Dr. Graf replied.

Kenny couldn't see why his help was needed. He asked, "Why doesn't the medical profession do it?"

"Well," Dr. Graf said, "we have to change the whole state law in order to have firemen trained to be paramedics, because they need to apply morphine in the first hour of treatment for a heart attack. And the Health and Welfare Code of the State of California states that only a doctor or a registered nurse can prescribe morphine."

So Kenny Hahn had to try first to change state law. He was told it would be impossible, but Kenny would not take "No" for an answer. He worked through red tape to gain support of his new bill allowing trained firemen to prescribe morphine in emergency situations. Finally, the bill passed through the California Assembly and the Senate, but it was opposed by the California Medical Association, as well as by the American Medical Association. The State Firechiefs Association was opposed also. They didn't want the firemen to practice medicine.

Then the supervisor got a call from Governor Ronald Reagan. "Kenny, I'm going to veto that bill you're interested in," he said.

"Governor, before you make your final decision," Kenny pleaded, "let me come up to Sacramento and explain to you how it works."

He went to Sacramento and talked to the governor. He explained, "The county fire department will cross all lines of the eighty-four cities in Los Angeles County. They will be able to reach eight million people. The county fire department will get the call. They will have a base hospital that will be able to monitor the person's heart attack right at the scene."

The governor looked at Kenny and said, "Did you say that they will cross all city lines?"

"Yes."

Governor Reagan signed the bill, even though so many opposed it. He said to Kenny later, "My own father died when city police ambulances wouldn't cross jurisdictional lines."

Imagine Mr. Hahn's joy then, at a paramedics reception after the first year, when twelve people who had been pronounced dead but were saved by trained paramedics came up to him and said, "Thank you." In 1985, in Los Angeles County alone, the paramedics responded to 101,000 calls for help.

Kenny is also responsible for a freeway telephone system that has helped countless stranded motorists in Los Angeles County. Again, Kenny was inspired by a need, and he responded with love and concern.

One day he was on the Harbor Freeway when he saw a woman climbing over the bank. Kenny pulled over and learned the woman had run out of gas and was stranded and lost on this busy, dangerous freeway. Kenny took her to a gas station, got her some gas, came back, and filled up her tank.

That experience convinced him that Los Angeles County needed emergency phones along the freeway system—one every mile. Now there are three thousand telephones on every freeway in the county. This is the only county in the United States that has emergency telephones. And already over five million motorists have used them.

Kenny Hahn—I am proud to call him a friend, because he shows his love by deciding to make others' problems his problem. He doesn't just talk about it. He does it—to the very best of his ability!

*Love*
*is*
*my decision*
*to make*
*your*
*problem—*
*my*
*problem!*

# THE *EXPRESS*-WAY EXPRESSES LOVE—BY DOING SOMETHING TO HELP!

Ralph Showers is another example of someone who makes others' problems his own. As a disabled farmer he is in the business of communicating the meaning of love to hundreds of mentally retarded young people and young adults. His organization, called Rainbow Acres, consists of three ranches, where ninety mentally retarded people are cared for by a staff of fifty, with many of the mentally retarded working to help pay their own way. Rainbow Acres has helped nine other ranches start across the United States, as well as one in Japan. The ranch does not take any government support and is becoming self-sufficient.

The man who built this tremendous organization was told when he was in the seventh grade that his IQ was 84—"dull-normal." The "experts" suggested that he not continue school, but his family reminded him that God had created him and had breathed life into him. If God believed in him, so did they.

Ralph did have a tough time getting through school. Yet he managed to get his undergraduate degree and then his theological education. He served as a pastor after he got out of seminary and was ordained in the American Baptist Church. He served churches in Hawaii, Arizona, and California. Then he had an intuition, a compulsion to acquire ten acres of land in Arizona.

He had no idea what he was supposed to do with the land other than to build a ranch on it. After he took the step of faith to purchase the land, the Lord gave him the dream of a ranch for the mentally retarded. Ralph began to work diligently on the dream. Then, in 1973, while Ralph stood atop a barn that was being moved to the ranch, he backed into a power line bearing 7,200 volts of electricity. His hands and arms were burned so badly that gangrene set in and both hands had to be amputated.

Today, Ralph has two hooks for hands. But he says that his handicap has actually been a blessing, because he now is able to work that much better with handicapped people and share with them and love them; he knows exactly what it means to be handicapped.

Ralph loves people who frequently have been forgotten by others. He sees their possibilities, what they can contribute to society. Approximately three out of every hundred people in America are mentally or physically handicapped. But Ralph believes that every person is created for a purpose, for a reason. And he has shown that it doesn't matter whether or not legs are lame, eyes are sightless, ears cannot hear, minds are slow, or hooks have replaced hands. Whatever the handicap might be, God has a purpose for each life!

I asked Ralph one day, "People with severe handicaps, are they happy?"

Ralph replied, "Oh, of course we have all the normal problems, the ups and the downs like everybody else, but I wouldn't exchange living with this group of people for anything on the face of the earth. There is simplicity; there's no question about it. But their faith, their excitement, everything about them is special, and it's a wonderful experience to love them and be loved by them."

It's possible for *all* of us to be a success at communicating love—*if* we will take the time to use the *express*-way! Yes, it means we become "God loves you . . . and so do I" people, "one-to-One-for-someone" persons!

Now, we'll *express* love! We'll see it! Say it! And show it!

# THE ROAD OF LOVE:
## PAY THE PRICE!
## USE THE
## *TOLL*-WAY!

*Real Love Compromises*

*"Love does not insist on its own way."*
1 Corinthians 13:5

**T**wo boys were trying to play on a hobby horse outside a department store. It was one of those horses where you put a quarter in a slot and the horse goes up and down. They were both trying to ride at the same time when one boy said, "You know, if both of us didn't try to get on at the same time, I could have a much better ride."

There's a lot of truth to that statement! And we adult drivers on the road of life could take a lesson from those boys. Too often we vie for the same spot on the road, each trying to pass the other. Our pride can't handle being in second place, yet not everyone can come in first.

This "push and shove" way of life will only lead to frustration and is quite dangerous. And unless we are prepared to take the *toll*-way, are willing to wait in turn at the gates, pay our dues, and graciously drive side-by-side with fellow travelers, we may find we're not even on the road of love.

We've reached a point in our world where unless we compromise, we're all going to be bruised over the same hobby horse, and nobody is going to have a decent ride. Many of us never learned to give and take, even after we grew up. We are guilty of thinking that we have earned a right to demand our own way—in marriage, in business, in parenting, in every life relationship. Many of us are guilty of acting like children, of stating through our actions, "I want what I want, when I want it!"

But Paul, in his love letter to us, gives us a clue on how to

411

secure lasting, happy relationships. He encourages us to give when we feel like taking. He encourages us to take the nobler route—the way of compromise. Although compromising appears to be the weaker stance I contend that it is really the stronger. Compromise requires a love forged from steel. It requires a deep, mature love to take the long view—to see beyond the momentary "high" of winning an argument and thereby winning the relationship.

This is a difficult concept for most of us to grasp, for we have been warned from childhood never to compromise. So-called "principles of success" often suggest that we must hold unwaveringly to our beliefs and our plans. We are taught that the laurels go to the strong. The victories go to the brave. The accolades go to the resolute. So we feel that we should fight for our rights. We should never back down.

Right? Sometimes. But not always!

I am a strong advocate of firm convictions, of being true to commitments, of climbing the mountain, of tunneling through the difficulties, but there are times when we must learn to compromise. Sometimes it is in our best interests, as well as others', to give a concession to our "opponents."

Where could we find an example of compromising love at work? Well, one place to look is in the Lennon home. As you know, the Lennon sisters, who sang on the Lawrence Welk television show, all come from the same family. The sisters who form the singing group are the four oldest of a family of eleven children. Yes, eleven! Mrs. Lennon is the mother of five boys and six girls.

Now, I've got to tell you, there's no way that a family of that size can live harmoniously, and there is no way that four sisters can sing so harmoniously unless there is a tremendous capacity to compromise.

The sisters say in their book, *Same Song, Separate Voices,* *

*Round Table Publishing, 933 Pico Blvd., Santa Monica, CA 90405.

that they sang from the time they were very little. They learned their harmonies from their father and his brothers who used to sing and rehearse at their house. At first the sisters sang mostly for church functions.

But one of the girls, Dee Dee, went to school with Lawrence Welk, Jr. He heard the girls sing one night and said, "Gosh, my dad has a TV show and he's looking for talent. I'm going to tell him about you."

A few weeks later young Lawrence called and said, "My dad's home in bed. He's sick with a cold and he can't get out. So come sing for him."

They did. That was around Christmas of 1955, and Mr. Welk had the girls sing on his Christmas Eve television show. The Lennons were on the show every Saturday after that for nearly thirteen years.

Can you imagine how much compromising it took for four different, individual teen-age girls to arrange singing schedules, taste in clothes, hairdos, even the choice of songs—not to mention the harmonies? Who would sing melody? Who would sing the solo line? Believe it or not, after all these years of working together and singing together, the sisters all still truly love each other!

Today they are all married and among the four of them have fourteen children. They still perform and need to make even more compromises, for now their schedules are even more complicated, the sacrifices more difficult.

I asked them once, "How do you do it?"

"We know a lot about harmony," they answered. "And the joy of harmony is that *you can't sing it by yourself.*"

Compromise is not easy. That's why we call it the *toll*-way. But I promise you, if you will pay the "duties" on this road of love, you will find that the journey was well worth the price!

## COMPROMISE IS LOWERING YOURSELF

The first "duty" on the *toll*-way is *lowering* yourself to give someone else an opportunity. *Love does not demand its own way!* There can be no community without compromise. You've met people with hardened opinions, iron wills, frozen viewpoints. This stance will only lead to loneliness, for I can assure you that nobody wants to be around people who can only see one point-of-view—theirs!

Frequently, these people mistakenly assume that their unwavering position is a sign of strength. When it comes to moral values, as we saw in chapter seven, that is often true. But many times, this single-minded view of life is nothing more than a disguised stubbornness.

The really *strong* persons are those who have self-denial at the core of their love. They are people who can give of themselves freely. They know how to go more than halfway. They can compromise when the going gets rough. For compromise is self-denial; it is backing down, backing off, and settling for less in the present moment to gain more in the end. Compromising is lowering yourself *only to be lifted.*

Retreating is sometimes the wisest way to advance. Compromise today; make up for it tomorrow. Give a little now. Regain it—and more—down the road. *Compromising is taking one step back in order to take two steps forward.*

I have a friend who claims that the complaint department is really the quality control department. A successful company or person must be humble enough to listen to constructive criticism and then to make creative changes. That's compromising for success. That's lowering yourself only to be lifted. There is a principle I have learned to live by, which I discuss at length in the *Be Happy Attitudes:* "I don't want my own way—I want to do what's right!" Compromising is being willing to lower yourself.

## COMPROMISE IS LOOKING BEYOND

The second "duty" on the *toll*-way is *looking*—looking for better ideas, new insights, broader views, brighter ways to help. This way of loving assumes that somebody else knows something you don't know. It is looking beyond the present moment to the big picture. Is there a tension or a problem in your marriage or a relationship? Maybe there is a disagreement between your boss and you? If so, perhaps you need to practice looking at the larger perspective. Compromise your feelings—your hurts, your sense of rejection, and your despair. Forget about them. Compromise is another word for humility.

## COMPROMISE IS LIVING WITH THE SPIRIT OF COMMUNITY

The first duty on the *toll*-way of compromise is *lowering* yourself. The second is *looking* to the bigger picture. And the third is *living* with the spirit of community. By that I mean a give-and-take attitude. Compromise is "living" with people, trying to understand and appreciate their ideas, even when you don't share their viewpoints.

Why is America unique among all the nations of the world? *Pluralism.* Every element is represented in this country. All religions are free to practice their faith.

Freedom! That's the trademark of our social fabric. But could this distinct quality also be a weakness? If every religious, ideological, sociological, cultural, ethnic, racial, and sexual group becomes self-centered to the point where "MY RIGHTS!" become more important than the spirit of loving and caring for one another, then we are in danger. "MY RIGHT" loses its MIGHT, when it turns into a FIGHT!

In other words, my freedom loses its moral power if it fails to move forward and outward with love! The plain and simple fact is that no one has a right to demand all of his rights all of the time! So compromise! Give and take! Be a part of a community. Get on the team!

You can imagine how important the art of compromise and a sense of community are when you manage a baseball team. And compromising, like managing, is possible when you can *look* for better ideas, *listen* to what your players are saying, and *live* with them, making room for their viewpoints.

I once asked my good friend Tommy LaSorda, manager of the Los Angeles Dodgers, what contributed to the success of his team. Here's what he said:

> Well, I think a manager has to be a leader, and I have thought a lot about which qualities are important in a manager. I found my answer in church. The priest talked about Solomon, who is the paragon of truth and wisdom. And the Lord went to Solomon and said that He appreciated all that Solomon had done for Him, and He wanted to give him a gift. God said, "Any gift that you would want, I would love to give to you." And Solomon thought a minute and said, "The greatest gift that you can give me is an understanding heart." I think that is one of the real qualities that a manager should have.
>
> You should understand how the players feel. You should understand that when a player pops up with the tying run at third base with less than two outs, no one feels any worse than he does. So if you have an understanding heart, I think you are able to get along a great deal better with your players.

It is no wonder that Tommy has been recognized more than once as manager of the year. He looks for the big picture; he listens to what his players are really feeling; he understands. These traits can't help but build a community spirit. A team will not excel if each member cannot compromise on his personal goals and rights.

Perhaps we can see now what compromise really is! Compromise is:

- *Learning* how to live abundantly, even when you don't get your own way.
- *Listening* to what others are saying and requesting. It is hearing their opinions, their views, and their interpretations—even when you don't agree.
- *Lowering* yourself to give someone else an opportunity.
- *Looking* for better ideas, new insights, broader views, brighter ways to help.
- *Living* with a give-and-take attitude. And it is . . .
- *Letting go!*

## LET GO AND LET GOD!

Compromise is letting God have His way in your life. Can't you sense it—that there is a God? That a divine destiny is operating in the universe? That there is a purpose for your life? That God has a road He wants you to walk—a road that will lead to genuine peace and authentic pleasure? Do you need to re-evaluate and review your values and your views and, perhaps, change or convert or compromise your long-held posture or position?

A chief executive officer of a major corporation said to me, "For years I've been motivated by fame and fortune. Now I'm asking myself three questions: (1) What do I really want to accomplish in my life? (2) If I keep living and working the way I am, will I succeed? (3) If I make it—will I really be satisfied and happy in the end?"

Those are three good questions for all of us to ask ourselves! And when you do, be prepared to *let go* if:

A. Your views or your values tear apart your precious human relationships.

B. Your lifestyle causes your faith in God to drift aimlessly, dangerously downstream.

C. Your habits or hobbies threaten your health of body and happiness of spirit.

You must be willing to let go of all disruptive and destructive patterns of thought and behavior.

Yes, compromising is letting God have His way and His will in your life. This may not be what you really want to do! But it is the difference between being moral and immoral. An immoral person is somebody who does what he wants to do, when he wants to do it, the way he wants to do it—whether it is right or wrong. That's immorality. By contrast, morality is doing what is right, even if you don't like it. This is the point beyond which you cannot compromise.

All of which leads us to an important question: "When do we compromise and when don't we?" I want to suggest four times when compromising is the wise choice, the loving choice!

## 1. Compromise When Your Losses Are Irreversible.

When I returned from Europe some years ago, there was a memo for me to call a friend, Pat Shaughnessy, a pastor in Phoenix, Arizona. The note said he was at a Los Angeles hospital.

I called right away. "What are you doing there?" I asked.

He replied, "I was on my way to Korea, standing at the Pan Am air center, when all of a sudden there was an explosion. Three people were killed. I was closest to the bomb, and suddenly I found myself lying on the floor. My right leg was blown off between the hip and the knee. Blood just gushed out. But I never lost consciousness. My first thought was, *Lord, if I have to go, I'm ready. But I don't want to. I enjoy preaching about*

*Jesus so much because Christ is such a wonderful person. My second thought was, My wife, I hope she won't be too hurt by what is happening to me.* Then, on the way to the hospital, they were pumping blood into me, and it was a mad scene. They said I wouldn't live, and I was wide awake. Then this thought struck me, *I don't need a right leg to preach the gospel!*"

Pat has compromised. He has accepted the loss of a leg. We all always need to look at what we have left, not at what we have lost. We must learn to compromise in the face of a hurt or a loss we cannot change.

Teddy Kennedy has certainly suffered some irreversible losses in his life, yet he has gone on. To help others who have been hurt or are going through agonizing losses, Senator Kennedy shares this poem:

### LET IT BE FORGOTTEN

Let it be forgotten,
As a flower is forgotten,
Forgotten as a fire
That once was singing gold.
Let it be forgotten,
For ever and ever—
Time is a kind friend,
He will make us old.

If anyone asks,
Say it was forgotten
Long and long ago—
As a flower,
As a fire,
As a hushed foot-fall
In a long forgotten snow. *

---

*Sara Teasdale, *Collected Poems of Sara Teasdale* (Macmillan: New York, 1966), 135. Reprinted with permission of Macmillan Publishing Company.

If you have suffered an irreversible loss, then be assured of this: Time will make the pain less harsh. It will not go away completely—no more than the memories will ever leave—but the pain will become bearable.

## 2. Compromise When Your Dignity Has Been Denied.

Compromise when your self-esteem has been scratched, when you, your position, or your performance has not received deserved respect or recognition.

Few people are more unhappy or more miserable than those who lack the humility to overlook personal affronts and insults—obvious or oblique, real or fancied, intentional or unintentional. Several illustrations come to mind.

Albert Schweitzer, the renowned, dedicated man who merited over fifty honorary doctorates, was one of the greatest men of our century. He built his hospital in what was then the Belgian Congo, and the natives normally would do anything for him. But one day when he needed to build a wall, he asked one tribal native to carry some wood. The native, who was busy reading a book, said, "I am sorry, Doctor, but I'm an intellectual now; I'm busy reading and intellects don't carry wood!" Dr. Schweitzer replied, "Well, I congratulate you! I always wanted to be an intellectual, but I never succeeded, so I'll carry the wood!" And he did!

At the height of the Civil War, Abraham Lincoln wondered how the war was going. Rather than ask General McClellan to come to the White House and report, he decided that he and the secretary of war would go to the general's house in the battle area. They made their way to the general's home and waited. Finally the general came in, walked right on upstairs to his room, and never acknowledged the president and the secretary. They thought he'd be back in a minute with cleaner garb, but he didn't return. They asked the maid to go upstairs and check on the general.

When she came down she was aghast! "I'm sorry, Mr. President," she said, "but he said to me, 'Tell President Lincoln I'm tired and that I've gone to bed.'"

The secretary of war said to Lincoln, "Surely you're not going to let him get by with that? You will relieve him, will you not?"

The president thought about it for a long time and, finally, when he broke the silence, said, "No, I will not relieve him. That man wins battles, and I would hold his horse and clean his shoes if it would hasten the end of this bloodshed by one hour."

Doesn't that remind you of Jesus Christ? He overheard His followers talking behind His back. "When Jesus is gone, who is going to be the top man here? You, Peter, you, John, or Thomas?" Do you know what Jesus did? He asked for a basin of water and a towel. And before they shared the first communion, He got down and started to wash their feet.

"Wait a minute," Peter said. "I should wash your feet. You shouldn't wash mine." But Jesus just moved from person to person and washed their dirty feet and wiped them with a towel.

You compromise if you teach somebody a lesson by helping them when you do not have to. Schweitzer hauled wood, Lincoln would have held the man's horse. Jesus washed the disciples' feet. Great men have revealed their greatness by showing when to help, to bow, to compromise.

## 3. Compromise When You're Wrong—But Too Proud to Admit It!

Some of the hardest words to speak are the same words that lead to joy and peace. These hard but happy words are: "You were right! I was wrong!"

How can you salvage your self-esteem when your pride has been shipwrecked on the rocks of a wrong decision? By proudly proclaiming yourself to be a normal, imperfect, yet loveable human being through statements like these:

- "I made a mistake!"
- "Forgive me."
- "Allow me to correct myself."
- "Thank you for permitting me the freedom to improve my position."
- "Thank you for respecting my right to correct myself."
- "I am honored that you would allow me the privilege of compromising my viewpoint in light of the growth I am experiencing now."

When your pride has been wounded because your position has been faulted, you can rescue your self-esteem by openness and honesty. So, when confession leads to compromise, your dignity is immediately nourished by your honesty. You are honored by your humility. You have extracted positive possibilities from your predicament.

In old England, when a man was to be knighted, the queen or the king tapped each shoulder with a sword, and he was declared to be a knight. But there's one thing every potential knight had to do: He had to be humble, to kneel, to bow, to compromise his pride. He had to kneel to be knighted.

Yes, compromise can be kingly! Your life can be crowned with joy and happiness if you discover the peace and the pleasantness that proceeds out of the heart of a humble person.

Compromise: I am knighted with honor and glory when I compromise *my* right in the face of *what's* right!

## 4. Compromise When the Rewards Are Heavenly—But the Price Is Horrific!

In explaining this principle, no life is more inspiring, illuminating, and illustrative than the life of Jesus Christ. And no single event in the life of Jesus stands out as dramatically as the crucial experience that occurred in the Garden of Gethsemane the night before Jesus was crucified.

The scene begins at supper. The twelve apostles are sharing a Passover meal with Jesus. Judas slips out to prepare to betray his Master. Jesus now leads His followers out into the garden to pray. He moves quietly into a secluded section where He can commune with God. He is fully aware that if He doesn't turn now, run away, escape, tonight He will be betrayed and tomorrow He will be crucified.

He is young, only 33 years old! He is alive! He has so much to live for! To stay in the garden will mean capture and crucifixion! Now comes the prayer of all prayers. Hear Him: ". . . Father, all things are possible for You. Take this cup away from Me; nevertheless, not what I will, but what You will" (Mark 14:36).

What visions now pass through His mind? Does He see millions, hundreds of millions, yes, a billion believers two thousand years down the road who will respect and reverence Him for His courage, His commitment, and His cross? Does He see the untold hundreds of millions of souls saved because of His sacrifice and His death? Does this heavenly reward prove enough to move Him to pay the horrific price?

This we know—He compromised His will to fulfill God's dream! The result? Betrayal. Trial before Pilate. Scourging in the morning. Crucifixion at noon. Death at mid-day Friday. But new life on Sunday! And today He is Lord over a kingdom of untold millions who share His life and His love.

Compromise can be kingly!

# THE ROAD OF LOVE:
## CONSIDER TAKING THE *SUB*-WAY!

*Real Love Forgives and Forgets*

*"Love is not . . . resentful."*
1 Corinthians 13:5

"**F**orgive *and* forget! That's impossible!"
She was actually angry at hearing my advice!
"Impossible! Impossible!" she repeated. She was a hurting woman, a relatively innocent victim of a cruel divorce. Her self-esteem was shattered. She was bitter—understandably so.

"Let's discuss it," I offered.

"I doubt if I can *forgive,*" she finally volunteered. *"Forget?* No way!"

"But it is possible," I repeated. "Listen . . ." She was listening, so I continued. "Let me ask you a question: Is it possible you are confusing reconciliation with forgiveness?"

There followed one of the longest pauses I have experienced in my years of pastoral counseling. "Forgiveness does not mean you have to approve his behavior! You could never do that! But forgiveness does mean you are going to put it behind you—and, yes—in practical terms—forget it! Which means you'll bury the hatchet and not leave the handle above the ground! But to forgive and forget does not mean you have to have a restored relationship! You don't even need to become friends. You just have to stop being enemies!"

Her whole body seemed to breathe a heavy sigh, and her face seemed to lose ten years of age! She suddenly relaxed, looking enormously relieved of a colossal burden! The turnaround had begun! Healing love was moving in. Result? She salvaged the respect and love of the rest of her close friends and family, for

427

they were becoming tired of her morbid, negative, unhappy side! Had she not learned to forgive and forget, the rest of her meaningful relationships could have been hopelessly poisoned and destroyed. The alternative to forgiveness is destruction beyond calculation.

Any fool can count the seeds in an apple, but only God can count the apples in one seed. The principle works with bad seeds, bad feelings, and bad thoughts just as it works with good seeds, good feelings, and good thoughts!

"I am going to choose to forgive! To let love come back!" she promised. Result? Several years later, she attracted a wonderful husband! Today her life is precious, glorious, and beautiful! More amazingly, she said to me recently, "Dr. Schuller, I ran into my ex-husband. And guess what—I didn't hate him anymore! The resentment is gone. My feelings are kind and pleasant." This all happened when she chose a positive attitude! You can, too!

Robert Frost once suggested that before we build walls, we should make sure we know what we're walling out and what we're walling in.

No wall is more impenetrable, more formidable than the wall of resentment. This silent killer of relationships is a common cause of divorce, split friendships, and broken partnerships.

So when relationships break up and the "traffic backs up," go *under* the wall of resentment. Take the *sub*-way to forgiveness.

## REMEDIES FOR RESENTMENT

The Apostle Paul says, "Love is not . . . resentful." That sounds noble, but in practical terms how do you handle the person whose lifestyle, whose behavior, or whose attitude toward you meets with your nonapproval? How do you handle the nonapprovable persons, experiences, or situations?

You have several options. At the shallowest level of

**Forgiveness
is a
snowplow:**
* **Removing the barrier**
* **Plowing through**
* **Tunneling underneath**
* **Opening the road—
to
love!**

nonapproval there is what I would call *reticence,* which means there's a silence about the whole situation or the person. You simply avoid the issue if possible. For example, in a meeting where someone has become angry and is ripping into another person, you might be quiet, wait for a pause, then abruptly change the subject.

The second reaction, a little more intense, is operating when you understand exactly what's happening and rather than avoid all confrontation through reticence you try *resistance.*

Instead of ignoring a tense situation, you may stiffen up and bristle within. But you want to do anything you can to try to keep yourself protected from an involvement with the "obnoxious" person. You hope the conversation can be terminated swiftly, perhaps even gracefully. But deep within yourself you've already made a judgment; you have your mind made up. You are disturbed by this person and the situation is now brimming with problems, obstacles, and difficulties. Reticence has been replaced by a more intense form of inner resistance.

There is also a third reaction, which is even more intense— *retreat.* In the setting of this tense meeting, you'll probably say to yourself, *Hey, I want to get out of here! And as quickly as possible!* You may make an excuse to split, or you may stop attending the meetings. You may even quit going to the organization, the church, or whatever it is. In a marriage, retreat may mean separation.

Sometimes, even though you long to walk away from a person or situation, retreat simply isn't an available option. You find yourself trapped. You're reticent, you're resistant, you want to retreat but you can't, and you'll probably react with the fourth level of nonapproval, and that's *rebellion.* This means, in the meeting I've described, you may interrupt the angry person and begin lambasting him for the way he is attacking the other person, the result often being an argument.

Rebellion is often expressed verbally, but it takes other forms as well. We all have our own instinctive or contrived, subconscious or conscious ways of rebelling, such as in our dress—consider the "hippies" of the 1960s and the "punkers" of the 1980s.

Nonapproval at its most negative level will result in *resentment*. Reticence? You can ignore it. Resistance? You can just play it away. Retreat? Take off! Rebellion? Get angry, verbally abuse someone, thumb your nose at authority! Resentment is the most dangerous reaction to a nonapproving experience or situation or person. It is the most dangerous because it is self-destructive. It is anger turned inward, outward, upward, and downward—all at the same time.

*Question:* Are you carrying resentments? How many fears, how many anxieties, how many worries are you suffering from because you will not forgive somebody who hurt you deeply? How many sunny days are turned gray by your angry mind— seething, quarreling in fantasy bouts with your adversary, who may be an ex-husband, an ex-wife, a relative, a neighbor, a customer, a client, or a clerk? Are you depressed and unhappy or even suffering from ulcers, high blood pressure, or heart problems because you will not forgive?

*Next question:* Are you developing wrinkles on your face that will become permanent creases, monuments to the fact that you spent most of your life thinking angry thoughts that twisted your expression into a permanent frown?

*Last question:* How many friends did you once have who no longer talk to you because you have developed a reputation of pouting, grumbling, and complaining?

This reminds me of the story of the monk who went to a monastery on a mountain in Spain. One of the requirements of this monastic order was that each monk must maintain perpetual silence. Only after two years was a monk allowed to speak, and then only two words. This was followed by two additional years of silence, two more words, and so on.

A young initiate had spent his first two years at the monastery and was called by his superior to make his first two-word statement. He said, "Bed hard." Two years passed. He got his second chance. His next two words were, "Food bad." Two more years passed. His next words were: "I quit!"

The superior looked at him and said: "It doesn't surprise me. All you've done since you got here is complain, complain, complain!"

This story brings a smile, but in all seriousness, none of us wants to go through life bearing the reputation of a grumbling, complaining, resentful person.

At one time or another all of us will face a situation that will "make our blood boil." We will find ourselves justifiably or unjustifiably angry. Yet Paul says that "Love is not resentful." What in the world can he possibly mean? An illustration from my childhood may help explain his meaning. Born and raised in northwest Iowa, I vividly recall the feelings of winter's first snow. The sight of snowflakes was wonderful. What we didn't appreciate were the blizzards, because these storms, fueled by driving winds of fifty to sixty miles an hour, often piled snow so high in drifts that the roads were impassable. We were marooned, unable to drive to the store and buy food. It was serious. One positive thing—there always is *something* positive—I did not have to go to school! When the storm ended I remember looking out of our farm house, half a mile down the road, to the hill where we could see the snowplow coming, cutting through the drifts, slicing the snow, chopping it up and blowing it in a huge, spewing stream into a ditch. After the snowplow came through, the road was open again, and we could go for our food. And I was obligated to return to my education.

Resentments are like snowdrifts, and forgiveness acts like the snowplow. Forgiveness, in the eyes of the non-Christian, is simply a matter of passive acquittal. But to the Christian, that's not it at all. Forgiveness is the snowplow, opening the road, removing the barrier, plowing through, or tunneling underneath, so that communication can be resumed and what people are trying to say can be heard again. We dialog and interchange; we move back and forth. Whether it's between God and myself or a person and myself, forgiveness is a snowplow.

We all make many mistakes. We all say things we do not mean and forget to say the things we should. Consequently, a lot of resentments can build up in just a day.

How do you handle them? We've shown how *reticence, retreat, rebellion,* or *resentment* don't work. Now let me give you the Christian option: *Repentance* and *forgiveness.*

In digging under the wall of resentments, in seeking sincerely to forgive, we are bound to run into some obstacles. After all, even a mighty snowplow will be slowed by huge snowdrifts. It's the same with Christian forgiveness.

## Obstacle #1: An Extreme Sense of Injustice

Odds are that if you're basically a decent person and yet are plagued by resentments, you probably feel you have been treated unfairly or thoroughly victimized. Your overpowering respect for justice gives birth to this resentment. Resentment, in a perverse fashion, becomes your way to mete out justice. That's not right. The Bible says, "'Vengeance is Mine. I will repay,' says the Lord" (Rom. 12:19).

That's that. At no point in the Bible does God ever command the Christian to execute that kind of justice against sins. He reserves the right to execute vengeance. We have to trust that He can do so in many ways that we cannot. In fact, we must trust that He is already executing justice.

I have often been helped by the biblical story of Joseph. He was sold by his brothers and became a slave in Egypt. The brothers had hoped they could kill him and get him out of the way. Instead he became a ruler. Hoping to kill him, they ended up through the providence of God crowning him. By the time he saw them again Joseph was able to say, "You meant evil against me; but God meant it for good" (Gen. 50:20).

Let justice be handled by the Lord. He knows how to take care of people. You can be sure that if you have been truly victimized, the person who has victimized you is already paying the price in his own conscience or heart or mind. You may say, "But, Dr. Schuller, I don't see any evidence of that."

Trust God. He has His own ways of executing justice. He is doing it. He can, He is, He will do a much better job of it than you or I can.

May those around us that we love be spared when we try to take justice into our own hands. God have mercy on your wife or your husband or your kids! I never have met a person whose personal form of executing justice changed him into a joyous, happy, beautiful human being in the process!

A man who was the victim of injustice once said to his pastor, "But wouldn't it be *man*-like of me to be angry?"

The pastor replied, "Indeed it would. But it would be *Christ*-like of you to forgive."

## Obstacle #2: Exaggerating Negative Experiences

We tend to emphasize the little negative events of life that get under our skin, and we forget all the little positive events of life that should fill us with joy, hope, and love. Any person who has hurt you does have many fine qualities, but chances are you can't see them. That's because we are all by nature negative thinkers. We see the wrong, and we don't see the good. That becomes an obstacle. We take a little detail and get hung up on it.

An artist was teaching his students how to paint. On a special occasion, he took them on an all-day trip to a particular hill where the sunsets were exceptionally beautiful. Just as the colors broke—purple, red, pink, orange, yellow, and gold—the teacher walked behind his students who were all intently capturing the artistic moment. To his disappointment he found one student who was diligently painting the shingle on a barn in the valley under the sunset. He had missed the glorious shading of sunset in favor of a shingle!

What's the point? Don't use a microscope to find the negative when if you'll just open your eyes you will be overwhelmed by a whole landscape of positive!

## Obstacle #3: Ignoring the Positive Possibilities in Negative Experiences

Every situation has some positive element in it. No person is totally bad. No situation is entirely hopeless.

I used to give lectures in which I took a piece of paper and drew a circle on it. Then I drew a straight line, and next to it added a curving line. I tacked the paper up and asked the class to tell me what they saw. The reactions were interesting.

"I see a straight line."

"I see a curve."

"I see a circle."

Some saw the objects and turned them into a work of art into which they read all kinds of meaning. In the process, many of them committed little Freudian slips, I suppose, but the point was that *no* student ever said, "I see a piece of paper!"

All they saw were the black marks! They saw the negatives; they didn't see the positives. Our first inclination in a potentially nonapproving situation is to see the negative and not the positive.

I shall never forget the night Mrs. Schuller and I were on the East Coast in a very prominent city where I was to deliver the Sunday message in a huge church the next morning. I had just come from an international trip only a few hours before. At the Geneva airport I had cashed two $50 traveler's checks and received two $50 bills in exchange.

I was preparing for my sermon in a hotel when I noticed that a particular movie was playing in the neighborhood theater. I had reason to believe the movie would give me some good sermon illustrations, so Arvella and I went to the theater. We stood in line, a long line, and after checking our watches we knew the movie was about to start. I didn't want to miss the opening, and at just two minutes before the scheduled starting time we arrived at the box office. I slid my $50 bill through the slot and the ticket teller passed back the two tickets. Then she paused, looked at the bill, and said, "I'm sorry. We don't take $50 bills."

"You can't reject it!" I said. "Do you know what that bill says? 'This is legal tender for all debts public and private.' You can't refuse it!"

"I'm sorry. We can't take it."

Now, never in my life have I been a public protester, but the line was getting longer and longer behind me, and it was beginning to drizzle. "I'm sure you can take it because it's a good $50 bill," I pleaded.

"I'm sorry. We *won't* take it."

The people behind us glared. I could feel the impatience of the crowd. Finally, the ticket teller said, "You've got your tickets."

"All right," I answered. "Thank you." And I walked in.

Suddenly, the ticket girl stuck her head out of the box office and yelled at the head usher, "That man didn't pay!"

I thought, *Oh, my gosh! I hope nobody recognizes me!*

The usher stopped me and asked, "What's the big idea!"

"She wouldn't take my $50 bill, and it's all I've got! I just left Geneva twelve hours ago, and I'm sorry. But watch where I sit, and you just check with the hotel and see if there is a Robert Schuller listed. Check out if they think he's honest or not. By the time I leave the theater, you'll have had time to check me out."

Unfortunately, halfway through the movie I had to step out to the rest room. I no sooner got in the men's room than there was that same usher! "O.K.," he said, "you are either a counterfeiter or the greatest con man I've ever met."

"Did you check the hotel?" I questioned.

"No!" he said sternly. "I don't have to. I can spot a con man a mile off."

"Look," I said, reaching for my billfold. "Here is the $50 bill. You take it, check it out, and when I leave the theater, give me $40 back, please. I want to go in and finish watching the movie." And I left him with the $50 bill.

When the movie was over and Arvella and I walked out, I couldn't find the usher. But I did see a man in a black coat who looked "official," so I said to him, "I'm looking for the head usher. He's got my $50 bill."

He looked at me with a frown and said, "Oh, so you're the guy with the $50 bill! We *don't take* $50 bills here."

"Well, I want my change, $40, or I want my $50 bill back," I persisted.

He reached into his pocket and with a hateful look on his face said, "Here is your blankety-blank $50 bill," and threw it on the floor.

I reached down, picked it up, and put it in my pocket. Do you know what? I was mad!

We walked out of the theater, and it was raining. We were three blocks from the hotel. Arvella said, "Bob, this is a great opportunity to practice what you preach. This situation is loaded with possibilities."

Frankly, I didn't feel like practicing what I preach. At that moment I did not even feel like preaching. I certainly didn't feel like looking for the possibilities. "Yeah? Like what?" I asked.

"Well, let's go back to the hotel, break the $50 bill, return to the theater, and pay them what we owe them. Then the usher will listen to a witness for Jesus Christ."

Suddenly, my resentment was plowed through. The possibility of sharing Christ's love overcame any anger I had felt. "O.K. Let's do it!"

We walked to the hotel, got the change for the $50 bill, and hurried back to the theater. We stood in the rain at the locked door and knocked persistently until the girl who ran the snack bar let us in. "Not you again?" she said.

"Please, may I see the head usher?" I asked.

Just then I saw the usher coming down the steps carrying his tuxedo. He was wearing his street clothes. "Oh, my God," he said, "not you again?"

"Yes, it is I again. I have come to pay you the $10 I owe you."

"Oh, you didn't have to do that," he said.

"Yes, I did." I said with a smile. "I owe it to you, and I want you to know that I am doing this for one reason: I claim to be a Christian, and it's very exciting trying to follow Christ in daily life. I want you—if you ever hear people say that 'Christians are all a bunch of hypocrites, that there's nothing to this Jesus Christ, and there's nothing to this God business'—I want you never to forget that there was once a man who came in dripping wet from a walk in the rain to pay his $10 because he was a Christian."

The usher's eyes were moist. He took the $10 and said, "Yes, sir. Thank you, sir. Good night, sir. I'm very sorry."

We smiled and shook hands.

To forgive doesn't mean that you erase the slate. Forgiveness means that you cut the road open, you dig under the wall, you move back and forth, and you love someone again! You don't just acquit the person. You see the possibilities and make them into something beautiful.

## Obstacle #4: Blinding Ourselves to the Positive Possiblities in Negative People

If you know someone who you cannot *like,* much less *love,* then remember: You are not alone!

As Frank Laubach, a great missionary statesman of the 20th century once said: "None of us loves perfectly, but Christ loves perfectly. No human being is totally perfect in love, but Christ is. Now, let's suppose you run into somebody you can't love. What do you do? Do you let yourself hate them? No. Do you tell yourself, 'I'm a Christian; therefore I'm going to love them.' *Yes!* Even though *it might not work,* don't surrender to your negative thoughts about the person. Of course not. You call in the expert, the authority—Jesus Christ."

Here's how Frank taught me to handle such a situation: "Put one hand up in the air, open your palm, and stretch out the other hand with a pointed finger aimed at your adversary. Now pray: 'Jesus Christ, You are perfect love. I am imperfect love. Because I'm imperfect I can't love that guy.' (Keep your finger pointed right at him! Aim at his heart!) 'Jesus Christ, will You please fall into the palm of my hand, flow down through my arm, through my elbow, through my shoulder, my chest, my heart, down my other arm, out of the end of my finger, and hit him, please? Hit him hard! Hit him gently! Hit him beautifully! You love him, Jesus! You can do it! I can't do it! But *You* can!'"

I explained Frank's method some years ago at the Crystal Cathedral. One man who heard me thought to himself, *Boy, Schuller's getting carried away again.* A week later he told me what had happened:

Monday morning I went to work remembering your sermon of the day before. The first person I saw coming into my store was the one salesman I could not stand. I saw him drive up to the curb and get out of his car. I was already in a bad mood. My secretary, who also goes to this church and had heard the same sermon, said to me, "Maybe you'd better try what Dr. Schuller talked about yesterday. Shoot him with prayers."

So before he got in I reached one hand in the air and with the other hand I pointed at him through the window. He was gawking at me as if I were nuts. (Later on he told me he thought I was going to change a light bulb!) But I was praying silently, *Jesus, I can't love that guy. But You can. Flow into my hand, through my arm, through my heart, and You love him, Jesus.*

The most amazing thing happened! I couldn't believe it. The man came up to me and said, "Good morning. How are you today?" I'd never heard him say it that way before. I looked at his face and saw that it had a countenance I'd never seen before. His eyes, that had always looked so nasty, now looked so sweet. It had worked! *I ended up loving this guy!*

A love that forgives casts out all kinds of negative forces. Christ's love can even tunnel under the obstacle of dislike. With Christ's love, it *is* possible to love—even the unloveable! It is possible to forgive—even the unforgivable!

Tragically, the daughter of Jim and Catherine Coyer was brutally murdered. The young man Michael, who killed Debbie, had grown up in the same small town, so he was no stranger. He was found guilty and sentenced to prison.

Five years after Debbie's death, Jim and Catherine moved to California and became members of the Crystal Cathedral. They met with me one afternoon and shared with me their story. Then Jim pulled out a letter and said, "Doctor Schuller, this was written from our heart."

I was so struck by the power of forgiveness and the immensity of love that was exhibited in this letter that I asked then if they would let me use it in a book. Generously, they agreed.

Dear Michael,

The words that follow are going to be the most difficult ones I have attempted to write. I have thought over them many times in the past, but never had the courage to put them on paper. Michael, I want you to know that I, with the help of our Lord Jesus Christ, do forgive you for the act which has so drastically changed our lives. The vacuum and the hurt still are very apparent and felt daily.

Debbie is still missed by many. Please understand that the act itself is the most abhorrent one possible, but because all of us are children of God, it is my Christian duty to forgive. Because I myself would want to be forgiven. Know that God loves you, and thus I love you as a brother in Christ.

> In Christ,
> James Coyer

No matter how obstinate the obstacle or how horrific the hurt—forgiveness is possible! It's really true, "I can do all things through Christ who strengthens me" (Phil. 4:13).

# THE ROAD OF LOVE:
# THE *HIGH*-WAY
# TO THE *GREAT*
# WAY!

*Real Love Believes the Best*

*"Love . . . believes all things."*
    *1 Corinthians 13:7*

**H**ave you ever been to the Dallas-Fort Worth airport? The roads that loop around the enormous, sprawling complex resemble high-speed highways. They are miles long and very confusing. On one of these loops, about two miles from the terminal I needed, all of a sudden, the rental car I was riding in stopped. So did my heart, for when I looked at my watch, I saw that in sixteen minutes our plane would take off. I couldn't let that happen, so I turned to my associate, Fred Southard, and said, "This is ridiculous. We *cannot* be stopped by a dead car! Come on!"

I opened the door, stuck my hand out, and put my thumb up like a hitchhiker. Amazingly, the first car that came by stopped. "Quick Fred, get in!" I said.

Fred grabbed the suitcases, I grabbed my briefcase and the tuxedos, and both of us ran across six lanes of traffic, carefully dodging the other cars and buses.

I am sure it must have been an interesting sight to see us galloping across the Dallas-Fort Worth highway. I opened the front door of the waiting car. The front seat was occupied by an empty child restraint seat. The back seat was covered with boxes, toys, and other items, but Fred squeezed in. I handed the luggage to him. The lovely young woman who was driving didn't even look to see who we were. She had impetuously, impulsively decided to help someone in trouble.

Thinking she might be frightened, seeing that two men were

445

climbing into her car, I said, "You can trust me. My name is Dr. Schuller."

She looked at me for the first time. Her eyes got wide! "Robert Schuller? You can't be!" she said. "You can't be Dr. Robert Schuller. Not hitchhiking on the Dallas-Fort Worth freeway! You can't be! I don't believe it! *Nobody* will believe it!"

"I am Robert Schuller!"

"If I tell anybody that I picked you up hitchhiking on the freeway today, nobody will believe it," she said, shaking her head.

"Oh, yes, they will. What's your name?"

"Joanne."

By then, she was staring at me and starting to run onto the curb.

"Just watch the road!" I said. Then I opened my briefcase and pulled out my newest book. Before handing it to her, I wrote, "To Joanne, I love to give people a lift myself."

I do love to give people a lift! I love to lift them to *faith* even when there's no apparent reason to believe. I love to lift them with *hope* even when others say, "Give up!" I love to lift them in *love* when they've been hurt.

It's all summed up in the verse in 1 Corinthians 13: "Love . . . believes all things" (v. 7). It's the "faith-hope-love" way to live: The *high*-way of life! And believe me, it's the way to go when you get hurt, when the bottom falls out of a marriage, when you are tempted to turn back and quit on love.

"I was the last to know," a woman said to me. "I feel like such a fool! Everybody knew he was betraying me—except me! I believed him! But that's the last time! I'm never going to believe anyone again!"

She wiped her eyes, squared her shoulders, and looked at me. I saw a hint of a cold, protective gleam in her eye. That scared me, for if she allowed a defensive shell to grow around her heart, she would certainly be doomed to a lonely life.

"You say you were a fool for believing in your husband," I

said, "but I say you made the smart choice, the choice to believe. As for me, I would much rather choose to err on the side of love than on the side of suspicion. I would far rather err on the side of faith than doubt, on the side of grace than retaliation. It's better to have loved and lost than never to have loved at all."

Suddenly, the cold gleam melted. A smile softened her hardened face. "Really?" she said. "I never thought of it that way. I guess I'm O.K. I guess I'm not a fool after all."

I never heard what the outcome for her marriage was, but one thing I am certain of—she chose to believe in love again! When she was tempted to turn her back on love, she chose to take the *high*-way, the way of love—regardless of the outcome.

The *high*-way of love is a love that believes the best!

## LOVE BELIEVES THE BEST!

When it comes to other people or any situation in life, we can assume the worst or we can assume the best. Most of us prefer to live safely and suspiciously. We assume the worst so we will be prepared when we hit rock bottom. We pride ourselves on being aware, alert to people who could take advantage of us:

- "Nobody's gonna pull the wool over my eyes!"
- "I'm nobody's fool!"

And so we live life looking over our shoulders, never really trusting anyone.

First Corinthians, however, recommends an alternate route. St. Paul suggests a love that believes the best about those we love; it is a love that jumps to *positive* conclusions. This is faith in others, and faith in love lifts us to the *high*-way of life!

Love without faith is meaningless. It is as flat, dead, and lifeless as a fallen soufflé—the opposite of a perfect soufflé—the delicate baked custard that rises like a golden cloud above its baking dish. I must admit—I have a "thing" about soufflés!

Some years ago in a spiritual experience, God said to me, "Schuller, in order to keep your body healthy, you have to run every day." And then He told me to eat right. For me that meant no cakes, pies, ice cream, breads, or butter. The only desserts my conscience would allow me were fresh fruits and baked soufflés. I reasoned that soufflés were so rare I wouldn't have to worry.

Soon after I went into a restaurant and ordered a soufflé, but they had never heard of one! I found out that only French restaurants serve them, so I immediately started picking out French restaurants. But I found that many of them did not bake soufflés, either. "God has a fantastic sense of humor," I laughed. "That's why he lets me eat soufflés—I can't find them!"

Recently, when Mrs. Schuller and I were returning from a ministry in Australia, we stopped over in Hawaii, and I began to prepare my Sunday sermon. I had what I thought was an inspiration for a great illustration in the message I was writing. We would find a French restaurant where I could order a soufflé. I planned to create a sermon illustration around this soufflé!

Arvella and I arrived at the restaurant and were seated at a quiet corner table. The waiter handed us the menu. A few minutes later he returned and asked if we were ready to order. Now, if you are going to order a baked soufflé, you have to order at the beginning of the meal because it does take a while to bake. I said to the waiter, "We'll begin by ordering our dessert. We will both have a soufflé."

"Oh," he exclaimed, "but we don't bake soufflés!"

Stunned, I said, "Of course you bake soufflés! I'm told this restaurant makes the best soufflés in Hawaii!"

"I'm sorry," he replied. "We don't bake soufflés."

"Please check," I begged. So he left and came back after a few minutes. "I'm sorry. We no longer bake soufflés."

"That can't be," I lamented. "This is very important to me. Please go back to the chef and ask him if he'll make us a soufflé. I know he can."

By this time the waiter was a little flushed, but he left again only to return and say, "I'm awfully sorry, but the kitchen is not making soufflés today."

I grasped the medal I wear around my neck and began to read aloud: *When faced with a mountain, I will not quit. I will keep on striving* . . . . May I talk to the *maitre d'*?" I pleaded.

"Yes," he answered and left.

The maitre d' was at our table immediately. He was a handsome, charming, debonair gentleman. "Sir," I explained, "we've come a long way just for a soufflé."

"I'm sorry, sir," he replied. "We can't make a soufflé for you."

I tried a different approach. "Look, I am desperately in need of anecdotal material. You see, I write books and talk on television. And I came to your restaurant specifically to get an illustration—all about a soufflé. Please, may I talk to the executive chef?"

The maitre d' threw up his hands. "Just a moment!"

Pretty soon, into the crowded dining room strode the executive chef, clad in a tall white hat and apron. He came right up to our table and stopped short. Suddenly his mouth dropped open, his eyes widened with the "I-know-you-I-see-you-on-television" look, and he said, "*Father* Schuller! What a surprise! I never miss you on television! So you're the one who's been asking for the soufflé!"

"Yes," I answered, "like only you can bake it!"

"I'll bake you a good soufflé!" he said.

We selected our entrée, and as we were finishing our meal, the chef himself entered and paraded through the crowded, gorgeous dining room, holding high a huge platter draped with beautiful napkins, covering two masterful soufflés! Golden toasted brown! They rose high out of their individual ceramic dishes like small, steaming, feather-light, upside-down angel food cakes! And to top it all the maitre d' announced: "Compliments of the house!"

There is no dessert quite like a baked soufflé! A good soufflé is like a bud that has opened to full bloom! Like a symphony with all instruments in a final massive chord of glorious harmony! Like seeing a person come out and blossom under the magic spell of *love*! Yes, "love is the soufflé of life!" *Faith gives love its life and life its lift!* I made these points in my next sermon.

There is nothing that can match a person whose life has risen to beautiful new possibilities for joy and happiness because of loving faith.

As a child I used to sing the old hymn, "Love lifted me . . . when nothing else could help, Love lifted me!" When you believe the best about others, when trust, admiration, and esteem are at the core of your attitudes, then miracles will happen!

## LOVE THAT BELIEVES THE BEST— REMOVES THE WEIGHT OF DOUBT!

What is it that weighs us down?

- Suspicion!
- Doubt!
- Fear!

These negative defenses hold us down and keep us from experiencing full, rich, rewarding love relationships. They hang over us like a cloud, blocking out the possibilities of love, keeping us from being happy, from loving, from being loved!

"Perfect love casts out fear." We've all heard this Scripture verse. But what in the world did the writer, John, mean when he said, "*Perfect* love"?

Well, I contend that none of us is perfect. But when we make a mistake, when we fail, the best way to correct the situation is to *believe* that life is not over and *have the faith* to try again.

In the same way "perfect" love is a love that has faith at its foundation. This faith can cut through the chain of fear that imprisons our heart. It can clear away the clouds of doubt and let the love shine through.

On one Valentine's Day I married a lovely young couple at a hotel in a distant city. After the wedding the four of us who had participated in the ceremony sat down with the couple in the hotel restaurant and shared the wedding cake with them. The young bride then opened her purse and said, "Dr. Schuller, I have a special gift for your wife. It's my way of saying thank you for marrying us."

Into my hand she placed a little jade elephant about an inch and a half long from the tip of its trunk to the tip of its tail. Around the two front feet of the little charm was a tiny golden chain.

"This little elephant symbolizes what my faith has done for me," she said. "I have been liberated from the terrible thoughts I had about myself and now see the beautiful possibilities God has for me and those I love."

She went on to remind me of how mighty elephants are controlled. Once a wild elephant is captured, the captors tie the end of a long chain around the elephant's foot. The other end is tied to a huge banyan tree.

The great elephant will pull with all its strength, but it can't budge the banyan tree. Finally, after struggling for days and weeks, when the elephant barely lifts its ponderous foot and feels the chain tightening, it drops its foot heavily to the ground because it knows that further struggle is useless. The elephant has surrendered to the chain.

At this point the trainers know the elephant is really trapped forever. For when they take the elephant and chain it to a little iron stake by a circus tent, the elephant never attempts to pull away because it still thinks it is chained to a banyan tree.

You are not chained to a banyan tree! Your problem is not insurmountable! You can repair and redeem a broken relationship if you will dare to cut through the chains of fear.

Face it—life will be dominated either by love and trust or by suspicion and doubt.

So, take a leap of faith. Dare to believe in others. Be a lifter, and you will find to your amazement that you, in turn, are lifted. You always feel great when you have helped someone. Love puts back what you give out. A believing love takes away the weights of doubt and gives you wings of faith.

## LOVE THAT BELIEVES THE BEST—GIVES LIFTING POWER UNDER THE WINGS OF FAITH!

When you take the *high*-way of faith, hope, and love, suddenly you are lifted above the problems, fears, and doubts. You have discovered a new perspective! You can see possibilities! You can imagine new solutions! You can anticipate happy endings! You become a possibility thinker and begin to practice the uplifting power of possibilitizing!

*Doubt Blinds You To Possibilities!*
*But Faith Opens Your Eyes To New Opportunities!*

Possibilitizing is *imagining,* it is *visualizing,* it is *praying,* it is *multiplying* mentally, it is *overcoming,* it is *anticipating*—in spite of the problems you encounter.

## Possibilitizing Is Imagining

Positive love will overpower the negative thoughts, so you will be able to possibilitize your way out of a tough situation by imagining that things are going to get better.

While lecturing in New York, I placed a telephone call to a young woman who told me how helpful the "Hour of Power" ministry had been to her. She told me, "A year ago I had major surgery, and it didn't look like I'd live. Your positive messages reinforced what my doctor was telling me. When I asked him, 'Do you think I'll ever walk again?' he looked at me intently and said, 'That's the wrong question. The right question is not do *I* think you'll ever walk again, but do *you* think you'll ever walk again?'"

Problems really have become serious when they distract your eyes from the goal. Constantly imagine that things are going to get better for you and the ones you love. Situations will not stay the way they are. If you imagine they're going to get better, you will be in a frame of mind to contribute to their getting better.

## Possibilitizing Is Visualizing

You must see the victory beyond the battle of the hour, see the ultimate reward instead of the pain, see the crown instead of the cross.

For years swimmer Steve Genter from Lakewood, California, trained for the Munich Olympics. He wanted to win so badly the 200-meter freestyle race. You may know what happened. One week before the big event his lung collapsed. The doctors said that would wipe him out, but Steve didn't agree. He looked beyond the moment. At his insistence surgeons cut his chest open, repaired the lung, and stitched him back up. When names were called for the event in Munich, Steve Genter stepped forward, his chest taped and stitched!

The starter fired his gun and Steve dove in. He was in the 100-meter turn of the 200-meter freestyle, in a neck-to-neck race with Mark Spitz, when he hit the pool wall and ripped his stitches open! This hurt his timing, but Steve kept swimming and finished seconds behind Mark Spitz! Steve came home from the Olympics with a gold medal, a silver medal, and a bronze medal!

I've studied human beings and I can tell you that when they look beyond the obstacle to the reward, they'll forget the pain.

Again and again in your life you're going to have problems, setbacks, rejections, disappointments, discouragements, and prayers that seemingly are not answered. God may seem to be deaf. You may even think that prayer doesn't work and that God isn't real and Christ isn't real. You'll run into a stone wall. You'll hit bottom.

Keep on possibilitizing! Keep believing!

## Possibilitizing Is Praying

"Play it down and pray it up." The sentence came into my mind, strong and forcefully—from God, I truly believe. I was flying from Korea to Sioux City, Iowa, to my daughter Carol's bedside, where I would have to face her for the first time since she had lost her leg. Facing me, sitting on the small fold-down seat, was a beautiful stewardess, elegant in her prim and polite uniform.

The seatbelt sign was still on. Her fingers were interlocked, her hands folded, resting on her knees. Suddenly, I noticed her *two* ankles, her *two* legs. Then I noticed the diamond ring and a wedding band on her left hand.

A horrible, negative thought came into my mind: *Would my*

*daughter, with a permanently severed limb, ever wear a diamond ring? A wedding band?*

The tears overwhelmed me. Then came God's message loud and clear, "Play it down and pray it up!" I believed He was telling me, "I love your daughter; I have a plan for her life; I will never stop loving her."

I cannot tell you how often since then with every passing year I prayed for God to give Carol a love that would more than compensate for whatever small part of her life she lost in that surgical room in Sioux City, Iowa.

Eight years later, those prayers were answered when in her wedding gown she walked elegantly down the aisle of the Crystal Cathedral to become the wife of a tall, handsome, kind man—Tim Milner—on March 29, 1986.

## Possibilitizing Is Multiplying the Results

Are you tempted to quit because you don't see the returns and the results? Sunday school teachers have quit at the Crystal Cathedral because they didn't think they were doing a good job; they couldn't see the results. Ministers have given up the ministry because they thought they were failing. I know salesmen who gave up because they thought they were bombing out. If only these people had kept on possibilitizing and mentally multiplying the possible results!

I am inspired by the story of George Smith, the Moravian, who from his early years wanted to be a missionary. He finally finished his preparation and traveled to Africa but was there just a few months before being expelled. He left behind only one convert, an old woman. He came back home and soon died, still a young man, literally on his knees praying for Africa, for the people he had come to love. Think of it! All of his life he prepared—he went—he spent only a few months—he came home and died. *But one hundred years later, that ministry to one old woman had blossomed into thirteen thousand happy Christians!*

Possibilitizing is multiplying what's going to happen!

## Possibilitizing Is Overcoming While You're Undergoing

Colleen Johnson, my wife's executive secretary, knows what it is to overcome when you feel overwhelmed. Colleen is originally from Philadelphia. She married when she was only seventeen years old. She and her husband had a little girl when Colleen was nineteen. When her little girl was only two, Colleen's husband died suddenly at the age of twenty-five.

Then she found out that she was pregnant—a widow with a two-year-old and another child on the way. Colleen turned to her older brother, a seminary student, for support. They became close, but nine months later he had a heart attack and died. Colleen told me later, "At that point I realized the Lord was the one I must hold on to—He was the faithful one."

The years passed, and Colleen was married again to a great guy, Jimmy Johnson. He was a Christian and loved children. Together they left Philadelphia and came to California. A year later they started attending and then joined our drive-in church. They had a son, Mark. Then, two years later Glenn was born. He weighed only three pounds and had several problems. The most severe was that he had no rectal opening, a condition which required surgery the day he was born. Then Colleen and Jimmy learned their son was mentally retarded. But he lived through the surgery and became a very special boy. He had a great spirit. He loved everyone and was always ready to hug and kiss.

Then Jimmy was diagnosed with cancer. In 1977 he went through two surgeries and the cancer went into remission. But in 1979 the disease flared again in the liver. Jimmy died just before Christmas of that year.

We all shared Colleen's loss. Jimmy's smile had been infectious, and his face had lit up the choir loft every Sunday.

With the help of her older children, Colleen carried on, working full time and caring for Glenn. Even though his vocabulary was limited, his darling little face lighted up like no other! But Glenn missed his daddy terribly. He asked repeatedly, "Has Daddy gone to the doctor? The hospital? When is he coming home?" It was not easy for him to understand what it meant when they told him his daddy was gone. Colleen once found Glenn in her bedroom, sitting on the bed, looking at a picture of Jimmy that Glenn had taken on Thanksgiving Day. The picture, amazingly, had turned out nicely framed and focused—one of Colleen's favorites of her husband. Glenn talked and sang to the picture for almost fifteen minutes. This incident apparently settled his mind concerning Jimmy, for he no longer questioned his father's absence.

Not long after that, Glenn joined his daddy in heaven.

Somehow, in spite of all the difficulties that Colleen faced, she remained a woman of faith. She never stopped smiling. She never stopped working. She never stopped loving.

When I asked her how she did it, how she could keep on smiling, she said, "That's the way I feel. I know that everything is going to work out. I have Someone that I can hold onto. I always have, and I always will. And I'll always smile."

## Possibilitizing Is Anticipating a Happy Ending

Are you tempted to turn back? Well, don't give up! *Don't quit when you're so close.* It would be a tragedy to come to the end of your life and have somebody say about you, "It's a pity he missed it. He quit just before he would have made it!"

We only have one chance to live this life. It would be a shame to throw away love and happiness because we're afraid that someday we'll lose the ones we love—afraid we'll get to the last page and discover a tragic ending.

What is a happy ending? Is it:

- "They lived happily ever after"?
- "They rode off into the sunset, two hearts intertwined forevermore"?

Listen to the following love story. Read it all the way to the end. Although at first you may not agree, it has, in my opinion, the happiest ending of all!

It happened years ago in a Midwest town. A wealthy man died leaving a rich and beautiful widow to mourn his passing. The pastor of their prestigious church was faithful in visiting the home to comfort the widow. He called the first week, then the second, and each week thereafter—month after month. His attention was deemed "unusual" by a few alert ladies of the town. Someone noticed that the shades were always drawn when he called at her home.

Rumors began to fly. Eyebrows were raised. A ruling elder was directed to look into the matter. The pastor's rounds were to be quietly and carefully monitored. On a given day he was seen driving up to her home. The elder was alerted by telephone. He headed for the pastor's study preparing to confront the reverend who, he was certain, would go from the widow's house to his private study in the church before he would go on to his own home and his wife in the manse.

An hour and more passed before the pastor opened his door and saw waiting for him a sober, serious, and suspicious elder. Even as the pastor entered he reeked with the rich fragrance of perfume!

The conversation was discreet but the elder's point was obvious—"You must stop calling on the widow, Reverend."

The pastor protested his innocence. Two weeks later the

Believe the best
about people!
And if
you're wrong,
you've only
made a
mistake
on
the side of love.

truth came out. The widow died! Now the pastor could tell the story. The woman had discovered that she had cancer just as her husband died. "When I'll need him most, on my road ahead, he will not be there! Pastor, help me!" she had pleaded. "Do not let me walk alone. And please, keep my illness a secret."

So each week the pastor had called—to pray, to comfort, to befriend.

"The light, it hurts my eyes, please draw the drapes." This had been her frequent request.

The last few weeks she had worn heavy perfumes to cover the unpleasant fragrances of medicines and the odors of her sickness.

The town gossips had believed the worst and were wrong! The pastor's wife always had believed the best about her husband and her best friend, the widow, and was right!

Love believes the *best*! So, when you are tempted to give up on love, to believe the worst, and to give in to suspicions, take the *high*-way to God's way of living! Have faith! Believe! You'll never be sorry you did!

# THE ROAD OF LOVE:
## MAKE IT *YOUR*-WAY

*Love! or Loneliness? You Decide!*

*"Love never ends."*
  *1 Corinthians 13:8*


**Now:**          It is time for *you* to take *action!*

**Recipe:**       At best, this book is only a *recipe.* But a recipe never fed anyone!

**Blueprint:**    Hopefully, this book is a *blueprint* for reconstructing human behavior and human belief systems. But no blueprint ever built anything!

**Road Map:**     Surely, this book is a *road map*—but a road map never took anyone anywhere.

Love, after all, is a choice. But consider the alternative: Loneliness!

## LONELINESS?

Many of you know her as "Dear Abby." Abigail Van Buren said to me privately one day, "Dr. Schuller, loneliness, the need for love, is the number one problem that faces people." We both agreed that the deepest of all needs is to be accepted, understood, yes, loved! The problem has not gone away. The need has not lessened. We all still long for love. Many of us suffer from the disease of loneliness.

Loneliness is caused by a battle between two persons who live

465

inside of you. One person reaches out for love, like a little child in a candy store grasping for candy. This person desperately, anxiously, almost hysterically, longs for love and understanding. But another self, like a father holding back a child's hand in a candy store, says to your "grabbing" person, "Look out! Don't grab so fast. You might get hurt. You might be rejected. You don't want to love and be rejected, do you? Love is a risky business. To love is to be vulnerable. To be vulnerable is to be accountable. To be accountable is to run the risk of being rejected. Rejection is the risk of all risks: You might end up hating yourself because others don't love you!"

And so the lonely person is the one who ultimately listens to fear instead of to faith. The lonely person is the one who chooses the safe road, who listens finally to the self that says, "Be careful. Don't take any chances. Don't make any commitments. Don't get involved. You might get rejected. You might get hurt."

If that's the voice you listen to, if that's the road you choose, you will have your freedom intact, but the *price* you will pay for your freedom from involvement is *loneliness*.

One reason our society is so infected with loneliness is that the spirit of selfish freedom is so widespread. We don't want to risk losing our freedom by running the risks of making long-term commitments. So there are those who say, "What's the use of marriage? It's only a piece of paper. Live together; love together. Then if the relationship cools, you can split, you can go your way, and nobody will get hurt."

The fallacy of such a notion is that the man loves the woman only as long as she's young. Then when the wrinkles come, he deserts her. And when she's old, nobody cares.

We have a lot of lonely people today because unwillingness to make permanent commitments results in temporary interpersonal relationships. When people are hurt, they react like infantile children who pack up their marbles, go their way, and find themselves free once again. Those people will wake up one day and discover that nobody knows them and nobody cares!

Unless you are willing to surrender some freedom to make permanent commitments, you must be prepared to pay the price—*loneliness!*

Love dissolves loneliness, but love has a price tag, too. The price tag of love is commitment to continuity. As I said to a young couple the other day, "The one thing that makes marriage more important than a piece of paper, a license, is the commitment. Marriage says, 'I love you today and always will love you, even when our skin is wrinkled, even when the muscles sag, even when the hair thins.' Believe it or not, that's when you're going to need love more than ever."

## WHERE ARE YOU?

If you've been afraid to make a commitment to love, if you've found that you are lost on the road of loneliness, if you would say to me if we met, "Dr. Schuller, I'm lost! I'm lonely! I want to get off!"—the first thing I'd ask you is, "Where are you? The road of loneliness has several paths. Before I can guide you or give you directions, I have to know where you're coming from."

Consider then the paths of loneliness; on which one are you?

### The Loneliness of Sinking

The threat of failure, of course, brings its own type of loneliness! What is greater? The loneliness of success or the loneliness of failure? When things aren't going right and you're facing bankruptcy or your marriage is falling apart, you have that sinking, failing feeling; you are lonely because you don't want to share your failure with others. Nobody wants to hear a loser cry. Yet, precisely, here is where we need help and healing for our hurt.

*Are you lonely in your sinking?* Reach out! Open up! Be honest! After all, as I have said in *The Be Happy Attitudes*, "If you're too proud or too afraid to let people know you're hurting, don't be surprised if no one seems to care."

## The Loneliness of Success

I don't know which is the worse. I have known both the loneliness of sinking and the loneliness of succeeding. There were two years in my ministry when my will to die was stronger than my will to live. I had dreams of a church with fountains and grounds where people could worship in their cars or inside the sanctuary. I had a vision for a tower with twenty-four-hour telephone counseling, a staff of great ministers, and a thousand volunteers who would do Christ's work. God had given me the whole dream. But the problems were momentous. Many times I thought the whole dream would dissolve. I was sure I was failing, but I couldn't get up in front of my church on Sunday morning and share my failures with my people. They had come for a lift themselves, and it was my responsibility to lift them, not lean on them. I felt the loneliness of *sinking*.

But I've also known the loneliness of *succeeding*. Think of it—when you succeed, who wants to listen to you? With whom can you share your victories? Most people will think you're boasting! So, in the wake of triumph, when everyone thinks you are on top and a great success, you may find yourself desperately lonely.

*Are you lonely in your success?*

Maybe you need to stop and remember that your success, if it is in your career, is nice—but it's really not all that wonderful in and by itself! After all, what is *real* success?

*Real* success is helping others, loving others, and being loved by them. *Real* success is building a family; it is sharing a smile or a meal; it is lending a hand. It is being interested in those around you who are real successes, too!

## The Loneliness of Struggling

This path of loneliness is characterized by uncertainty; you don't know if you're sinking or succeeding. You do know you're struggling! You don't want to publicly admit you have problems or to show your weaknesses. You are reticent to display imperfection, so you strive to keep up a strong front. You don't want to expose the fact that you've got problems.

*Are you lonely in your struggling?*

First of all, it's important to acknowledge that every person in this world has problems. As Dr. Norman Vincent Peale once said in the Crystal Cathedral, "Everybody has problems. The only person who doesn't have problems is dead. Anybody who is really alive has problems."

I would add—anyone who is alive is someone who dares to get involved. A person who is getting involved is taking risks. And a person who is taking risks *will* have struggles! But isn't it better to be struggling and alive—a full-fledged member of the human race—than to be "dead" with boredom and loneliness?

## The Loneliness of Striving

God gives you a dream. Should you tell people? There is the fear of what people will say, especially if you think big. Will they laugh and say, "Who do you think you are that you can be that person? Who do you think you are that you could amount to something? Boy, has something gone to your head! Wow, are you an egomaniac!" The fear of such ridicule drives many of us to strive *alone* to reach our dreams.

There is occasionally a legitimate fear that your ideas and your plans might be stolen by someone else. You may have to be protective of your concepts until you have an option, a copyright, or a patent. But isn't there usually at least one person you can trust who would love to hear your dream?

*Are you lonely in your striving?*

Perhaps you need to be reminded of the efforts of Dr. Howard House and Dr. William House. As I said in chapter seven, the House brothers developed the cochlear ear implant, which has been revolutionary in restoring hearing to children. Both of these men have impressed me with their willingness to share what they've learned with the medical community at large. They have not sought government aid for their work. It has all been private enterprise because their primary aim is to make their inventions and discoveries available to help as many people as possible. The Institute has no patents. I can assure you these men are far from lonely!

## The Loneliness of Searching

Who has not known the loneliness of searching between two choices, searching for the best alternatives, searching for the right decision. In the final analysis, you *alone* make most of the decisions in your life. No one can make them for you. This part of your life will always be separate from the part of your life that interacts with others.

Most of us live in interpersonal relationships, acting and reacting to the challenges, instincts, and impulses of the people around us.

There is another part of your life that you live totally alone. You were born alone. Even if you are a twin, both of you were born individually—alone. When you learned to walk, you learned to walk alone. When you learned to talk, you learned to talk alone. True, there were those who guided, supported, and sustained you. But *you* did it—*alone*!

When you must make the great decisions—your career or profession or whom you will marry—you make them alone! Your father doesn't make them, your mother doesn't make them, your friends don't make them. You do! Others may advise and attempt to persuade or dissuade, but in the final analysis, you must search through the discussions, arguments, reasons, pros and cons and decide!

*Are you lonely in your searching?*

Why not consider meeting my good friend, Jesus Christ. He will walk with you in your times of *searching* . . . as well as in your time of separation.

## The Loneliness of Separation

For all of us there comes the time when we will die. That is another moment that you will go through alone. There will be those who will stand by you. They will be supportive and helpful, but you will die alone. All alone. *Unless* you have a very special friend.

A few years ago, I sat at the bedside of a lovely woman. She had cancer and had taken every form of chemotherapy and radiation treatment. But after all this, the doctors told her that she only had a short time to live.

I sat by her side, held her hand, and repeated to her the words my mother found so helpful on her deathbed:

"Fear not, for I have redeemed you;
I have called you by your name;
You are Mine.
When you pass through the waters,
I will be with you;
And through the rivers, they shall not overflow you.
When you walk through the fire, you shall not be burned,
Nor shall the flame scorch you.
For I am the Lord, your God." (Isa. 43:1–3)

*Are you lonely in your separations?*

The river, the fire, the flame of separations—of losing loved ones, whether through death or divorce—need not consume you. You will not be overwhelmed if you have the Lord, your God, to *lead* you through! To *walk* you through! To *carry* you through!

### The Loneliness of Sinning

No failure is more depressing than moral failure! It defies calculation—how much loneliness and alienation is related to secret sins harbored in human hearts. Who dares to expose their hidden shortcomings? Who is not naturally inclined to cover up and conceal their private iniquities? What stress does this loneliness place on our emotional system? And what is our salvation? Is there a safe release? Can confession liberate us from the bondage of guilty isolation?

"No" and "Yes." "No"—confession is destructive if it exposes our worst self to persons who could use it against us. "Yes"—if confession is made humbly, honestly, and hopefully to someone who loves us totally, trustfully! That Person to me is Jesus Christ! That's why I call Him Savior!

## LOVE OR LONELINESS? YOU DECIDE!

Wherever you are on the road of life, even if it be on any of the paths of loneliness, you can choose, you can decide where it is you want to go. Your final destination is in your hands. So stop! Quit blaming your loneliness on:

- Parents
- Ex-spouses
- Hurtful, deceitful lovers
- Critical teachers
- Harsh employers
- Two-faced "friends"
- Cold, isolated society

Instead, start! Begin to believe in *love!*

It's true that loneliness permeates our world. But so does love! We only need to choose which we want to look for, which we want to have.

You can choose to be lonely, or you can choose to love and be loved! It all starts when you choose to accept God's love for you.

## *ANYBODY* CAN FIND LOVE!

The late Corrie ten Boom inspired me with a thought years ago: "No problem is too big for God's power; no person is too small for God's love."

One day, when two of our girls were quite young, Mrs. Schuller and I took them to our cabin high in the California mountains. Gretchen, our youngest, came to me one morning and said, "Daddy, in our Bible school our teacher said that if you take a pine cone and put peanut butter on it and you sprinkle it with birdseed, the birdseed will stick to the pine cone, and you can hang it in a tree for the birds to eat."

"You don't have to go through all that," I answered. "We've got some birdseed here in the cabin. Just put it out on the deck. The birds will come and eat it."

She did as I suggested. She sprinkled the birdseed along the railing of the deck, and sure enough, the blue jays came and gobbled it up. Next the squirrels came, chased the blue jays away, and finished every crumb of birdseed.

"I still think I should put the seed on a pine cone with peanut butter," my daughter persisted. It sounded like a nice project, so I agreed to help her.

We went for a walk in the woods, and under one of the great old trees in the forest we found some pine cones and took them home. I tied a rope to the very top prong of the cone so that I could hang it from a branch of a tree. Then we got out the peanut butter. It was a mess trying to spread peanut butter all over the wood scales of the pine cone.

Then Gretchen sprinkled the birdseed on, and sure enough, it all stuck to the peanut butter. We took it outside and hung it on a branch, right on the tip so it hung down, drooping on the branch like a too-heavy ornament on the tender tip of a Christmas tree.

"Gretchen," I said, "you should tie it in the middle of the branch, where the branch is stronger."

"No," she said, "I'll tie it here at the end."

So she left it hanging there on the end. Pretty soon the blue jays came, but they just flew around and didn't dare to land on the pine cone, because it was weaving back and forth and looked too unsteady for them. They didn't dare to sit on it. They stood on the branch, but when they couldn't begin to get at the cone beneath them, they flew away in disgust.

Pretty soon the squirrels came. They had smelled the peanut butter. Up the tree they went and onto the branch. I can still see one of them running down the branch until it started to bend, then backing off fearfully and running back down the trunk of the tree. What a lesson in frustration! He went back up another branch, trying to approach it from another direction, but he never got within two feet. Finally, he ran off.

"Gretchen," I said, "it's a sublime failure. They can't eat it." And then something wonderful happened. All the *little* birds started coming. They came and literally walked down the rope and nibbled the food from the top so they wouldn't get their feet dirty with the peanut butter. It was an amazing sight! Then more little birds came. One very resourceful, "possiblity thinking" winged creature grabbed the bottom of the pine cone where there was no peanut butter with his feet and ate from the bottom. So, the *little* birds had their feast. And the big blue jay and the squirrel were unable to take the food from the little ones.

This illustrates the good news I have for you! As far as the food for your heart is concerned, God has set things up in such a way that the lonely people can always get what they need, the love their hearts hunger for! *Anybody* can find the road of love.

Love is not a chance! It is a choice!

Love is not luck! It is an election!

Love is not a result of fate! It is a result of faith!

Love is not a result of luck, environment, or genetics. It is the result of a decision! You mistakenly may have assumed that the people who find someone to love them are the lucky ones. Or they're the ones who were raised in a family environment that stimulated love. Or they are the people who were born with loveable personalities.

This is a myth! Don't let it keep you from finding love for yourself, for the truth is that love *is* a choice! It is an act of faith. It is a cognitive decision to believe in others, to believe in yourself, and to believe in the love of God.

## ACCEPT THE LOVE THAT ENDS ALL LONELINESS!

You can travel around the world and meet Christians in every country. And when you talk to them about their faith, the conversation will quickly focus on the life and person of someone named Jesus of Nazareth, who lived two thousand years ago. When you ask them what Jesus means to them, you will get many different answers because Christians have different concepts of Jesus Christ. But if you will listen at a deeper level, you will conclude that they all agree about one thing: *Christ is Love!*

A remarkable unique quality of Christ's life was that He was *Love Incarnate.* And that makes the difference! No other religious leader claimed to have the authority from heaven to forgive sins. And the scars in His palms give him enormous credibility! He had love! He lived it! He died because of love! And He rose again in love! This quality of love makes all the difference in the world! And I want to help you to see that if you choose to put Christ's love at the central core of your life, a rising power within you will change everything!

If you "by *chance*" encounter love, you might question if it is real love. But if you encounter somebody who has *chosen* to love, then you will have found *real* love, a love that ends all loneliness!

It matters not who you are, where you are coming from, or where you have been. If you are a mother, a business person, a teacher, a lawyer, a criminal, or a prostitute, you can find real love! It doesn't require wealth, or education, or connections with powerful people. It doesn't require talent, intelligence, or even beauty to be loved. It only requires choosing to believe and accept the fact that God loves you—just the way you are!

I met her in Hawaii. I shall never forget her, for she became for me the symbol of hurt, despair, and loneliness. I was in Hawaii resting and being renewed after the busy Christmas season at the Crystal Cathedral. I love to walk a particular beautiful, unpopulated beach there. The white sand is dotted with graceful coconut palms; the tropical breezes caress my skin with their balmy warmth. The sun's hot rays seem to draw all tension from me. Time on this beach is very therapeutic for me.

One day while walking this beach, I carried with me a copy of a previous book of mine, *Tough Minded Faith for Tender Hearted People,* and a notebook in which I could jot down my thoughts. I walked to the rocks, as I often do, for I am seldom recognized or interrupted there.

I enjoyed a wonderful time of meditation, reading, and writing, and then I waded through the shallow, gently rippling surf on my way back to my room. Two women were wading in the water about twenty feet away.

Suddenly, one of them called out, "Are you on television?" I said that I was.

Coming closer, she asked, "Are you an actor?"

"No. I give speeches."

"What do you speak about?"

I motioned to the books I was holding in my hand and said, "I speak about the same stuff as I write about. I write books."

"What are you writing a book about?"

I noticed that this young woman had a tattoo on her shoulder and her eyes were empty. "I'm writing a book entitled, *Be Happy—You Are Loved!*"

"What does that mean?"

"That means that happiness in life is not based on the money you earn or the clothes you wear; it matters not where you live or what you do; it matters not what happens to you. Even if you've experienced tragedy or triumph, you *can* be happy for one reason—you are loved!"

She gave me a skeptical look at that point, so I quickly continued, "Every person has value. Every person has worth."

She looked down at the sand. I could tell she didn't believe a word I was saying. Suddenly, I had an idea; I think it was heaven-sent. I said, "Say, you know I often interview people for my books. Could I interview you?"

"Well, I guess that would be O.K."

I started off with what I thought was a safe question: "What do you do?"

She just looked at me. When she failed to answer my question, I asked, "Don't you have a job? Don't tell me you are retired at such a young age?"

"No," she replied, "but what I do, people don't normally talk about."

"What could that be?"

She hesitated and then said, "Do you really write books?"

I turned the copy of my book over and showed her my picture on the back.

She didn't bat an eye. She said, "I am a prostitute."

Whatever answer I had expected—it surely wasn't this.

She hastened to add, "I am not a street girl. I am a call girl."

I decided to continue the interview for I truly wondered how a girl could end up like this. Here is the story as she told it to me:

She was twenty-eight years old, white, born and raised in Atlanta, Georgia. There she got her RN degree, married, and had a baby. She and her husband divorced, so she went to Honolulu to find a new life. As she explained it to me, she and her girlfriends went to bed with guys anyway, so why not charge them for it?

"Are you proud of your work?" I asked.

Not prepared for her answer, I was shocked when she said, "Yes, I am proud of it. I'm the best. I earn the most money."

I challenged her claim by asking, "How do you know? Do you report it to the government?"

"No."

"Do you know what the other girls get?"

"No."

"So if you are not ashamed of what you do, then why don't you brag about it?"

Her silence was as close to an admission that I would get that deep down she had some feelings of shame that she would not admit to herself, much less to a stranger.

The next question I asked was, "What about morality? Does that enter in?"

"I don't think I am doing anything immoral. The people who are killing are immoral. I don't kill people."

"Next question: What about religion? Do you have any?"

"No."

"Have you ever been to any kind of synagogue, church, or temple in your life?"

"Yes. Twice. Sunday school in Atlanta."

"Another subject: Jesus Christ. What do you know about Him?" I shall never forget her answer. I still almost tremble at it.

"Jesus Christ . . . I think He lived and died, didn't He?" she said.

"Is that all you know about Him?"

"That's all I know."

I was stunned! Shocked! Here stood a young woman who only two years earlier had been a nurse, married, the mother of a baby in Atlanta, Georgia. Today she was a call girl in Honolulu, and all she knew was that Jesus was someone who "lived and died, didn't He?"

Before I left she said, "I would like to read one of your books."

I gave her the one that I was holding. "My name is Robert Schuller. I'm on television. Read the book. Watch me on TV. I think you might just love what I say, because I will tell you more about Jesus Christ."

By now her whole manner had changed. Her cold, tough shell seemed to melt. An openness, an attractive humility, an appealing vulnerability seemed to take over. I added, "And you just might discover for the first time in your life what love really is."

She took the book and said, "Thank you. Maybe I'll see you again someday."

I pray every day that she will read and she will watch and she will listen and she will open her heart to the One who will teach her about love. It would be my greatest joy to meet her again some day, to hear her say, "Remember me? I'm the call girl you interviewed. I have found Jesus! I have found real love for the first time in my life!"

In the meantime I will be haunted by her description of Jesus Christ as someone who "lived and died, didn't He?"

Jesus Christ was much more than just a man who lived and died. He was much more than just a prophet. He was God come to earth as a man to die on a cross to tell us how very much God loves us.

Dr. William Glasser, whose book *Reality Therapy* has been

helpful to many people, has a sentence that I find very, very significant: "Every [person] needs one essential friend." I would add: If you've got that, then you've got a cure for loneliness.

Each one of us should have one friend so intimate that we can expose ourselves completely without fear of rejection, without fear we will be shamed! Without fear that someday we'll be exposed! Where can you find a friend you can trust like that? I have such a friend. His name is Jesus Christ. He is that one essential friend.

You will never get lonely as long as there is one person who loves you with a love so great that you know you don't have to be a phony around Him. You don't have to play games. You don't have to wear a mask. You don't have to pretend. He loves you anyway. He will never condemn you. He will never scold you. He will never belittle you.

I can go to Him and confess all my sins—of thought, word, and deed—and know that He will put His arms around my shoulder and love me anyway:

- I can go to Him in the Loneliness of Striving—He will *encourage* me!
- I can go to Him in the Loneliness of Searching for Alternatives—He will *guide* me!
- I can go to Him in the Loneliness of Struggling and Sinking—He will *support* me!
- I can go to Him in the Loneliness of Succeeding—He will *rejoice* with me!
- I can go to Him in the Loneliness of Sinning—He will *save* me!

Well, then—Love or Loneliness?—it's your choice! The secret of happiness is so simple: Become a "God loves you . . . and so do I" person! Accept Jesus Christ as your Savior and best Friend. Become a "one-to-One-for-someone" person.

Now let me give you a final blessing—this prayer:

May the Lord touch your heart with his finger
of love and leave a fingerprint no one can rub off.
                                                    *Robert Schuller*